THE BANK OF ENGLAND AND THE GOVERNMENT DEBT

The Bank of England and the Government Debt recounts the surprising history of the Bank of England's activities in the government securities market in the mid-twentieth century. The Bank's Governor, Montagu Norman, had a decisive influence on government debt management policy until he retired in 1944, and established an auxiliary market in government securities outside the Stock Exchange during the Second World War. From the early 1950s, the Bank, concerned about inadequate market liquidity, became an increasingly active market-maker in government securities, rescuing the commercial market-makers in the Stock Exchange several times. The Bank's market-making activities often conflicted with its monetary policy objectives, and in 1971 it curtailed them substantially, while avoiding the damaging effects on liquidity in the government securities market that it had feared. Drawing heavily on archival research, William A. Allen sheds light on little-known aspects of central banking and monetary policy.

William A. Allen is a Visitor at the National Institute of Economic and Social Research. He worked at the Bank of England from 1972 to 2004, serving as a senior official in the Gild-Edged Division from 1982 to 1986.

STUDIES IN MACROECONOMIC HISTORY

Series Editor
Michael D. Bordo, *Rutgers University*

Editors

Owen F. Humpage, *Federal Reserve Bank of Cleveland*
Christopher M. Meissner, *University of California, Davis*
Kris James Mitchener, *Santa Clara University*
David C. Wheelock, *Federal Reserve Bank of St. Louis*

The titles in this series investigate themes of interest to economists and economic historians in the rapidly developing field of macroeconomic history. The four areas covered include the application of monetary and finance theory, international economics, and quantitative methods to historical problems; the historical application of growth and development theory and theories of business fluctuations; the history of domestic and international monetary, financial, and other macroeconomic institutions; and the history of international monetary and financial systems. The series amalgamates the former Cambridge University Press series 'Studies in Monetary and Financial History' and 'Studies in Quantitative Economic History'.

Other Books in the Series

Eric Monnet, *Controlling Credit: Central Banking and the Planned Economy in Postwar France, 1948–1973* (2018)

Laurence M. Ball, *The Fed and Lehman Brothers: Setting the Record Straight on a Financial Disaster* (2017)

Rodney Edvinsson, Tor Jacobson and Daniel Waldenström (eds.), *Sveriges Riksbank and the History of Central Banking* (2017)

Peter L. Rousseau and Paul Wachtel (eds.), *Financial Systems and Economic Growth* (2017)

Ernst Baltensperger and Peter Kugler, *Swiss Monetary History since the Early 19th Century* (2017)

(continued after Index)

The Bank of England and the Government Debt

Operations in the Gilt-Edged Market, 1928–1972

WILLIAM A. ALLEN

National Institute of Economic and Social Research (NIESR)

CAMBRIDGE
UNIVERSITY PRESS

CAMBRIDGE
UNIVERSITY PRESS

University Printing House, Cambridge CB2 8BS, United Kingdom

One Liberty Plaza, 20th Floor, New York, NY 10006, USA

477 Williamstown Road, Port Melbourne, VIC 3207, Australia

314-321, 3rd Floor, Plot 3, Splendor Forum, Jasola District Centre, New Delhi - 110025, India

79 Anson Road, #06-04/06, Singapore 079906

Cambridge University Press is part of the University of Cambridge.

It furthers the University's mission by disseminating knowledge in the pursuit of education, learning and research at the highest international levels of excellence.

www.cambridge.org
Information on this title: www.cambridge.org/9781108469524
DOI: 10.1017/9781108605830

First published 2019
First paperback edition 2019

A catalogue record for this publication is available from the British Library

ISBN 978-1-108-49983-5 Hardback
ISBN 978-1-108-46952-4 Paperback

Cambridge University Press has no responsibility for the persistence or accuracy of URLs for external or third-party internet websites referred to in this publication, and does not guarantee that any content on such websites is, or will remain, accurate or appropriate.

Contents

Figures

Tables

Boxes

Preface

When I joined the staff of the Bank of England in 1972, equipped with a masters' degree in Economics, I was assigned to the Economic Intelligence Department, which was the Bank's main repository of economic expertise. Yet what seemed to be the Bank's most important functions were performed without reference to the Economic Intelligence Department. Those functions were its operations in financial markets: the domestic money market, the gilt-edged market and the foreign exchange market. Why was that? Was it simply that a mystique been created, perhaps to protect the positions and self-esteem of those involved and exclude *parvenu* economists, or perhaps to maintain secrecy? Or did performing the functions require knowledge beyond that which had been imparted to the economics students of that time?

The purpose of this book is to describe the history of the Bank of England's operations in the gilt-edged market, and to suggest possible reasons why they were at times conducted in a way which most economists found quaint and incomprehensible, and which led to a conflict of objectives. The evidence is patchy, as will be explained, and I am sure to have missed some interesting episodes. Nevertheless I believe that I have produced enough evidence to alter the perception of debt management and monetary policy during the period.

I am grateful to many people for helpful discussions about the subject over many years, comments on earlier versions of the book, and for general encouragement, which in many cases was unconsciously provided. They include the late Derek Allen, the late Sir Nigel Althaus, Michael Anson, Lord Armstrong of Ilminster, Angus Armstrong, Rex Baldwin, Jagjit Chadha, Victoria Chick, Tony Coleby, the late Lord Cromwell, Roger Daniell, Jonathan Davie, Sahil Dutta, the late John Fforde, Kenneth Garbade, the late Lord George, Graeme Gilchrist, Charles Goodhart,

Tony Hibbitt, Rob Jones, Jim Juffs, Olwen Myhill, George Nissen, Margherita Orlando, Brian Peppiatt, the late Patrick Phillips, Ian Plenderleith, Jessica Pulay, Clifford Smout, Sir Robert Stheeman, David Wilkie, Peter Wills, participants in seminars at Cass Business School, the Debt Management Office, the London School of Economics, and the National Institute of Economic and Social Research, and the archivists of the Bank of England and the National Archives.

I am especially grateful to Anthony Hotson, Susan Howson, Richhild Moessner, Rodney Offer and Jeremy Wormell for reading the entire manuscript and making helpful suggestions, and to Susan Howson for provoking me to look closely at the events of 1940. None of the above necessarily agrees with anything I have said in the book, nor is responsible for errors or misinterpretations that I have perpetrated.

Above all I am grateful to my wife Rosemary for her remarkable tolerance and encouragement.

1

Introduction

Government securities are an essential item of equipment for an effective state. They enable governments to borrow to finance expenditure which cannot immediately be paid for out of taxation or accumulated savings. In the past, such expenditure was often for the conduct of wars. Britain was able to raise more money than France to fight the Napoleonic Wars because it had better arrangements for government borrowing. Governments which could not borrow have often resorted to creating money, which its citizens are forced to accept as payment, leading to serious inflation; that is why wars are frequently accompanied by inflation.[1]

At the end of the Napoleonic Wars, in 1815, the British national debt was 214% of gross domestic product, according to present-day estimates of GDP. By 1913, the ratio had come down to 28%.[2] There had been no significant price inflation in the meantime, the gold convertibility of the pound having been restored in 1821. The reduction in the debt ratio was achieved through the combination of economic growth and a sustained balanced budget. Britain's already-strong credit standing was further enhanced.

The First World War increased the debt/GDP ratio to 140%, and there was considerable inflation: the cost of living index rose by 120% during the war. Owing to deflationary policies and slow economic growth, and despite balanced budgets, the debt ratio did not fall back after the war: by 1939, it was 153%. Economic management during the Second World War relied

---

[1] On the Napoleonic Wars see Ferguson (2001, p. 180); also Bordo and White (1993), Sargent and Velde (1995) and Bernholz (2015, ch. 6), who presents a complete theory of inflation.

[2] Source: Bank of England, 'A millennium of data', www.bankofengland.co.uk/research/Pages/datasets/default.aspx, tables A29 and M6.

heavily on controls over prices and borrowing. The cost of living index rose by 31% during that war, and the debt/GDP ratio had risen to 259% in 1946.

Since the First World War, government borrowing has been a routine feature of peacetime economic management. Large amounts of government debt are outstanding, and large amounts need to be borrowed each year, not only to finance ongoing deficits but also to refinance maturing debts. Thus in the financial year 2016/17, official government bond sales were £147.6 billion, or about 7.5% of GDP. Roughly half of this borrowing was accounted for by the refinancing of maturing debt. Failure to sell these bonds would have led to creation of near-money assets of the same amount, increases in inflation and inflationary expectations, and the destruction of the government's monetary policy. For this reason, governments are reliant on the existence of markets in which their bonds can be sold, as are central banks, which could not otherwise achieve their price-stability objectives. Market liquidity – the ability to buy and sell easily – matters a lot. It makes government securities more attractive to investors; and it thereby enables governments to borrow more, and more cheaply.

This book is largely the story of how the market for UK government bonds – known as gilt-edged, or gilts – developed in the middle of the twentieth century, of how the monetary authorities tried to compensate for its deficiencies, and of how they overcame the unintended consequences of their actions. Specifically, it is about official intervention by the British monetary authorities in the secondary market for gilts from 1928 to 1972. Its main purpose is to describe how the intervention was conducted and to what ends.

The Bank of England, which was the agency responsible for government debt management, was motivated not only by immediate needs to sell gilts to finance the government, but also by the desire to maintain the liquidity of the gilt market. The latter became more difficult during and after the Second World War, when the quantity of gilts outstanding exploded, and the capacity of the commercial market-makers could not keep up. The Bank's operations, which were conducted in great secrecy, led to conflicts with monetary policy. These were partly resolved in 1971.

The Bank went to great lengths to ensure the continued presence of commercial market-makers. In 1931 it acted as lender of last resort to the Stock Exchange jobbers, and on several occasions in the 1950s and 1960s it subsidised them to keep them in business. During the 1950s and 1960s, the Bank played a much larger role itself as a market-maker in gilt-edged than has generally been appreciated.

The role of central banks as 'market-maker of last resort' has been discussed extensively in the context of the crisis of 2008–09. This study shows that, long before that, the Bank of England had acted as the market-maker of last resort – and perhaps at times of first resort – for a protracted period, and demonstrates that market microstructures can have important macroeconomic implications.[3]

There are already several accounts of debt management in Britain in the twentieth century,[4] to which the present account should be seen as a supplement. My main contribution is to say more about official operations in the secondary market, and to draw attention to the under-appreciated connection between the microstructure of the gilt-edged market and monetary policy.[5] It is based on looking at what the Bank of England did, as well as what it said.

The account begins in 1928, when the Treasury currency notes which had been introduced in 1914 were absorbed into the Bank of England note issue, and the consequent massive enlargement of the assets of the Issue Department of the Bank provided it for the first time with the resources to intervene in the gilt market on a substantial scale.[6] It ends in 1972, partly because the Competition and Credit Control programme of 1971, which

---

[3] Recent discussions of central banks acting as market-maker of last resort, in the context of financial crisis, can be found in Buiter and Sibert (2008, pp. 171–8), Tucker (2009) and Mehrling (2011).

[4] They include Wormell's book (1999) on 1900–32, Howson's paper (1988) on 1932–51, and Sayers' book (1956) on 1939–45. In addition, the successive histories of the Bank of England by Sayers, Fforde and Capie (1976, 1992 and 2010 respectively), Howson's accounts of British monetary policy from 1919–38 (1975) and 1945–51 (1993), Nevin's account of the mechanism of cheap money (1955), Dow's history of macroeconomic management from 1945–60 (1964), my own account of British monetary policy from 1951–59 (Allen, 2014), the accounts of the 1960s by Cohen (1971) and Tew (1974), and Needham's account of post-1967 monetary policy (2014) all have plenty to say about debt management. And there is the Bank of England's reporting of its own activities in its *Quarterly Bulletin* and elsewhere.

[5] The work of Ranald Michie (1999) and Bernard Attard (2000) on the history of the Stock Exchange has been invaluable in the writing of this book. Attard's paper describes the conditions in which the jobbers worked and of the relationships which developed within the Stock Exchange. It is partly based on his fascinating project on the jobbing system of the London Stock Exchange undertaken under the auspices of the Centre for Metropolitan History at London University, shortly after the Big Bang of 1986 ended single capacity in the Stock Exchange and, with it, the distinction between brokers and jobbers. Records of interviews with individual jobbers can be found at www.history.ac.uk/projects/research/jobbing (last accessed 28 March 2016).

[6] The accounts of the Bank of England are divided into two parts, the Banking Department and the Issue Department. The Issue Department's only liabilities can be Bank of England notes.

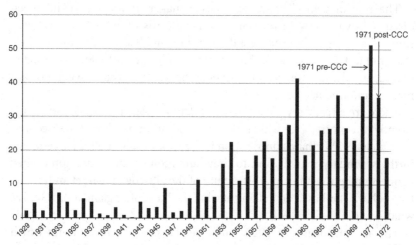

Figure 1.1 Issue Department Secondary Market Turnover with Market Counterparties
(Percentage of Outstanding Gilts), 1929–72

curtailed the Bank's intervention in the gilt market, represents a natural break point, and partly because I joined the Bank of England staff in 1972, and do not believe in writing the history of events in which I was personally involved, even if only peripherally. Intervention nevertheless continued after 1972 until 1986, when Big Bang in the London Stock Exchange led to greatly increased liquidity, and ultimately made it possible for gilts to be sold by auction with no need for official intervention (Figure 1.1).[7]

---

[7] It was not until more than a decade after Big Bang that all primary market sales of gilts were conducted by auction, but it was the increase in market liquidity that Big Bang created that made auctions possible. For an early assessment of the liquidity effect of Big Bang, see Bank of England (1989).

2

Price and Quantity Discovery, Market-Making and Liquidity in the Gilt Market

Standard economic theory cannot readily accommodate the concept of market liquidity. In models of perfect competition, prices depend on the supply and demand schedules of the participants in the economy, none of whom is important enough to have a perceptible effect on the market price and all of whom therefore take prices as given: they are price-takers, not price-makers. In the models, as Kenneth Arrow pointed out, 'there is no one left over whose job it is to make a decision on price.'[1]

The job is, in fact, entrusted to a *deus ex machina*: Walras' auctioneer is assumed to inform all traders of the prices at which all markets are going to clear. This always trustworthy information is supplied at zero cost. Traders do not have to wrestle with situations in which demands and supplies do not mesh; all can plan on facing perfectly elastic demand and supply schedules without fear of ever having their trading plans disappointed. All goods are perfectly 'liquid', their full market values being at any time instantaneously realizable. Money can be added to such models only by artifice.[2]

The lack of realism has serious consequences. According to one influential interpretation, the target of Keynes' attack on 'classical economics', and its inability to explain mass unemployment, was its assumption of instantaneous market-clearing, and its failure to explore the processes of price and quantity discovery, in particular in the labour market.[3] Much modern macroeconomic theory has been devoted to surmounting, or circumventing, the theoretical difficulty posed by the absence of a procedure to determine prices in models of a perfectly competitive

[1] Arrow (1959, p. 43).
[2] Leijonhufvud (1981, p. 6). The reference is to Léon Walras's *Éléments d'économie politique pure*, first published in 1874.
[3] Leijonhufvud (1968).

market.[4] Obviously, it is logically impossible to draw inferences about the optimality, or otherwise, of the quantity or price of market-making services provided in a free-market economy from theories that assume that such services are available at no cost.

In real-life financial markets, market-makers are the parties that are always ready to deal.[5] They fill, after a fashion, the vacancy identified by Arrow. Such was the structure of the gilt-edged market. Market-makers are willing to quote prices (bids and offers) at which they will buy and sell. They provide to inquirers, free of charge, options to buy or sell up to a certain amount at the quoted prices; if a market participant wants to buy or sell more than that amount, then he or she will have to find additional bids or offers, which may be less attractive. The term 'market liquidity' refers to the ease with which large amounts of a particular asset can be bought or sold; 'ease' embraces both the amount of time it takes to complete the transaction, and how close the transaction price is to the price ruling in the market just before the transaction was undertaken.

Market liquidity depends on the amounts for which market-makers are willing to quote, the number of market-makers, and the spread between the bid and offer prices, which provides the reward which the market-makers receive for their services. The market is not in equilibrium as long as the market-makers are holding unwanted positions, but it is in a kind of near-equilibrium as long as the market-makers' positions are not too far away from what they want. The near-equilibrium is continually disturbed as new bids and offers are made, including, in the case of gilts, new issues by the government. It is also disturbed when new information emerges which affects the valuation of the asset in question: for example increases in Bank rate often led to immediate large falls in gilt prices. Of course the market-makers are exposed to risk: if they have a positive inventory of an asset whose price falls, they will lose money; likewise if they have a negative inventory of an asset whose price rises (they can acquire a negative

---

[4] Backhouse and Boianovsky (2013) provide an excellent account of the work. Kregel (1995) notes that the accounts of price formation developed by Walras and Marshall in the nineteenth century reflect the contemporary methods of trading employed in the Paris and London stock exchanges, respectively; the Paris exchange used a procedure akin to a periodic *tâtonnement*, whereas trading in the London exchange was continuous (as is common practice today), with temporal gaps between buying and selling orders being bridged by the intervention of professional jobbers. He concludes that the difference does not lead to theoretical diversity: 'There thus appears to be a substantial similarity between Marshall and Walras' (p. 463).

[5] Foucault, Pagano and Roell (2013) give a lucid partial-equilibrium account of the economics of market-making and market liquidity.

inventory by borrowing an asset and then selling it, leaving themselves obliged to buy the asset back and return it to the lender). The spread between bid and offer prices includes a charge for bearing these risks.

Plainly the behaviour of market-makers depends on the anticipated behaviour of other market participants. If market-makers believe that others are willing to buy and sell substantial amounts of the financial asset in question in response to small price changes, they will feel more confident in quoting prices themselves. Thus market liquidity depends not only on the market-makers themselves, but also on the community of active dealers.[6] Indeed, the distinction between market-makers and active dealers is often unclear.

It is possible to imagine a near-perfect government securities market in which the government, or any other party, can sell as many securities as it wishes, at a time of its choosing, and at a price very close to the price prevailing before the sale. Such a market has existed in the United States for many years, perhaps since the 1970s, and in the United Kingdom after Big Bang in the Stock Exchange in 1986.[7] This book, however, is concerned with the period 1928–72, when the UK government securities market was nowhere near perfect. The characteristics of the market at that time, compared with the imaginary ideal, had seriously adverse macroeconomic consequences.

There is no comprehensive body of evidence on the liquidity of the gilt-edged market in the period. No continuous records survive of the amounts for which the market-makers' bids and offers were good. As regards bid-offer price spreads, until November 1965 the *Financial Times* published two closing prices for each gilt-edged stock; these may be presumed to have been bids and offers reported at the end of the trading day.[8] The spreads as at (or near) 11 September each year (date chosen at random) from 1945–65 are shown in Figure 2.1, calculated as a percentage of the price of the stock in question. A tendency for spreads to widen is observable, except in the case of short gilts.

The evidence given to the Radcliffe Committee on the working of the monetary system, and to the Parker Tribunal on the alleged Bank rate leak of 1957, provides a lot of information on the liquidity of the gilt-edged market

---

[6] Hicks (1989, p. 10) talks of an 'inside market' between buyers and sellers.

[7] It has not always existed in the United States: see Garbade (2012), and Box 8.1.

[8] The words 'stock' and 'bond' are used interchangeably in this book. Gilts were normally known as 'stock' in British parlance during the period under review, except when they were in the form of bearer instruments, when they were known as 'bonds'. In American parlance, 'stock' denotes equity.

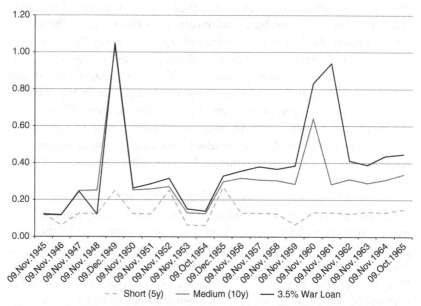

Figure 2.1 Dealing Spreads Quoted in the *Financial Times*, Around 11 September, 1945–65 (%)

in the late 1950s. The internal records of the Bank of England, and of the Government Brokers, Mullens and Co, give qualitative indications of how it developed in the 1960s. The Bank's archives contain detailed quantitative information on the Issue Department's transactions, and on the discount houses' holdings of gilts, which I have transcribed onto spreadsheets and made available on the internet.[9] The gilt prices which were published each day in the *Financial Times* and *The Times* newspapers can be found in their digital archives. And in 1964, the Stock Exchange began to collect and publish statistics of turnover in gilts. Turnover is not the same as liquidity, but it is suggestive. This book describes, among other things, how the Bank of England became the principal market-maker in gilts in the 1960s. The share of official transactions in total turnover is a revealing indicator of how far it had progressed by the mid-late 1960s, and of how far it withdrew from market-making in 1971, when the conflict with monetary policy had become intolerable.

---

[9] The data are available at cambridge.org, niesr.ac.uk, bankofengland.co.uk, eh.net and researchgate.net. See Appendix B for more information on sources.

Market-makers supply liquidity by quoting prices, or limit orders, at which investors can trade. Market orders – orders to deal at the best available price in the market – are executed against standing limit orders, and 'effectively decrease the available trading options, and, as such, consume liquidity.'[10] At least from the 1950s onwards, the Bank of England seems to have executed its transactions by responding to bids and offers from the jobbers, thus providing liquidity – e.g. it made tap stocks available at prices which were known in the market.[11]

The work of Benos and Wetherilt suggests a measure of liquidity provision which can be applied to the Bank of England's activities in the gilt market. If the Bank systematically sold gilts when yields fell, and bought them when yields rose, it would be supplying liquidity. In Benos and Wetherilt's language, it would for example be contributing offers of gilts to the market at times when offers were being consumed by others because demand was rising. If the Bank's purchases and sales were unrelated to yield changes, it would be a consumer of liquidity; and if the Bank were systematically to sell when yields rose and to buy when yields fell, it would be a destroyer of liquidity. The scale of its liquidity supply or destruction can be measured by the amount it bought or sold for a given yield change, and this can be estimated by regression analysis; this is done in Chapter 13.

---

[10] Benos and Wetherilt (2012, p. 345).

[11] Confusingly, the word 'tap' has two different meanings in the history of the gilt market. 'Tap stocks' in and just after the Second World War were gilts issued continuously at a fixed yield, directly to investors, in response to the flow of demand. 'Tap stocks' in peacetime were stocks of which the Issue Department held a large amount as a result of its underwriting activity, and which it was willing to sell in response to bids from the jobbers in the Stock Exchange. The reference here is to tap stocks in the latter sense.

3

Government Securities and the Structure of the Stock Exchange

Government securities had been dealt in on the Stock Exchange from the inception of a permanent national debt after the Glorious Revolution of 1688.[1] From 1909 until Big Bang in 1986, the London Stock Exchange insisted on 'single capacity'. Member firms had to be either brokers, who could deal with ultimate investors but could not trade with those investors from their own portfolios, or jobbers, who could trade from their own portfolios but only through brokers. Single capacity was made obligatory in 1909, and it was supplemented in 1912 by a rule requiring brokers to charge their clients according to a minimum scale of commissions. These rules were regarded as a means of ensuring that investors could have an impartial source of advice from brokers, who could not offload unwanted positions of their own onto their clients, and that prices quoted to clients were based on all the bids and offers in the market, not just those available to an individual firm.[2]

Although gilts could be and sometimes were dealt in outside the Stock Exchange, the Bank of England dealt nearly exclusively on the London Stock Exchange, and, not being a member, was obliged to deal through a broker. Its broker, the Government Broker, was the senior partner of Mullens and Co, a stockbroking firm.[3] The structure is illustrated in Figure 3.1.

The market-makers were thus the jobbers. Until the late 1960s, jobbing firms had to be partnerships, and the partners had unlimited liability. This

---

[1] Morgan and Thomas (1962, ch. 1).

[2] Morgan and Thomas (1962, pp. 145–7, 153–4), Kynaston (1983, pp. 252–62), Michie (1999, pp. 115–21) and Attard (2000, pp. 8–9).

[3] Mullens and Co had previously been known as Mullens, Marshall and Co, and Mullens, Marshall, Steer Lawford and Co. Wainwright (1990) provides a history of the firm and of the various individual Government Brokers.

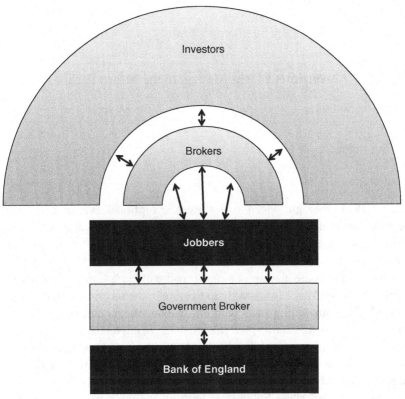

Figure 3.1 The Structure of the Gilt-Edged Market in the Stock Exchange

made it difficult to assess their creditworthiness, since the wealth of the partners was not publicly known, and many partners transferred assets to their wives or other family members to reduce their contingent liabilities.

4

Government Debt Management before 1928

Before 1914, new gilt-edged issues were exceptional events; each one required legislation. The Bank of England participated in government debt management as issuing house and registrar, but it was not the Treasury's only collaborator. For example Rothschilds and Morgans participated with it in the placing of a new tranche of 2½% Consols in 1901 to finance the Boer War.[1] Its capacity to operate in the secondary market was limited. The Bank of England's accounts had been separated into two parts in 1844 by the Bank Charter Act, the intention being to assure what would now be called financial stability by regulating the note issue according to the size of the gold reserves. Thus the Issue Department, whose only liabilities were banknotes, was constrained to hold gold bullion or coin (or, within limits, silver bullion) as backing for the note issue, save for a limited fiduciary issue which could be backed by government securities. At the end of 1913 the fiduciary issue amounted to £18.45 million, out of a total note issue of £52.32 million. Other banks' rights to issue notes were severely circumscribed. The Banking Department was initially intended to be managed, like any other bank, in the interests of the private shareholders, except that it could not issue notes. It acted as the government's banker, and at the end of 1913 held £11.2 million of government securities, which it had acquired in exchange for its note-issuing privileges and for the periodic renewal of its charter. It was willing to extend credit to the government when it was needed by providing deficiency advances and ways and means advances, and by buying Treasury bills. In practice, the

---

[1] Osborne (1926, vol. 1 p. 380). This document is a lengthy history of the activities of the Bank of England from 1914 to 1921. It was edited by J.A.C. Osborne and completed in 1926, and is available on the Bank of England Archive internet site (archive reference BOE M7/156). Wormell (1999, pp. 30–9) provides a full account of Boer War gilt issues.

scope for discretionary intervention in the market for government securities by either department of the Bank of England was limited.

The scale of credit that the government needed changed completely in the First World War.[2] 'As soon as the 3½% War Loan had been floated [in November 1914] and the Bank found that they had to take up an enormous subscription, it became their policy to dispose of all their securities other than government issues, and even of the pre-War holdings of some of these, in order to conserve their resources and be able to place them wholly at the disposal of the Government.'[3] Government borrowing during the war proved very expensive.[4] As the expected duration and cost of the war increased, yields rose and successive bond offerings had to carry increasingly high coupons. Moreover, when making new and higher-yielding issues, the Treasury offered the holders of the earlier issues the right to convert into the new ones at no, or not much, penalty. The result was that by March 1919, £2.0 billion of outstanding gilts, or 45% of the total, consisted of the high-coupon 5% War Loan 1929–47.

The capacity of the Stock Exchange to make a market in gilt-edged was impaired after the First World War. The close pre-war relationship between the money market and the Stock Exchange was ruptured when at the outbreak of war members of the Stock Exchange did not receive remittances due from Continental Europe and could not repay loans that the banks had previously considered safe:

Another activity that had generated much activity on the London Stock Exchange [before 1914] was buying and selling in response to money market conditions. Banks and other institutions in London, with money temporarily unemployed, readily employed it by lending to brokers and jobbers. In turn, these, either on their own account or through lending to other members, used the funds to purchase and hold securities, profiting from the yield differential between short- and long-term interest rates, with fluctuations in one being readily transmitted to the other. It was this role that had made the members of the London Stock Exchange so vulnerable on the outbreak of war, as so much of their activity required a high degree of trust among the individual participants. Bankers and others had to believe that not only could they employ remuneratively whatever idle funds they possessed but also that such loans would be quickly repaid when asked. Otherwise they would be more reluctant to lend, would lend less, would charge more and would be more ready to

---

[2] The financing of the First World War has been described by Osborne (1926), Morgan (1952), Sayers (1976) and Wormell (1999); all but Morgan had access to the official archives.

[3] Osborne (1926, p. 243). The 3½% War Loan was redeemable in 1925–28 and should not be confused with the later 3½% War Loan 1952 or after.

[4] Morgan (1952, pp. 106–12).

withdraw from the business. Conversely, brokers and jobbers had to know that the securities they purchased and held could be quickly sold at little loss if loans were recalled. Otherwise, they would be reluctant to undertake the activity. Inevitably, the war, with its closure of the Stock Exchange and its moratorium on loans, undermined the trust that had underpinned the relationship between the money and securities market.[5]

On the outbreak of the First World War, 'as part of the Government's crisis programme of assistance for financial institutions, the [Stock Exchange] Committee [for General Purposes] made enquiries of members and found that the London Stock Exchange owed £81 million and the provincial exchanges £11 million. Just under half of this was due to the London joint stock banks, and the rest to other financial institutions, including merchant banks and the London offices of overseas banks.' It was estimated that the banks had lent £250 million in all against the collateral of Stock Exchange securities. Gross domestic product in 1913 is estimated to have been £2,411 million, and commercial banks' assets at the end of 1913 were £1,205 million, Therefore the Stock Exchange members' debts represented 3.4% of GDP and 7.6% of bank assets, and loans collateralised by Stock Exchange securities might have been a tenth of GDP and a fifth of bank assets.[6]

Some historians attribute the decreased post-1914 market-making capacity of the Stock Exchange in gilts to the rule requiring cash settlement rather than account-day settlement. 'Dealing for the account' meant dealing for settlement on the next fortnightly account day, on which deals made in the previous fortnight were settled. Account dealing had made it possible to take positions for a limited period without putting up any cash. It was banned when the Stock Exchange reopened in January 1915, having been closed since 31 July 1914, just before war broke out, and the ban was maintained after the war for gilts.[7]

This [post-war] instability in the market for long-term government securities was partly due to the instability of economic and political conditions and to changes in monetary policy. It was accentuated, however, by changes in the organisation of the market. In the nineteenth century dealings had been largely for the account and there was a large amount of speculation which had a strong stabilising effect on

---

[5] Michie (1999, pp. 245–6).

[6] Morgan and Thomas (1962, p. 155), Sir John Clapham, in Sayers (1976, Appendix 3, p. 43), www.measuringworth.com (last accessed 27 January 2018), and Sheppard (1971, table (A) 1.1). Withers (1910, p. 104) also describes the 'large business' of bank lending to the Stock Exchange. Odlyzko (2016) draws attention to the importance of the Stock Exchange in the money market in early Victorian times.

[7] Morgan and Thomas (1962, pp. 223–4).

prices. The insistence on cash settlements during and after the war reduced this stabilising force, and it was further weakened by the fact that the volume of securities in the market had grown far more than the resources of the jobbers.[8]

Whatever the explanation – and there may well have been several, including the massive issues of long-term debt during the First World War – the shape of the yield curve changed permanently in 1914. The average differential between the yield of Consols (and its predecessors) and Bank rate had been minus 73 basis points on average between 1756 and 1914. Between 1918 and 1939, before the onset of inflationary expectations and the accompanying uncertainties, it was plus 38 basis points.[9]

The circumstances surrounding the issue in and after 1914 of £1 and 10 shilling Treasury notes to supplement the Bank of England note issue, whose minimum denomination was £5, are well-known.[10] Treasury notes were the liability of the Currency Note Redemption Account (CNRA), and the corresponding assets were gold coin and bullion, silver coin, government securities, deposits at the Bank of England and Bank of England notes (see below). The CNRA used its assets to intervene in the gilt market: it underwrote new gilt issues, subsequently selling them in the secondary market, and bought gilts approaching maturity, so as to spread out through time the impact of the redemption on the government's cash flow.[11]

The issue of Treasury notes was a transparent evasion of the Bank Charter Act of 1844 and a flagrant violation of the principles of the gold standard. Getting rid of them was part of the restoration of the gold standard, which was a cardinal objective of post-war monetary policy.[12] It was achieved by the Currency and Bank Notes Act 1928.[13] The amalgamation of the two note issues involved transferring the assets and liabilities of the CNRA to the Issue Department of the Bank of England, and enlarging the fiduciary issue accordingly. The Bank of England began to issue both £1 and 10 shilling

---

[8] Morgan and Thomas (1962, pp. 190–1). No evidence is cited, but Morgan and Thomas had access to the 'minutes, sale books and other records' in the possession of the Stock Exchange Council.

[9] Bank of England, 'A millennium of macroeconomic data for the UK', www.bankofengland .co.uk (last accessed 27 January 2018). Unless otherwise specified, references to Consol yields refer to 2½% Consols.

[10] See Morgan (1952), Sayers (1976) and Roberts (2013).

[11] See Howson (1975, Appendix 2) and Wormell (1999, pp. 704–8).

[12] See Moggridge (1972) and Sayers (1976, chs. 7 and 12) for more information about the return to the gold standard and the amalgamation of the note issues.

[13] The delay of more than three years between the re-institution of the free export of gold in 1925 and the amalgamation of the note issues was intended to allow time for the authorities to learn what level of reserves would be adequate and what level of the fiduciary issue would be required. See Sayers (1976, ch. 12).

notes.[14] At the time of the amalgamation of the two note issues on 22 November 1928, the Treasury note issue was £285 million, and the Bank of England issue was £181 million, of which just £20 million represented the fiduciary issue and the rest was backed by gold.[15] Very roughly £50 million of Bank of England notes (my estimate) was held by the CNRA, so that the total of banknotes outstanding was less than the sum of the Treasury and Bank of England note issues by that amount. The Issue Department became much larger, and the fiduciary issue increased from around £20 million to £260 million.

The amalgamation had been undertaken as part of the restoration of gold, but it incidentally provided the Issue Department with resources, equal in amount to the fiduciary issue, that enabled it to intervene on a substantial scale in financial markets, so that the Bank of England had much more power in financial markets.[16] The 1928 Act regulated the Bank's use of its new power: it provided that the revenues of the Issue Department would be paid over to the Treasury after deduction of costs, and the Bank agreed in negotiation that the Treasury should be kept fully and constantly informed about the Issue Department's operations. The Bank also undertook to 'act in personal consultation with the Treasury' in managing the Issue Department.[17] The Treasury naturally decided new issues and conversion operations, and the Bank's role was advisory: the extent of its influence fluctuated over time, but the Bank seems usually to have had plenty of discretion in secondary market operations. The present study is largely about how the Bank used its discretion; governance is discussed in more detail in Chapter 14.

---

[14] It had issued £1 notes between 1797 and 1821. It had never before issued 10 shilling notes.

[15] Source: BOE C1/76.

[16] Sayers (1976, p. 295) reports that soon after the return to gold, the Chancellor (Churchill) had refused to allow the Bank to use securities from the CNRA for the purpose of sterilising an influx of gold. So the Bank probably welcomed its new power and influence, even if its arrival was an incidental consequence of the Act.

[17] Mahon–Secretary of the Treasury, 27 July 1928, BOE G14/25. The letter, and relevant clauses of the 1928 Act, are reproduced in Box 14.1.

5

The Gilt Market and the Issue Department 1928–39

5.1 The Size of the Issue Department's Gilt Holdings

The Issue Department more than doubled in size when it absorbed the Treasury note issue in November 1928, and the fiduciary issue was multiplied by 13 times. At the end of the year, about one-sixth of the Issue Department's assets were gilts, and they were mainly of short maturities (Table 5.1):

The Bank of England had no grand new plan for managing the assets which it inherited from the CNRA; initially, it simply managed them in much the same way as they had been managed hitherto. The Macmillan Committee, reporting in 1931, recommended that the Bank should be ready to manage its assets in order to influence the difference between short and long-term interest rates.[1] In the event, the Bank influenced long-term interest rates through the War Loan conversion, in which operations in the market played a relatively small part (section 5.6); thereafter, until 1940, its operations do not appear to have been guided by any interest rate objective.

The Issue Department's total gilt holdings fluctuated from 1928 to 1939 as shown in Table 5.2.

The fluctuations can be explained broadly as follows; fuller explanations are provided below:

a. The increase between the end of 1928 and the end of 1932 reflected the heavy incidence of maturities, which the Issue Department

---

[1] Macmillan Committee (1931a, para. 359).

Table 5.1 *Issue Department Assets, 31 December 1928 (£m)*

	As at 31 December 1928[a]	Inherited from CNRA 22 November 1928
Bullion	152.4	0
Gilts (nominal value)	70.9	41.4
4½% Treasury 1929	17.2	16.2
5½% Treasury 1929	2.3	2.3
5% National War Bonds 1929	2.6	2.3
3% Exchequer 1930 (due 01/01/1930)	0.3	0.3
5½% Treasury 1930	0.3	
4½% Treasury 1932/34	25.3	
4½% Treasury 1934[b]	3.6	3.6
4½% Conversion 1940/44	0.5	0.5
5% War Loan 1929/47	0.7	
4% Funding 1960/90	5.3	5.3
4% Consols 1957 or after	8.1	5.4
3½% Conversion 1961 or after	2.9	2.9
3% Local Loans	1.9	2.2
Commercial bills	2.5	
Treasury bills	188.9	185.1
Ways and Means advances	1.1	
Note issue	412.3[c]	285.5[d]

Source: BOE C1/76, NA T284/1.

Notes

[a] The recorded totals of gilts, Treasury bills and commercial bills in the Issue Department add up to slightly more than the fiduciary issue of £260 million; the apparent discrepancy is no doubt explained by the difference between book and nominal values of gilts.

[b] 4½% Treasury 1934 could be redeemed at par on 1 February in any year from 1927 to 1933 if either the Treasury or the holder gave notice in January of the preceding year. £75.5 million of the £164.4 million issued was repaid before 1934 in this way.

[c] Out of the total note issue as at 31 December 1928, £32.1 million was held in the Banking Department of the Bank of England.

[d] This is the amount of currency notes outstanding as recorded in the Bank of England daily account book. It was well above the maximum of £244.94 million allowed by the 'Cunliffe rule' of 1919, but the excess will have been accounted for by Bank of England notes held by the CNRA: for further explanation, see Howson (1974, p. 94), Sayers (1976, appendix 7, p. 62) and Peden (2000, p. 152). In calculating the new fiduciary issue, £6 million was deducted on account of the imminent replacement of UK currency notes in Ireland by Free State notes.[2]

bought before they were due for redemption, and of new issues, which the Issue Department underwrote (sections 5.2 and 5.3).

[2] Statement by A.M. Samuel, Financial Secretary to the Treasury, HC Deb. 14 May 1928 vol.217 cc. 700–1.

Table 5.2 *Issue Department Gilt Holdings, End of Years
1928–39 (£m)*

End of:	Issue Dept gilt holdings (nominal)	Fiduciary issue
1928	70.9	260
1929	93.6	260
1930	136.4	260
1931	164.8	275
1932	222.5	275
1933	168.8	260
1934	60.2	260
1935	247.7	260
1936	118.4	200
1937	38.4	220
1938	67.2	230
1939	62.3	580

Source: Bank of England daily account books, BOE C1/76–87.

b. The increase in 1935 was mainly the result of the underwriting of 2½% Funding 1956/61 (section 5.2).
c. The decreases in 1933 and 1934, and in 1936 and 1937 reflected the sterilisation of inflows of gold (section 5.7).
d. The decrease in 1937 also reflected the Bank's reaction to the losses which the Issue Department had sustained on its gilt holdings as yields rose (section 5.8).

5.2 New Issues

There was a succession of new gilt issues in the period 1928–39 (Appendix C), intended to refinance maturing issues, to keep down the amount of outstanding Treasury bills against the pressure created by gold and foreign exchange purchases (section 5.7), and later on, to finance military spending.[3] The authorities' phobia about Treasury bills has been aptly characterised as a 'floating debt complex' or a 'funding complex', which had been partly motivated by the Treasury's post-war experience of not being able to renew bills and being driven to rely on advances from the Bank of England,

[3] Wormell (1999, pp. 574–84 and 606–8) provides a full account of the issues made in 1928–32.

which were thought to be inflationary.[4] It might have been expected that, by the 1930s, this fear would have receded, but it persisted.[5]

The Issue Department underwrote all the issues, and sold the stock it had thus acquired gradually in the secondary market over a period. Market liquidity was not considered sufficient to support auctions with no minimum price, and the Bank acted as issuing house and underwriter.[6] With some exceptions, new gilts were issued by fixed-price tender, or by a conversion offer in which a fixed amount of the new issue was offered in exchange for each £100 of the old one, sometimes accompanied by a cash bonus.[7]

Thus, for example, 3% Funding 1959/69 was issued in April 1934. The issue price was £98 per £100 nominal, and the nominal amount issued was £152.4 million. The Issue Department underwrote the issue and acquired £95.5 million (of which £20 million was fully paid, the remainder 48% paid).[8] The Issue Department sold the majority of its holding as shown in Table 5.3.

These secondary market sales, which averaged £8.7 million a month, were made during a period of rising gilt prices. Later issues had to be sold at times when gilt prices were falling: for example, 2½% Funding 1956/61, first issued in December 1935, and 2¾% Funding 1952/57 in November 1936. The Issue Department acquired £160.2 million of the 1956/61s on application, four-fifths of the amount offered, and it took 20 months to sell them, during which time the market price fell by 12.1% from the issue price. The Bank later described this as 'the first notable failure of Government borrowing'.[9] There were occasional purchases during the sale period, which suggests that the Bank responded in some degree to market conditions; nevertheless the average monthly rate of sales was £8.0 million, not much less than in the case of the 1959/69s. And it took the Bank only nine months, until August 1937, to sell off the £60.1 million of 1952/57s (three-fifths of the total) that it had picked up at the tender; during the period, the market price fell by 6.8% from the issue price. This suggests that the Bank was disciplined in maintaining the pace of secondary market sales even when prices were falling: it acted mainly as a price-taker and did not (as it had done

---

[4] Nevin (1955, pp. 149–54), Howson (1975, pp. 9–17, 99), Sayers (1976, ch. 6A).
[5] Clay (1957, p. 460).   [6] Yeomans, 'New issues', 29 October 1937, BOE C40/419.
[7] 4% Treasury 1934/36 (October 1930) and 3% Treasury 1933/42 (April 1932) were sold by minimum price tenders.
[8] Amounts of stock bought or sold are quoted in nominal amounts, unless otherwise specified. '48% paid' means, in this case, that the buyer had to pay £50 per £100 of stock at a later date.
[9] Bank of England, 'Government borrowing', 8 January 1946, NA T233/434.

Table 5.3 *Issue Department Transactions in 3% Funding 1959/69,*
May 1934–February 1935

Month	Net sales (£m nominal)	Average sale price (£, excluding accrued interest)
May 1934	1.9	98.10
June 1934	6.9	98.47
July 1934	14.9	98.27
August 1934	12.1	98.47
September 1934	12.2	98.80
October 1934	16.9	99.43
November 1934	18.5	100.78
December 1934	0.5	103.51
January 1935	0	
February 1935	2.6	104.40

Source: BOE C40/580 and 581, author's calculations.

in converting War Loan; see section 5.6) attempt to be a price-maker. In all cases, sales were made outright, rather than (as in the 1950s and later) against purchases of other stocks.

Many new issues were made, by long-established practice, in partly paid form, and the initial instalments were in some cases as low as 5%. The Bank of England's willingness to facilitate such a high degree of leverage suggests that its reputation for financial conservatism during this era is not fully warranted.

As an experiment, 2½% Conversion 1944/49 was offered for sale by auction at weekly tenders between March and May 1933, with no minimum price, before a fixed-price cash offer in September.[10] The Issue Department bid both at the weekly tenders and at the September cash offer. The experiment was regarded as unsuccessful and was not repeated. Further details are provided in the box at the end of this section.

The Issue Department also underwrote other issues, such as New Zealand Treasury bills (December 1931), London Electricity Board guaranteed debentures (July 1935 and January 1937), African Railway Company guaranteed debentures, International Power and Paper Company of Newfoundland guaranteed mortgage debentures (both October 1935), Railway Finance Corporation guaranteed debentures (January 1936) and a New Zealand government bond issue (August 1939).[11]

[10] Howson (1975, p. 97 and 1988, p. 243).
[11] The purchase of New Zealand Treasury bills in December 1931 occurred at a time when the public finances of New Zealand were in a parlous condition, and was urged on the government by the Bank of England Governor, Montagu Norman, in order to avoid

BOX 5.1 **The Experimental Sale of 2½% Conversion 1944/49**

The stock was first issued in March 1933. The initiative came from the Bank of England, whose motive, as usual, was to reduce the total of outstanding Treasury bills, which had been enlarged to finance purchases of gold and foreign exchange by the Exchange Equalisation Account, to pay off the residue of 5% War Loan which had not been converted, and which would be further enlarged by forthcoming gilt maturities.

The Bank proposed an unusual issuing technique, which was to offer the new bonds for sale weekly at a tender which would be integrated with the normal weekly Treasury bill tender. Thus at the first tender on 24 March, the Treasury offered up to £45 million of Treasury bills and the new bonds in total, of which not more than £5 million would consist of the new bonds.

The experiment was judged a failure. As Sir Richard Hopkins, the Second Secretary of the Treasury, later explained to the Chancellor of the Exchequer, Neville Chamberlain:

When this issue by tender was first started some weeks ago, there was great difference of opinion in the market as to the price they were worth. On the first tender the bond went at a price – well over £94 – which surprised us & which was in fact far too high.

Though we tried for some weeks to hold the position we never recovered from this false start. Most of the bonds taken have in fact been taken by the Bank and the Bank cannot sell them while they are still on weekly offer.

A week ago we put the price down by 10/- on the previous week (to £93.9/-) hoping to get a new start. But the general trend has since continued against us.

5.3 Forthcoming Maturities

The redemption of government securities involved a large repayment on a single day. This could be problematic for the management of the money market, particularly in the days of the gold standard, when a surplus of funds could lead to depletion of the gold reserves. Therefore maturities

a default in London by a dominion (Norman–Hopkins, 1 December 1931, NA T160/480). Drummond (1981, ch. 5(1)) describes New Zealand's financial problems of the 1930s. On Newfoundland, see Mayo (1949).

BOX 5.1 (cont.)

Yesterday the tenders were only for £m8 and the prices offered ranged down to £92.2/-.
We decided to take most of what was offered, at an average price of £92.9/- a drop of £1 on the previous week. But we did not put up any for tender next week.[12]

Hopkins' explanation reveals an inhibition about selling bonds at falling prices at successive tenders, but it is certain that weekly tenders will from time to time produce such a result. The Bank bought £34.2 million of the £55 million sold at the weekly tenders, and a further £0.3 million in the market in April, while the tenders were continuing.[13] It sold all or nearly all its holdings before the conventional tender offer took place in September.

At the conventional tender, the 1944/49s were offered for cash at a fixed price of £94, or in exchange for 4½% Treasury 1934 (Appendix C). £108.5 million were sold for cash and £43.0 million by exchange; the Bank was responsible for £87.2 million and £18.4 million of these amounts respectively. The Bank had sold the holdings it had thus acquired by June 1934.

There had been experiments in selling gilts by weekly tender in the 1920s. A review in 1937 concluded that the method had 'not in recent years proved successful'.[14]

were often anticipated by making conversion offers to investors, inviting them to exchange the maturing stock for a new, longer-dated one.

In addition, the Bank of England routinely purchased gilts approaching maturity, so as in effect to spread the burden of repayment over a period, and to allow itself the option of accepting any conversion offers for them. For example 4½% Treasury 1932/34 was called for repayment on 1 December 1932. The amount outstanding was £140.4 million at the end of March 1932, and it was reduced in October 1932 by a conversion offer into 2% Treasury 1935/38. The Issue Department had bought £6.0 million,

---

[12] Hopkins–Chamberlain, 27 May 1933, NA T160/497 F13380/1.
[13] The figure of £55 million comes from Hopkins' note cited above, and from Pember and Boyle (1950). However, there can have been only 10 weekly tenders between 24 March and 26 May, so more than £3 million bonds must have been offered at one or more tenders.
[14] Yeomans, 'New issues', 29 October 1937, BOE C40/419.

Table 5.4 *Issue Department Transactions in 4½% Treasury 1932/34,
March–November 1932 (£m)*

Month	Amount converted into 2% Treasury 1935/38	Net purchases by Issue Department
March 1932		−5.9
April 1932		2.5
May 1932		22.9
June 1932		1.4
July 1932		1.6
August 1932		5.2
September 1932		9.1
October 1932	73.2, of which 20.0 converted by Issue Department	1.8
November 1932		0.1

Sources: Pember and Boyle (1950), BOE C40/580, author's calculations.

net, from the market between January 1930 and February 1932, together with a further £14.7 million from the CRND. Official transactions from March 1932 are shown in Table 5.4.

The amount to be repaid on the maturity date was £66.6 million, of which the Issue Department held £42.2 million, leaving £24.4 million to be repaid to the market and the CRND.

Purchases could begin quite a long time before maturity. For example the Bank began buying the 1932/34s, the first optional redemption date of which was 1 February 1932, in May 1930. And it bought substantial amounts of 5% War Loan 1929/47 from November 1929 onwards, in anticipation of a conversion offer. Until 1932, most of the Issue Department's secondary market purchases were of stocks approaching maturity or possible conversion.

5.4 Emergency Financing for the Jobbers

The United Kingdom suspended the gold standard on Monday 21 September 1931, ending the convertibility of pounds into gold at a fixed price. Bank rate was increased from 4.5% to 6%. On 19 September, with exquisitely unfortunate timing, the gilt market had coincidentally been opened for its first Saturday session since April 1917. Prices fell very heavily: for example 5% War Loan fell by $1^5/_8$ points, and some undated stocks fell by 1¼–1½ points, net on the day; intra-day falls were larger. Dealing spreads widened: at one time, a three-point margin was quoted in 3½% Conversion 1961 or after, and a point in 5% War Loan.[15]

The former stockbroker Marcus Colby recalled these events, at the age of 86, in his interview with Bernard Attard in 1990:

> When we went off the Gold Standard, all the jobbers in the Gilt-Edged market were insolvent ... in those days if the Gilt market went up or down a sixteenth there was almost a crisis. And it went down about five points. It had never happened before, and there was a terrific thing; there was a kind of moratorium in the Gilt market in those days for a bit, and the Bank of England stepped in. It all came out in the end alright. But actually at that day I believe every single jobber was insolvent in the Gilt market.[16]

There was no moratorium on settlements, but the Stock Exchange was closed on Monday and Tuesday, presumably to allow time for the solvency of member firms to be assessed. Did the Bank of England 'step in', and if so, how? The records show that it did. On the Monday, when Saturday's transactions were settled, the Banking Department of the Bank of England lent £2.2 million to the Government Broker's firm, Mullens, Marshall, Steer Lawford and Co. The loan was repaid the next day. That next day (Tuesday), the Bank lent £750,000 to a large gilt jobber, Francis and Praed. The £750,000 was repaid after a week, when Francis and Praed borrowed £250,000 for another week, at the end of which they repaid in full. All of the loans were collateralised. These operations were unusual; at that time the Bank did not normally lend to the gilt-edged market.[17] They were not, however, specially mentioned in the minutes of the Bank of England Court or Committee of Treasury. My interpretation is that the normal sources of credit to the gilt jobbers were insufficient, or had dried up, and the Bank made the loans to enable the jobbers to settle purchases made on Saturday 19 September. The first loan was made to Mullens for on-lending to the gilt jobbers; all but Francis and Praed were able to repay the next day. The Bank thus provided liquidity support, though not capital support.

In addition, on 30 September the Bank provided an emergency liquidity facility to the discount house Smith St Aubyn against £2,250,000 of gilt collateral, of which the initial £100,000 could be left unsecured for one

---

[15] FTHA, 21 September 1931.

[16] Interview with Marcus Colby, CMH. Gilt prices did not fall quite as much as Mr Colby remembered.

[17] This is implied by the answer given on 28 November 1929 by Sir Ernest Harvey to the Macmillan Committee, Q28 (Macmillan Committee, 1931b, reproduced in Sayers, 1976, Appendix 21, p. 121).

night 'to meet their immediate needs'.[18] The fact that the loan was needed implies that the gilts could not all be readily sold in the prevailing market conditions. It was a condition of the loan that Smith's book must be drastically reduced and that the firm should be strengthened by amalgamation or otherwise. The Bank was evidently unwilling to buy the gilts outright itself. Nor, however, was it willing to let the firm fail, even though the source of its distress seems to have been over-exposure to gilts, which were not its main business. Details of all the operations are given in Appendix A.[19]

In later years, e.g. 1952, 1957, 1964 and 1967 (see below), the Issue Department rescued market-makers from financial distress after sharp increases in Bank rate by buying gilts from them at prices above the post-rate rise market levels. Examination of the Issue Department's records shows no evidence of any such rescue operation in September 1931 (Appendix A).

5.5 Other Operations

This section describes some of the Bank's other market operations.

5.5.1 Dealings with the Commissioners for the Reduction of the National Debt[20]

In the early days after the transfer of the CNRA's assets to the Issue Department, the Issue Department made steady off-market purchases from the Commissioners for the Reduction of the National Debt, mainly of long-dated issues (especially 3% Local Loans and 4% Consols), which it later sold in the market. These operations ended in February 1932 (Table 5.5).

From the initiation of Local Loans stock in 1887 to the last issue in April 1931, £431.7 million had been issued, three-quarters of it directly to the CRND. Between the beginning of 1929 and the last issue, the CRND was allotted £51.8 million of Local Loans, and its sales to the Bank were part of a programme of selling long gilts (Table 5.5). The proceeds helped the CRND to finance the development of the telephone network and to make advances to the Unemployment Fund.[21]

---

[18] Committee of Treasury minutes, 30 September 1931, BOE G8/60.

[19] The Bank also reduced its surplus margin requirements for lending to the discount market against Treasury bills, from 3% to 2%. Peppiatt, 'Discount market', 12 September 1955, BOE C42/3.

[20] The National Debt Commissioners and their functions are described in Box 5.2.

[21] Source: Pember and Boyle (1950).

Table 5.5 *Issue Department Transactions with CRND, 1929–32 (£m)*

Stock	Purchases from CRND	Sales to market (net)
4½% Treasury 1930/32	21.2	
4½% Treasury 1932/34	20.0	
3% Local Loans	86.5	67.4
4% Consols 1957 or after	24.0	24.0
Other	9.8	

Source: BOE C40/579, 580.

5.5.2 Making Markets in Illiquid Stocks

The Bank was willing to buy stocks which were not particularly liquid. An example was 2½% Treasury 1937, which had been offered in August 1933 in lieu of cash repayment to holders of a dollar bond issued in the United States in 1917.[22] Only £30.2 million was issued. The Issue Department did not deal in it until August 1934, but between then and December 1935 it bought £11.4 million, over a third of the entire issue. It sold £7 million to the CRND in February 1936, and bought £1.3 million in the four months before the stock matured on 1 February 1937.

5.5.3 Transactions with Bank of England Customers, Notably Overseas Central Banks

Many countries, notably British dominions and colonies, held their reserves in sterling, and in return had access to the London capital market.[23] Their central banks or currency boards needed sterling assets to hold in their reserves and were natural investors in gilts; moreover most or all of them were customers of the Bank of England. Their gilt transactions with the Bank of England are, I suspect, among those that are separately identified in the files by the fact that they did not incur expenses, such as brokers' commissions, in the monthly returns that the Bank provided to the Treasury.

---

[22] The bond was issued to private investors before the United States entered the war and was therefore not part of the post-war negotiations about inter-governmental war debts described by Self (2006).

[23] Drummond (1981, ch. 1.1).

5.5.4 Jobbing

The monthly returns that were sent to the Treasury show that the Issue Department acted as a jobber, notably in recent issues of which the Department had recently sold out all or nearly all of the amounts that it had acquired by underwriting. This activity has not as far as I am aware been recorded by other historians of the period, and I have not found any discussion of it in the archives, other than the bare transaction records.

For example, by the end of September 1933, the Bank had nearly exhausted its holdings of 3% Conversion 1948/53, which had been issued the previous November. Between October 1933 and June 1938, the Bank traded extensively in the stock, buying in total £37.8 million and selling £37.9 million. These operations appear to have been profitable, according to my rough calculations. Another example is 4% Consols 1957 or after, of which a tranche of £73.0 million was issued in March 1932 in a conversion offer. The Issue Department had held £4.3 million at the end of February, and acquired £55.4 million more by conversion. By the end of May, it had sold all but about £12 million of its holdings. Between June 1932 and September 1938, it bought £27.8 million and sold £37.6 million.

BOX 5.2 The National Debt Commissioners

The description of the National Debt Commission below consists of extracts from 'War administration of the National Debt Commission, 1939–1945', February 1946 (BOE C40/438).

The Commissioners for the Reduction of the National Debt – now commonly called the National Debt Commissioners – were established in 1786 by the National Debt Reduction Act of that year (26 Geo. III c.31). The first appointment comprised the persons holding for the time being the offices of Speaker, Chancellor of the Exchequer, Master of the Rolls, Accountant-General of the Court of Chancery (now Paymaster General of the Supreme Court)[24] and Governor and Deputy Governor of the Bank of England. The office of the Chief Baron of the Exchequer was added in 1808 and replaced in 1880 by that of the Lord Chief Justice ... It would seem that the real business was even then conducted by, or through the agency of, the Secretary and Comptroller General, the principal officer of the Commissioners, whose salary was, until 1854, charged upon the Consolidated Fund. At any rate that is the present

---

[24] From 1873 to 1925 the Paymaster General.

BOX 5.2 (cont.)

position, the Comptroller General acting, in major matters after consultation with officers of the Treasury and the Bank, who ordinarily represent the acting Commissioners, and communicating where he thinks fit – e.g. when he thinks it desirable to be fortified by superior direction – with the Chancellor and other active Commissioners.

The original function of the Commissioners was to administer the Sinking Fund established by the National Debt Reduction Act, 1786; and it was hoped that the inclusion among them of persons not identified with any political party, beside the chief financial Minister of the Crown, would secure the steady and regular reduction of the debt.

Needless to say this object was only partially fulfilled. Parliament retained the right of modifying its own decisions, and, though the Commission remained permanently in existence, financial exigencies deprived the standing provision of funds, made by the Act of 1786, of the permanence which had been contemplated. On the other hand from time to time opportunities were taken of placing other and additional funds at the disposal of the Commissioners . . . .

It is, perhaps, unnecessary here to observe that the increasing cost of war has time and again more than nullified the reduction of debt secured in the interval of peace.

The principal instruments for the reduction of debt are the Old Sinking Fund – i.e. any excess of revenue over expenditure in the preceding financial year; the New Sinking Fund – any unappropriated balance of the Permanent Debt Charge voted annually; the sale of annuities, (the stocks surrendered on a purchase, or, where the sale is made for cash, stock purchased with that cash, being cancelled); specific Sinking Funds devoted to the regular purchase and cancellation of particular stocks; unclaimed dividends, stock and redemption moneys; and donations and bequests, which in some instances are considerable.

A separate function of the Commissioners is the holding of public or semi-public funds of various kinds. This arose naturally out of the position of the Commissioners in relation to the Bank of England and the Stock Exchange. The first such fund was that of the Trustee Savings Banks (1817) followed by the Friendly Societies (1819) and, on its establishment, the Post Office Savings Bank (1861). These funds were followed by others resulting from the action of particular Government Departments, and culminating in the large National Insurance Funds of the present day. It is still however the case that some funds apparently similar to those entrusted to the Commissioners remain in the hands of other Government Departments. Legislative proposals now before Parliament provide for vesting in the Treasury a power of giving directions to the Commissioners as to their administration of certain of these funds.

5.6 The War Loan Conversion

The War Loan conversion of 1932 was the most important debt manage-ment operation of the inter-war period. In 1919 there were £4,482 million of gilts outstanding, of which no less than £2,011 million consisted of a single stock, 5% War Loan 1929/47.[25] Bearing in mind that the govern-ment intended to, and did, restore the gold standard, this was extremely expensive borrowing and a heavy burden on the public finances. By 1932, the size of War Loan had crept up to £2,085 billion, mainly as the net result of a series of conversion offers, in which investors were given the option to convert out of or into other stocks. Fortunately, the government had a call option from 1929 onwards, but the size of the stock – it was equivalent to about half a year's GDP – was such that the operation was bound to be risky and difficult. Converting War Loan successfully from a 5% coupon stock to a 3½% coupon stock with no final redemption date (1952 or after) was a major part of the cheap money policy that followed the departure from the gold standard in 1931. It was largely the achievement of the Bank of England Governor, Montagu Norman and his deputy, Sir Ernest Harvey.

A conversion of War Loan to a lower coupon had been widely expected, in the light of the economic depression, the suspension of the gold stan-dard, and Chamberlain's statement in Parliament that

I do not see any reason why, in the absence of any serious disturbances in other countries with which we have close commercial relations, there should not be for some time to come a continuance of the present situation, in which money is both cheap and plentiful . . . [26]

Nevertheless the yield of 3.5% offered on the new stock was lower than had been expected. The yield of 2½% Consols at the close of business on 30 June 1932, just before the conversion announcement, was 3.78%; the day after the announcement it was 3.58%, and a month after it was 3.44%. The change of 20–35 basis points can be taken as a rough indication of the unexpected component of the reduction in yields.[27] Chamberlain's statement is an example of forward guidance on interest rates, and shows that forward guidance, far from being a recent innovation, was in fact used

[25] Morgan (1952, table 10). Strictly speaking, the offer was an offer to investors to have their holdings of War Loan continued, but with modified conditions, including a lower coupon.

[26] HC Deb. 09 May 1932 vol. 265 c. 1673.

[27] Reinhart and Rogoff (2009) include the War Loan conversion in their table of domestic government defaults, but they are quite wrong to do so. The government had the option to redeem after 1929, and holders were not obliged to convert. See Weale (2010).

in the very earliest days of unfettered post-gold standard monetary policy.[28]

The conversion reduced government expenditure on debt interest by about £30 million a year, or 0.6% of GDP, and it lengthened the average maturity of the government's debt by replacing a dated stock (1929/47) with one having no final redemption date.[29] The saving of debt interest was widely welcomed, because it eased the constraints on other government spending; nevertheless the immediate fiscal and debt management effects were if anything deflationary.

The offer was open from July to September 1932. Conversions attracted a bonus of £1 per £100 nominal of stock converted if they were registered before 31 July, and 5 shillings (25p) of commission was paid to agents such as banks and stockbrokers. Extensive propaganda and 'moral suasion', together with an embargo on other issues enforced by the Bank of England, were deployed in support of the conversion. The embargo was partly removed in stages between August 1932 and January 1933, but foreign issues remained subject to control without any statutory basis, and in 1936 Chamberlain established a Foreign Transactions (Advisory) Committee to advise him 'both generally upon the scope of the restriction and also upon particular applications' in order 'to protect sterling exchange against sudden and dislocating strains.'[30]

There are already comprehensive and authoritative accounts of the conversion operation.[31] The conventional view is that the extent of the yield reduction involved a degree of 'price-making' by the authorities: they did not simply follow the market, but to some extent led it to where they wanted it to go. It can hardly be doubted that the experience of the War Loan conversion was influential in the setting of maximum yields for wartime issues in 1940, and in the attempt to get yields even lower in 1945–47 (see Chapter 6, 6.2 and Chapter 7, 7.2 and 7.3).

The conventional view has been challenged by some historians, who assert that the scale of the fall in yields can be explained by the fact that the interest saving held out the promise of cuts in income tax, which would

---

[28] Of course the term 'forward guidance' was not in use in the period covered by this book: as far as I know, what we now call forward guidance occurred, but was not the subject of economic analysis. I use the term in the absence of anything better.

[29] It was redeemed in 2015.

[30] HC Deb. 07 April 1936 vol. 310 cc. 2601–3. Sayers (1976, appendix 30) reproduces documents on the regulation of capital issues in London from 1915 to 1939.

[31] Nevin (1955, pp. 92–108), Sayers (1976, ch. 18B) and Wormell (1999, ch. 19).

enable pre-tax bond yields to fall without reducing post-tax yields.[32] The challenge is not credible, however. For one thing, the annual interest saving of £30 million represented only about 8% of the yield of income tax and surtax, so that even if all of the savings had been used to reduce income tax rates, the reduction would have been very modest.[33] And in any case, it would have been quite unrealistic, in the circumstances of widespread unemployment and dire poverty, to expect that the interest savings would be devoted to income tax reductions. In the event, income tax rates, which had been increased in September 1931, were not reduced until 1934, and then only a little.[34] In the conversion operation, the authorities acted as price-makers, not price-takers.

Official transactions in the secondary market, though larger than in most years, were notably modest in relation to the size of the conversion operation, and largely incidental (Table 5.6 shows transactions in War Loan). Indeed, they had to be modest, as the Issue Department's maximum gilt holding (£275 million at the time) was only a small fraction of the size of War Loan.[35] They included the famous purchase in July of £25 million of War Loan from the Midland Bank, which was unwilling to convert more than £5 million of its holdings of £30 million.[36]

The Bank was a seller as well as a buyer of War Loan, as Table 5.6 shows. And the Issue Department's operations in all gilts excluding forthcoming maturities between July and September amounted to net sales of £49.4 million (there were no new issues). The net sales were intended to sterilise the effect on domestic markets of the heavy purchases of gold and foreign exchange that were taking place at that time (see section 5.7), but they probably impaired the prospects of the conversion. Money market operations were expansionary, however. Bankers' balances in the Bank of England (head office) averaged £80.1 million in the second half of 1932, when the conversion operation was under way, compared with £68.1 million in the first half.[37]

There were severe delays in processing transfers in July 1932, as small investors sold their holdings of unassented 5% War Loan in response to demand from professional investors, which was inflated by the bonus that

---

[32] Capie, Mills and Wood (1986, p. 1122).

[33] Surtax was additional income tax levied on incomes above £2,000 a year, at increasing marginal rates.

[34] The basic rate of income tax was cut in 1934/35 by 10%, from 25% to 22.5%, and the highest marginal rate fell by 3.8%, from 66.25% to 63.75%.

[35] Wormell (1999, p. 616). Sayers (1957, p 53) was mistaken in suggesting that the Bank 'made large purchases of medium- and long-term bonds'.

[36] Sayers (1976, pp. 443–5) and Wormell (1999, p. 618).

[37] Source: BOE C1/80, author's calculations.

Table 5.6 *Bank of England Transactions in 5% War Loan 1929/47, July–November 1932 (£m)*

	Issue Department		Banking Department	
	Purchases	Sales	Purchases	Sales
July	36.7	23.6	11.6	4.5
	1.0 (assented)	3.6 (assented)		
	3.0 (assented after purchase)			
August	2.6		0	7.1
September		9.4 (assented)	5.5 (assented)	
October	5.0	1.5 (assented)		
November	2.0		2.4 (assented)	
Total	50.1	38.0	19.5	11.6

Sources: BOE C40/580, C1/80.
Note: 'Assented' stock was stock whose owners had agreed to convert, but which had not yet been converted; the conversion did not take place until 1 December.

was offered for conversions before the end of the month. The London Stock Exchange ruled that settlements could be delayed, but that meant that jobbers who bought War Loan could not know when it would be delivered. In order to maintain the functioning of the market, the Bank agreed both to buy unassented War Loan and to lend unassented War Loan from its own portfolio to the jobbers to facilitate settlements.[38] The loan transactions are not shown in Table 5.6.

After the War Loan conversion, the main objective of government debt management policy was to reduce the amount of Treasury bills in circulation. This meant continued sales of gilts, in order to finance the cash repayment of around £164 million of 5% War Loan, as well as purchases of gold and foreign exchange by the newly created Exchange Equalisation Account.[39]

5.7 Sterilising Gold Flows

In the vain attempt to maintain sterling on the gold standard in August and September 1931, the government and the Bank had borrowed the equivalent of £132 million, short-term, in New York and Paris. To repay

[38] Sayers (1976, p. 443) and Wormell (1999, p. 619).
[39] Nevin (1955, ch. IV), Howson (1975, pp. 92–9 and 126–33), and Howson (b1980).

these loans after the pound had left gold, they needed to sell sterling for gold and foreign currencies; in addition, the government wanted to keep sterling cheap in order to stimulate the economy. World gold production increased, and there was large-scale dishoarding from India and China, as the world gold standard gradually collapsed after 1931.[40]

After 1 July 1932, the innovation of the Exchange Equalisation Account (EEA) provided for automatic financing of UK official purchases of gold and foreign exchange by means of sales of Treasury bills. Until then, however, purchases made by the Issue Department had to be financed either by an increase in the note issue, or by running down other Issue Department assets. Between the end of September 1931 and the end of June 1932, the note issue and the bullion held in the Issue Department barely changed. However, during the same period, the external borrowings of £132 million were largely repaid out of purchased gold and foreign exchange.[41] Meanwhile, official gilt sales to the market were £149 million net, or £257 million excluding the Issue Department's purchases of forth-coming maturities, which continued during the period.[42]

When the EEA began operations, it had an endowment of £150 million of sterling.[43] Because its purchases of gold and foreign exchange were automatically financed by the sale of Treasury bills, they did not affect the balance sheet of the Bank of England, and the mechanism was therefore thought to insulate domestic monetary policy from flows of gold. However, the accumulation of reserves caused the total of Treasury bills in the market to increase; and the main objective of debt management policy after 1932 was to restrain the total of Treasury bills (section 5.2). Thus purchases of gold (EEA plus Issue Department) were sterilised in practice not by three-month Treasury bills but by gilts – a much more durable form of sterilisation, which might be called super-sterilisation – as well as by the rising banknote issue (Figure 5.1).[44]

In both 1933 and 1936, the EEA's accumulated purchases of gold exhausted its sterling resources, and gold was transferred to the Issue Department, in exchange for sterling assets, in order to enable the EEA to continue its purchases. The reductions in the fiduciary issue that

[40] See, for example, Bank for International Settlements (1939, ch. III).
[41] Sayers (1976, p. 420, note 3) says that the Banking Department also bought £10 million of foreign currencies in October 1931, and used £5 million for debt repayment early in November.
[42] Sayers (1976, p. 428) says that the sales were of the Issue Department's short-maturity gilt holdings, but the monthly statements sent to the Treasury show otherwise. It is true that £106 million of the short, 3% Treasury 1933/42 were sold net, but there were also net sales of £55 million of 4% Conversion 1940/44 and £61 million of 4% Consols.
[43] Howson (1980, p. 9).   [44] Lees (1953).

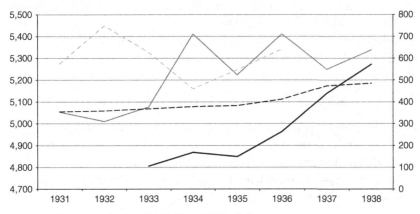

- — Gilts outstanding ex official holdings (31 March, lhs)
- – – Treasury bills in market (31 March, rhs)
- — Cumulative sterling cost of gold accumulation from end of June 1932 (31 March, rhs)
- – – Banknotes in circulation (31 March, rhs)

Figure 5.1 Gilts and Treasury Bills Outstanding, the Note Circulation, and Gold
Accumulation (£m), 1931–38
Sources: gilts and Treasury bills outstanding: Howson (1975, Appendix 2 table 1); gold:
United Kingdom (1951), author's calculations; banknotes in circulation: Bank of
England daily account books, BOE C1/79, 80.

occurred in 1933 and 1936 were the consequence of these transfers of
gold.[45] The gold purchases could have been financed by an increase in the
sterling capital of the EEA, but that would have required Parliamentary
approval. The gold transfers were £70 million and £114 million in 1933 and
1936 respectively, whereas the reductions in the fiduciary issue were only
£15 million and £60 million respectively, apparently because the public
demand for banknotes was rising fast as the economy recovered. Thus the
scope for gilt operations was not reduced *pro tanto* with the influx of gold.
Nevertheless, it is clear (Table 5.2) that net sales of gilts to the public in
1936 were made necessary by that year's reduction in the fiduciary issue.
Contrariwise, the increase in the fiduciary issue in 1939 reflected the
transfer of gold from the Issue Department to the EEA.

It would have been technically possible in 1933 and 1936 to maintain the
scope for gilt operations by leaving the fiduciary issue unchanged, increasing the note issue, and parking the excess of banknotes in the Banking
Department. The Banking Department could have financed the acquisition

---

[45] See Howson (1980) for a full account of the EEA's operations in the 1930s.

of notes by selling Treasury bills to the EEA, to replace the gold which the EEA had transferred to the Issue Department. This was not done, probably because Norman regarded it as important for confidence in post-gold-standard sterling to keep the fiduciary issue down.[46]

5.8 Rising Yields and Losses, 1935 Onwards

From 1935, bond yields increased as the economy recovered. The yield of 2½% Consols increased from 2.71% at the end of 1934 to 3.70% at the end of 1939, while the price of 3½% War Loan fell from 108⅝₆ to 93⅞₆.

The Issue Department, as a holder of gilts, faced losses which caused the Bank considerable anxiety:

Whenever the half-yearly revaluation shows a loss the Fiduciary Issue is uncovered for a period varying according to the amount of the loss and the income available for replacement.

The present figures show an uncovered position of approximately £7¾ million which, on the present basis of income and expenditure, will take five years to work off. However, the position may be worsened by further depreciation of securities and/or by future 'underwriting' of new Government issues.[47]

Not surprisingly, the size of the Issue Department's gilt portfolio and the scale of its dealing activities contracted sharply from 1937 onwards (Table 5.7). There were large sales of a range of gilts (net £6.6 million) in January 1938, probably intended to clear the decks and reduce risk, after which transactions were much sparser than hitherto. The Issue Department continued to underwrite new issues and to buy forthcoming maturities, but its other activities were reduced in scale or stopped altogether. The Bank was anxious for the Treasury to make good the deficiency in the Issue Department, and would not have wanted to weaken its case by involving the Issue Department in extraneous activities that might add to its losses. After lengthy correspondence with the Treasury, Norman received from the Chancellor, Sir John Simon, a carefully drafted latter in May 1938, which included the following:

---

[46] Clay (1957, p. 460).

[47] Peppiatt, 'Issue department securities', 9 April 1937, BOE G14/25. The losses would have been much larger had the Issue Department not run down its gilt holdings so much in 1936 and 1937. They could have been eliminated by revaluing the gold in the Issue Department, which was still valued at its Gold Standard price, but this was not done. They were revealed to the public in an article by Oscar Hobson in the News Chronicle, 'Why no profits from bank note issue last year?', 1 September 1938.

Table 5.7 *Issue Department Gilt Turnover, 1930–39 (£m)*

Year	Issue Dept purchases from secondary market	Issue Dept sales to secondary market	Net secondary market sales	Secondary market turnover	Secondary market turnover as % of stock of gilts
1929	42	71	28	113	2.1
1930	81	165	84	245	4.4
1931	45	68	23	113	2.1
1932	243	315	72	558	10.2
1933	136	282	147	418	7.4
1934	77	189	112	266	4.7
1935	74	55	−19	129	2.2
1936	113	215	102	329	5.7
1937	59	219	160	278	4.7
1938	36	35	−1	71	1.2
1939	30	13	−17	43	0.7

Sources: BOE C40/579 – 582, Pember and Boyle (1950), author's calculations.

I have now come to the conclusion that, while the precise contingencies which have led to the present state of affairs were not envisaged by those responsible for framing the 1928 Act, it was never intended that losses sustained from time to time in respect of securities held in the Issue Department should be for account of the Bank, and this I now confirm. It seems to me clear that, apart from the special circumstances that the losses on sales of investments have arisen from transactions made in the interests of H.M. Exchequer, it must follow as a general principle that the Exchequer which takes the profits (which I am aware in past years have been large) should also ultimately bear any losses, and I therefore agree that, in so far as the profits of the Department do not cover any such losses, they are to be regarded as the responsibility of H.M. Government.

However:

... there are no funds at the disposal of the Treasury which could be utilised in adjusting the present position. We shall have to rely therefore upon the accruing profits of the Issue Department to reduce the deficit over a period of years.[48]

The Bank of England did not provide any support to the market while yields were rising. Edward Holland-Martin expressed the Bank's attitude to market support uncompromisingly in 1939:

[48] Simon–Norman, 30 May 1938, BOE G14/25.

Mr. Francis, of the National Debt, telephoned to enquire what our policy was with regard to supporting the market in times of weakness. He stated that the Government broker had asked him yesterday whether he would be willing to give some support to the market: he had enquired of the Treasury who had told him that they did not concern themselves with the market position but that if he wished to take any action he must first consult the Bank.

I informed him that it was never our policy to support the market though it might be that on rare occasions when the weakness of the market appeared to be artificial, to give the Government broker discretion to purchase even a small amount of stock might have an effect quite out of proportion to the amount of money involved. I said, however, that if at any future time the Government broker suggested that some action of this kind would be useful, he should communicate with the Bank before any decision as to policy was reached.[49]

Turnover was exceptionally low in 1938 and 1939 (Table 5.7), no doubt because of the concern about losses described above, and perhaps also because, with the threat of war growing, the Bank was anxious to avoid creating any impression that it might be willing to provide market support. The policy as described by Holland-Martin in March 1939 was more austere than earlier in the decade.

The problem of the shortfall in the value of the Issue Department's assets was overcome by the Currency and Bank Notes Act 1939, which provided that any losses would be made good by a transfer of assets from the Exchange Equalisation Account. This was an act of pure obfuscation, since the EEA was not published in any detail. The Act also provided for the gold in the Issue Department to be valued at current prices, rather than the historic gold standard price.

5.9 The Structure of the Market

The main market for gilts was in the Stock Exchange, as it always had been. In 1938/39, there were 344 jobbing firms on the Exchange (equities as well as gilts), with 1,127 partners in all, an average of 3.3 partners per firm.[50] Nothing is known about their capital resources, as they all had to be partnerships or sole traders. The market must have been fairly robust: the jobbers managed to withstand the trauma of 1931 and the post-1935 fall in prices without any capital support. The largest gilt jobber was Francis and Praed, followed by Wedd Jefferson and Co. and Akroyd and Smithers. Even in the 1930s, though, the jobbers were concerned about competition

---

[49] Holland-Martin, untitled, 29 March 1939, BOE C40/437.　　[50] Michie (1999, table 7.1)

from the discount market.[51] Discount houses, which had originally been dealers in bills of exchange, financed by short-term deposits, had been the leading financial companies in London in the mid-late nineteenth century, but their dominance had been undermined, first by the reduction in the supply of inland bills of exchange, and later by the collapse of international trade which accompanied the onset of the Great Depression and which decimated the supply of international trade bills.[52] The discount houses were left with Treasury bills to deal in, but keeping the Treasury bill issue down was an objective of official policy, and the competition for the remaining supply was intense, so the potential for profit was meagre. Therefore the houses were anxious to find new sources of profit and it is not surprising that they took to gilt dealing.[53]

Discount houses had invested in gilts since the 1920s:

Bill business was not proving very lucrative at that time, and one or two of the larger units looked around for some more profitable use for their borrowings, and made one or two modest purchases of British Government short-dated bonds.

Little came of this movement in the early 1920s but gradually the seed took root and the plant developed. There was, initially, a marked reluctance on the part of lenders to take bonds as security, and it was not until after the financial crisis of 1931 that their general use as security became recognized by the banks and countenanced by the authorities.[54]

The Bank of England remained unwilling to lend to discount houses against gilt collateral until after the outbreak of war in 1939.[55]

The London clearing banks made large investments in gilts during the 1930s. Their holdings went up from £358 million at the end of 1929 to £905 million at the end of 1936.[56] They do not appear to have acted as market-makers, however. The use of short-term borrowing to finance gilt holdings by both the discount market and the clearing banks represented a partial repair of the rupture between the gilt market and the money market that had taken place in 1914 (Chapter 4).

---

[51] Michie (1999, pp. 215 and 248).
[52] On the decline of inland bills of exchange, see Nishimura (1971).
[53] King (1972), Scammell (1968) and Fletcher (1976) provide histories of the London discount market.
[54] Goodson (1962, p. 33). There was an ample supply of short gilts in the 1920s.
[55] Sayers (1976, p. 541).
[56] Source: Sheppard (1971, table (A) 1.8). This investment accounted for the entire increase in their assets over the period.

5.10 Minimum Prices and the Outbreak of War

Minimum gilt prices had been imposed in the First World War when the Stock Exchange reopened in January 1915, because of the jobbers' wish to avoid there being any record of transactions at prices which would compel them to write down the value of their assets.[57] In June 1938, in pre-war contingency planning, minimum prices were discussed, inconclusively, between the Stock Exchange and the Bank of England.[58] Shortly before the agreement at Munich between Chamberlain, Daladier, Hitler and Mussolini on 29 September 1938, which endorsed Germany's annexation of parts of Czechoslovakia, gilt prices fell heavily, market liquidity dried up and minimum prices were reintroduced, at the unilateral initiative of the jobbers:

> These [the principal gilt jobbers] proposed to draw up to-night a list of minimum prices below which they (jobbers and the market) would mutually agree not to deal. This action was unofficial and was designed to safeguard their position in the event of bad news to-night: it was hoped that it would not be necessary to put it into force.
>
> The Committee proposed to support this action if necessary by making use of their power to exponge [sic] markings below the agreed minimum prices.
>
> If this system is put into operation it will be done to-morrow for one day's trial and if it proves satisfactory the Committee may agree to a subsequent system of minimum prices.[59]

It seems clear that, as in 1915, the jobbers wanted minimum prices to protect their capital against the risk of a serious fall in the gilt prices recorded on the Stock Exchange, which they would have used in valuing their assets. As it was, the collapse of gilt prices just before Munich 'was enough to wipe out the whole of the published capital and reserves of the Clearing Banks'.[60] After Munich, gilt prices rose and the minimum price agreement lapsed.

Minimum prices were discussed again in spring 1939. As in September 1938, the initiative came from the Stock Exchange; the

---

[57] Wormell (1999, p. 69).

[58] Cobbold–Chairman of General Purposes Committee, Stock Exchange, 7 July 1938, BOE C40/422. On the First World War, see 'Summary of measures taken in 1914 on outbreak of war', BOE C40/422, and Osborne and Allport (1950, p. 1513). See also Sayers (1976, pp. 578–81).

[59] Holland-Martin, 'Stock Exchange', 26 September 1938, BOE C40/422. 'Bad news' meant no agreement. At the opening of business on 26 September, the spread between selling and buying prices of War Loan was five points (TDA, 27 September 1938).

[60] Clay (1957, p. 463). The banks also had unpublished reserves.

Bank of England and the Treasury were sceptical though acquiescent, and they made it clear to the Stock Exchange that 'the Treasury saw no possibility of preventing a black market outside the Stock Exchange.'[61]

The German-Soviet non-aggression pact, signed in Moscow on Wednesday 23 August 1939, made it seem much more likely that Britain and France would go to war with Germany. On the next day:

At the outset dealers in the gilt-edged market refused to make prices pending consultation with the [Stock Exchange] Committee as to the best method of meeting what threatened to be a difficult position. In the event it was decided about midday to establish minimum prices at the lower level of the double quotations given in the Stock Exchange lists of the previous day.[62]

Again, the initiative came from the jobbers. The Chairman and Deputy Chairman of the Stock Exchange told Norman of the decision at 12.30pm, immediately after the Bank of England Court meeting, and Norman recorded in his diary: 'We don't interfere now – but don't let prices freeze up & make dealings impossible (because prices absurd).'[63]

At the Court meeting, which began at 11.30am and which must therefore have coincided with the decision on minimum prices, Bank rate was increased from 2% to 4%. The increase was a last-minute decision, and had not been expected in the market.[64] The decision on minimum prices was therefore taken in ignorance of the Bank rate move. Minimum prices froze the gilt market in the Stock Exchange, but over the next few days longer-dated gilts moved above the minima. The market was frozen again from 7 September, when it reopened after the outbreak of war, until mid-October, when the recovery was helped by the reversal of the Bank rate increase, which occurred in two stages (4% to 3%, and 3% to 2%), and was completed by 26 October. I have detected no sign of any official purchases of gilts, but bankers' balances at the Bank of England head office were generally higher after late August than before (Figure 5.2), suggesting that the Bank was indirectly stimulating demand for gilts by providing ample funds to the banking system.

---

[61] On the attitude of the Treasury and Bank of England, Osborne and Allport (1950, pp. 1516–17), and papers in the Bank of England archive, e.g. Phillips–Catterns, 28 April 1939, BOE C40/422; on the black market, Cobbold, 'War measures: Stock Exchange', 1 May 1939, BOE C40/422.

[62] 'Stock Exchange', *The Times*, 25 August 1939, TDA.

[63] Norman diaries, 24 August 1939, BOE ADM34/28.

[64] Sayers provides extensive accounts of the Bank rate increase in his histories of wartime financial policy (1956, pp. 156–9) and of the Bank of England (1976, pp. 573–5).

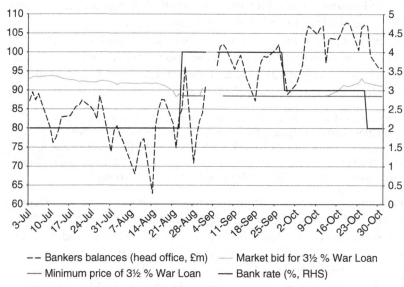

-- Bankers balances (head office, £m)   —— Market bid for 3½ % War Loan
—— Minimum price of 3½ % War Loan   —— Bank rate (%, RHS)

Figure 5.2 Bank Rate, Bankers' Balances, and the Price of 3½% War Loan,
July–October 1939
Sources: bankers' balances: BOE C1/87; War Loan prices: TDA, FTHA;
Bank rate: Bank of England website.

It is not too much to say that the gilt jobbers tried to force the authorities to do whatever was necessary to get gilt prices up: the government could not afford to have the gilt market frozen for an extended period. The jobbers took the risk that an alternative market would develop outside the Stock Exchange, however, and that is what happened, as the discount houses became more active traders in short gilts, with official encouragement (Chapter 6, 6.3).

6

Government Debt Management and the Gilt Market in the Second World War

6.1 Financial Controls

When war broke out, statutory controls on finance and commerce were imposed by the Defence (Finance) Regulations 1939. Purchases of foreign exchange and gold, the export of bank notes and securities, and loans to non-residents, all required official approval. Foreign exchange was made available for approved purposes at a fixed exchange rate, and foreign currency receipts had to be surrendered for sterling. The controls were later extended to non-resident holdings of assets in the UK.[1] Privately owned gold and balances denominated in specified 'hard' currencies were requisitioned by the government, and securities marketable outside the UK had to be registered and were subject to being taken over by the Treasury. All capital issues, not just foreign ones, were subject to Treasury consent, and the Foreign Transactions (Advisory) Committee was given wider responsibilities and renamed the Capital Issues Committee.[2] Statutory controls of varying degrees of restrictiveness were to remain in force until long after the war.

6.2 Debt Management

It was widely accepted in pre-war contingency planning that, in the event of war, the debt management mistakes that were thought to have been made in 1914–18 should not be repeated. In April 1939, Henry Clay of the Bank of England had recommended measures to facilitate government

---

[1] Osborne and Allport (1950, pp. 321–59, 714–30).
[2] Osborne and Allport (1950, p. 1528).

borrowing during wartime. The influential J.M. Keynes set out similar ideas in articles and letters in *The Times*.[3] Clay's recommendations included the following:

a. Requiring insurance companies to invest accruing cash, and non-financial companies to invest undistributed profits, in new government issues.
b. Maximum interest rates on deposits in banks and building societies.
c. 'Maximum rates of interest for medium and long term issues by H.M. G. to be fixed at the outset and adhered to for all subsequent issues.' And ' . . . avoid the practice followed in the last war of giving better terms to lenders in successive issues.' 'No conversion rights' (in the First World War, gilt buyers had been able to convert at low cost into later issues made at higher yields).[4]
d. 'Tap issues to be to be put out (say one of medium-term and one of long-term) with an intimation that H.M. Government does not intend to borrow subsequently at any higher rates . . . '[5]

These ideas were largely implemented, though not all immediately. Norman recommended that the government should rule out any increase in gilt-edged interest rates after the first wartime issue, but Sir Frederick Phillips of the Treasury had long thought that in 'the last resort we have got to get the money' and that 'if the saver prefers to give up saving rather than accept a low rate of interest we can do nothing but raise the rate of interest.'[6]

Pre-war issuing practices continued into 1940. In January, £350.3 million of 4½% Conversion 1940/44 was called and 2% Conversion 1943/45 offered in exchange. Conversions amounted to £245.3 million, of which £65.1 million were by the Issue Department.[7] The discount houses were told that they had to convert all their holdings, but they would have been unable to finance the conversion stock at an interest rate low enough to

---

[3] For example, 'Crisis finance – an outline of policy', 17 and 18 April 1939, and 'Borrowing by the state', 24 and 25 July 1939, TDA. Keynes recommended a maximum interest rate of 2.5%.

[4] Clay, 'Borrowing in War-Time' and 'Notes on War Finance', 14 April 1939, quoted by Osborne and Allport (1950, pp. 72–6). Osborne and Allport provide a full account of the general debate on the domestic financing of the war in their chapters II (pp. 72–104) and V (pp. 154–7).

[5] Memorandum of 18 April 1939, quoted by Osborne and Allport (1950, p. 156, footnote).

[6] Peden (2000, p. 317); quotation from note by Phillips dated 26 April 1939 is in Osborne and Allport (1950, pp. 82–3).

[7] Author's estimate.

provide an adequate margin, and the Bank bought £4.55 million from them.[8]

The reasons why an interest rate of 3% was chosen for the first long-term issue of the war are not evident from the archives. The Bank of England's internal historians say that 'An interest rate of 3% had always been contemplated', but provide no further information.[9] The issue for cash of 3% War Loan 1955/59 at par was conventional, in that the prospectus published on 5 March specified the amount to be issued, subscriptions were invited a week thence, on 12 March, and the subscription lists were closed on the 13th. The Bank of England ensured that the banking system had plenty of cash.[10] However, there was the risk that yields would rise, as they had done in the First World War. When the Chancellor, Sir John Simon, announced the new issue in Parliament on 5 March, he was asked about the yields of future issues. He had not been warned to expect such a question, and he declined to undertake that no future issue would be made at a higher rate.[11] He thereby ignored one of Clay's recommendations. Of the £302.5 million issued, £115.7 million was bought by the Issue Department and £29.7 million by the CRND.

The result was regarded as a failure, at a time of grave military peril. It could easily be attributed to the risk of rising yields, though I have found no documents making such an attribution. That risk would be reduced if the government announced its yield objective and if the minimum price levels that had been established in August 1939 (Chapter 5, 5.10) were adjusted upwards, and re-set at levels consistent with yields only a little higher than the government's objectives. Minimum prices could thereby be transformed from a device designed to protect the jobbers into an instrument of government debt management policy – a form of forward guidance.

The initiative for a rise in minimum prices came from Norman, who had overcome his earlier scepticism, but it was opposed by Treasury officials, especially Phillips, who was alarmed by it. According to Phillips, Norman's arguments were:

---

[8] Osborne and Allport (1950, pp. 100–1, 1324). The purchases from the discount market were made by the Banking Department. The Bank's instruction to the discount market to convert nearly caused Gillett Brothers to go out of business (Sayers 1968, pp. 117–19).

[9] Osborne and Allport (1950, p. 95).

[10] Bankers' deposits in the Bank of England were £122 million on 5 March, compared with an average £87 million and standard deviation of £5½ million in February.

[11] 'Statement by the Chancellor of the Exchequer' and 'Notes for possible supplementaries', 5 March 1940, NA T160/990 F16782, Sayers (1956, pp. 198–201), HC Deb. 05 March 1940 vol. 358 cc. 209–10.

a. that gilts would recover more quickly from any setback if there were minimum prices at a fairly high level;
b. that a substantial fall in gilt prices 'would put many City institutions into an embarrassed condition, owing to the effect of that fall on their balance sheets.'
c. If gilts became unsaleable owing to minimum prices, holders needing money urgently could rely on their bankers for advances.[12]

Phillips was concerned that in a market frozen by higher minimum prices, new issues would be difficult or impossible, and that minimum prices could not be effectively policed. In an extreme situation, the government would have to choose between reducing minimum prices and tolerating a frozen gilt market for the duration of the war.[13]

The Chancellor, Sir John Simon, was unable to make a decision. The matter was decided by the Prime Minister, Chamberlain, whom Norman persuaded after meeting him alone.[14] Neville Chamberlain may be regarded as the pioneer of forward guidance, having issued it in both 1932 (Chapter 5, 5.5) and 1940.

Accordingly, minimum prices were re-set, and the Chancellor, when announcing the result in Parliament after an unusually long delay on 18 March, provided the forward guidance that he had refused on the 5th:

The policy of the Government is to aim at stability of interest rates and to secure that the yields offered on future loans, whatever their type, shall, after making due allowance for such factors as the periods of the loans, be in agreement with the level of interest rates established by the terms of the recent 2 per cent. Conversion Loan and of the 3 per cent. loan just issued. In these circumstances I welcome the action taken to-day by the committee of the London Stock Exchange in announcing a revised list of minimum prices for Government securities. The new minima bear a closer relationship to existing prices than those fixed on the outbreak of the war and may be taken as evidence of the desire on the part of the authorities concerned to co-operate in the policy of maintaining interest rates at the present level.[15]

Despite this forward guidance, the Issue Department sold only very small amounts of the new War Loan before the end of June, the market being set

---

[12] Phillips, 'Minimum prices', 13 March 1940, NA T 177/55.
[13] Phillips, 'Minimum prices', 13 March 1940, NA T 177/55.
[14] Peppiatt, 'Minimum prices', 5 February 1940; Norman, 7 February 1940; BOE C40/422; Norman's diary, 14–15 March 1940, BOE ADM34/29; Clay (1957, p. 470); Sayers (1976, p. 587). Wicker (1969) describes the analogous debate in the United States, which took place in 1941–42.
[15] HC Deb. 18 March 1940 vol. 358 cc. 1648–9.

back by the German invasion of Belgium and the Netherlands on 10 May.[16] And during June, after British armed forces had been evacuated from Dunkirk and when France was overrun by Germany, secondary market prices fell to the new minimum levels for a time (see below). These alarming circumstances might have led the government to abandon the 3% interest ceiling. But it did not panic, thanks, according to Sayers, to the growing influence of Keynes and other economists. The gilt market recovered: 'the war news ceased to get any worse, the nation gathered new courage, and the Governor of the Bank inspired some buying by the institutional investors.'[17] There were no unusual gilt purchases by the Bank (Issue or Banking Department), and no unusual increase in bankers' balances at the Bank of England.

The strategy thus survived. The government introduced Treasury Deposit Receipts in July, giving it the power to require the banks to place deposits of specified amounts with the Treasury for six-month terms, thus providing a fall-back in case sales of gilts and other debt instruments were insufficient.[18] TDRs could be regarded as addressing Phillips' objection to a maximum interest rate for gilts: the government did need the money, but if all else failed, it could now compel the banks to provide it, by means of an instrument which was less liquid than Treasury bills.[19]

The government pressed on with its gilt programme but changed its technique. From June 1940, new gilts were sold continuously 'on tap' directly to the public. When a new issue was announced, no maximum amount was specified, and there was no pre-announced closing date for applications.[20] The yields were fixed, and, in announcing the first tap issue (2½% National War Bonds 1945/47) on 24 June, the Lord Chancellor (the former Sir John Simon) made it clear that the yield was 'on exactly the same general interest level' as the 3% War Loan.[21] Each issue was offered at par. The authorities waited to re-enter the long market until the turn of 1940/41, when they issued 3% Savings Bonds 1955/65 and 2½% National War Bonds 1946/48 at the same time as they closed the 1945/47s.

---

[16] It had sold its holdings by the end of October 1941, including £40 million to the CRND.

[17] Sayers (1956, pp. 201, 204). This may have been a reference to Norman's intercession with the insurance companies (see below).

[18] HC Deb. 04 July 1940 vol. 362 cc. 1033–4W.

[19] Osborne and Allport (1950, pp. 139–40), Sayers (1956, pp. 220–5). I have found no direct link in the archives between the increase in minimum gilt prices and the introduction of TDRs.

[20] As already noted, the word 'tap' has slightly different meanings when applied to issues during and immediately after the war, and to peacetime issues.

[21] HL Deb. 25 June 1940 vol. 116 c. 668.

Norman told the British Insurance Association early in January 1941 that
the 3% Savings Bonds 'had been designed particularly to meet their needs,
since it was realised that the continuance of loans on a 2 or 2½% basis only
would have jeopardised the fulfilment of their long term commitments.'[22]
From then until the end of the war, there were always two issues available
on tap – a short/medium and a long. Each issue, when it was withdrawn,
was replaced with a slightly less attractive one: the same yield, but a longer
maturity.[23] Thus the yield curve shifted very gradually downwards and the
public was put under continuous pressure to invest in gilts before the terms
got worse. Keynes called it the 'Sibylline books' principle.[24]

Short-medium National War Bonds, yielding 2.5% for maturities eventually stretching to 1954/56, were on offer more or less continuously from
June 1940 to December 1945, and long-term Savings Bonds, yielding 3%
for maturities beginning with 1955/65 and ending with 1965/75, from
January 1941 until December 1945. Issues of National War Bonds ranged
in size from £426 million to £810 million; Savings Bond issues were rather
larger, ranging from £713 million to £1,057 million (Appendix C). None
was more than half the size of the First World War loan.[25]

The strategy ran the risk that the war would go on so long that the policy
of gradually lowering the yield curve would become unsustainable, as it did
when pushed too far after the war (Chapter 7, 7.3). Long-term yields fell
from 4.1% at the minimum price levels in force at the end of September
1939, to a little more than 3% in early 1942; they then increased gently until
Autumn 1944, when they fell back below 3% as the military situation
improved (Figure 6.1).[26] And over the six years 1940–45, net gilt sales
were £5.8 billion net, or 37% of the government's current account deficit.
Treasury Deposit Receipts raised £1.6 billion, Treasury bills £3.1 billion,
and Ways and Means advances £0.2 billion.[27]

Moral suasion played a role in the turnaround in the gilt market from June
1940. On 25 June, the *Times* said that 'large subscription to the new issue of
bonds [the 1945/47s] is as much a duty and necessity as the intensive

[22] Osborne and Allport (1950, p. 91). Insurance companies bought £93 million of the £713 million of 1955/65s that were issued (Osborne and Allport, 1950, p. 171).
[23] See Sayers (1956, p. 206), Howson (1988, p. 252). The gradual lengthening of the maturities of successive issues was noted by *The Times* when the successor to the 1945/47s was announced. No doubt *The Times* had been carefully briefed. See 'City notes', 28 December 1940, TDA.
[24] Keynes, 'War loan policy', 19 November 1940, NA T175/118.
[25] See Sayers (1956, ch. V) for a fuller discussion.
[26] Sayers (1956, pp. 200–3) discusses the risks.
[27] Source: Osborne and Allport (1950, p. 130).

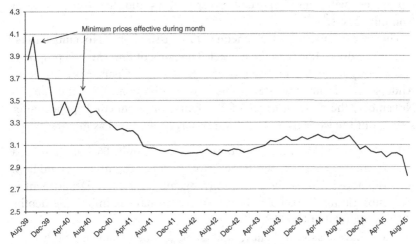

Figure 6.1 2½% Consol Yields, 1939–45

productive effort which munition and aircraft workers are now making.'[28] Insurance companies had not bought much of the March 1940 War Loan, and on 27 June Norman wrote to the chairman of the British Insurance Association enjoining his members to invest the net amount of the annual growth of their funds in government securities. The association issued investment guidance to its members in January 1941, after further discussion.[29]

During the war, the Issue Department continued its routine purchases of stocks approaching maturity. It had sold nearly all of its holdings of 3% War Loan 1955/59 by October 1941. The government's objectives in the bond market were to keep yields low and maximise sales; it might have been thought that this would mean that the Issue Department needed to support the market at times, but the Issue Department's net purchases were generally small; the Banking Department also made a few small purchases.[30] From time to time, there were 'savings weeks' in which the public was exhorted to buy national savings instruments or gilts; for each week a target was set and the results announced. It was thought desirable, as propaganda, to announce that the targets had been met or exceeded. On occasions when this was not in fact the case, investing institutions or the commercial banks were pressed to make up the difference. Initially the Bank of England resisted pressure to subscribe itself. It later relented, but subscribed only modestly to wartime

---

[28] 'City notes', 25 June 1940, TDA.   [29] Osborne and Allport (1950, pp. 90–1).
[30] On the Banking Department purchases, see Osborne and Allport (1950, pp. 1324–5).

tap issues, with one important exception, as did the National Debt Commissioners.[31]

The exception was 1¾% Exchequer 1950, issued on 7 November 1944, and priced out of line with the market. The Bank of England had proposed a 2% coupon, but had been overruled by the Chancellor, Sir John Anderson.[32] From the start, sales were disappointing, and on 23 November, the Chief Cashier of the Bank, Sir Kenneth Peppiatt, after setting out the week-by-week sales thus far, commented as follows:

1. ... This makes the disappointing total of only £6½ million in a fortnight, of which the Issue Department accounts for £1 million. [Footnote: Under the present arrangement the Issue Department is subscribing £500,000 a week.] Today we have plumbed the depths with a total of £20,000.

2. We have reason to believe that there will be certain relatively substantial subscriptions in due course from such people as the Railway Trust Funds and Courtaulds. Moreover, when –
   a) the Market recovers from its recent indigestion,
   b) the banks get over the end of their year; and
   c) the Bond becomes a 5-year maturity, we shall no doubt see subscriptions from various quarters, including the Discount Market and India.

3. However that may be, the results published weekly in the meantime can have nothing but a discouraging effect on potential subscribers. And the purpose of this note is to enquire whether for a time we should not consider each Tuesday (the end of the published week) making additional subscriptions for account of the Issue Department in order to make a better showing.[33]

Peppiatt's proposal was accepted. By 27 March 1945, the Issue Department had £141 million out of £199 million then in issue, and when the tap was closed on 12 June it had £225 million out of £327 million.[34]

In 1943, the Issue Department began acquiring long-dated gilts from the CRND and selling them into the market, thereby lengthening the average maturity of the debt held by the public. The CRND received in exchange gilts approaching redemption. The total of long-dated gilts

---

[31] Osborne and Allport (1950, p. 155).
[32] Catto–Eady, 10 October 1944, Peppiatt, 13 October 1944, Eady–Catto, 24 October 1944, BOE C40/450.
[33] Peppiatt–Governors, '1¾% Exchequer Bonds 1950', 23 November 1944, BOC C40/450.
[34] Osborne and Allport (1950, p. 186).

passed from the CRND to the Issue Department to the market in this way was £366 million over the three financial years 1943–44 to 1945–46.[35] As a *quid pro quo* for being able to draw on the CRND's gilt holdings, in 1946 the Issue Department transferred to the CRND £100 million of 1¾% Exchequer 1950 in exchange for Ways and Means Advances, accompanied by a promise that the Bank would repurchase the bonds if the CRND needed cash: this provided the CRND with the assurance of liquidity.[36]

The war was financed much more cheaply than that of 1914–18 (Chapter 4). The difference partly reflected better planning, including the immediate recognition that the war might be a long one, and the greater ruthlessness of the state in asserting and exploiting its monopoly power in the bond market and its power over the banks.

6.3 The Structure of the Gilt Market

By using the tap technique during the war, the government circumvented the secondary market in gilts. Continuous tap sales absorbed savings as they accumulated, and there was no need for intermediaries to perform a warehousing function, holding gilts that had been issued by the government until demand emerged from the investing public. And the yields of tap issues were fixed by government decision, so that the need for intermediaries to assist in price discovery was limited. The role of the secondary market was confined to that of providing a forum where investors could buy and sell from and to each other, subject to the various restrictions that were in force in the Stock Exchange, including minimum prices.

The Stock Exchange languished. Turnover (not just of gilts) 'appears to have peaked in 1936/37 and then fallen to half that level by 1938/39. With the outbreak of war turnover fell further, reaching half its prewar level by 1940/41. It was only after that date that turnover began to pick up, through [*sic*] not returning to its 1930s peak until after the end of the war, and then only in nominal terms.'[37] Many of the people who had worked in the market before the war were in the armed forces. By 1945, the number of jobbing firms (equities as well as gilts) had fallen to 254 from 344 in 1938/39: this did not reflect concentration into larger units: the average number of partners

---

[35] 'War administration of the National Debt Commissioners 1939–45', February 1946, BOE C40/438. Detailed statistics are provided in a note by Francis, 8 August 1945, BOE C40/438. Earlier in the war the NDC had been a buyer of long gilts, in order to boost their income.

[36] Holland-Martin–Yeomans, 23 January 1946, BOE C40/438, Francis–Holland-Martin, 6 March 1946, BOE C40/438.

[37] Michie (1999, p. 302).

per firm was barely changed at 3.4.[38] In December 1944, *The Times* noted the shortage of capital in the Stock Exchange partnerships, particularly among the gilt-edged jobbers, and the difficulty of building it up.[39] Moreover, the jobbers Wedd Jefferson complained in 1944 that much business in short-dated gilts (under two years) was by-passing the Stock Exchange because the brokers' minimum commission of 0.125% was too high. It was instead being done by the banks and discount houses.[40]

Short gilts were very good business for the discount houses, which thereby prospered during the war. The government's interest rate policy 'ensured a steadily rising market for bonds … Running yields on bonds were as high as 2½ per cent as against call money at 1¼ from the clearing banks', and the houses could borrow even more cheaply from other banks.[41]

Norman used his considerable influence in the 1930s and early 1940s to strengthen the financial foundations of the discount market, through mergers and capital increases.[42] As already noted, before the war the Bank would not lend to discount houses against gilts, but it began doing so soon after war broke out.[43] A little later, Norman warned the discount market that 'any rights of Dis Mkt to have accommodation here are on approved Bills – not Bonds.' In other words, the Bank reserved the right to refuse to lend against bonds – an unsubtle warning against over-exposure to gilts.[44]

By 1942 Norman had concluded that the discount market could play a useful role as market-makers in short gilts: 'the limited resources of the Stock Exchange partnerships had proved insufficient to deal with the increased [wartime] turnover.'[45] It is not surprising that Norman had reached this conclusion, as in 1937 he had set £300,000 as the minimum capital resources for discount houses, while the resources of the Stock Exchange jobbers were unknown to anyone except the partners.[46] And the jobbers' unilateral decisions to impose minimum prices in 1938 and

---

[38] Michie (1999, Table 7.1).

[39] 'City notes: Stock Exchange capital', 18 December 1944, TDA.

[40] Michie (1999, p. 307).

[41] Scammell (1968, p. 227). See also Fletcher (1976, pp. 58–61).

[42] Clay (1957, pp. 465–6), Sayers (1976 ch. 20E), Scammell (1968, pp. 210–17), Fletcher (1976, p. 51).

[43] Sayers (1976, p. 541). The procedures had been worked out in pre-war contingency planning (Item 1 of agenda for Committee of London Clearing Bankers' Chief Executive Officers, enclosure A, 31 July 1939, BOE G1/39).

[44] Norman's diary, 28 September 1939, BOE ADM34/28.

[45] Osborne and Allport (1950, p. 48).   [46] Sayers (1976, p. 543).

1939 might well have caused Norman to regard them as unreliable, though I have seen no direct evidence of this. It seems likely that much of the secondary market in short gilts migrated away from the Stock Exchange during the early years of the war.[47] During 1942, Norman told the Chairman of the Discount Houses Committee that 'the 4 or 5 big Cos [companies] ought to be ready to deal in their wares at <u>any</u> time: to be free jobbers in <u>short</u> Bonds: to be recognized as such. – it ought not to be only U.D. Co [Union Discount Company]'[48] And, reviewing the year 1943, the Principal of the Bank of England Discount Office reported that 'As regards general policy the market know that they are expected, within the limits of their capacity, to act as jobbers in short bonds and they have been given the necessary dealers facilities here.'[49]

The larger discount houses established themselves as effective jobbers in the last two years of the war:

In the big houses ... the jobbing function has become highly developed. In the professional circle it had long been known that the big discount companies could often absorb or supply larger lines of stock than the stock market could easily handle, and could at times quote finer prices. Professional business, therefore, often came direct to such houses, without passing through the Stock Exchange. Much of it also came 'direct' through stockbrokers, although in 1944 the Stock Exchange Committee ... made a rule that brokers must not thus by-pass the stock market jobbers unless it was certain that they could get a better price outside the 'House' [Stock Exchange] than within it. Now, therefore, a stock-broker who obtains a quotation in Lombard Street [discount market] must always give the jobbers a chance to better it before he confirms the order – but the confirmation often comes.[50]

During the war, the discount houses' gilt books grew both in size and in average maturity: between the end of 1939 and the end of 1945, the houses' holdings of bonds with more than a year to redemption rose from £77 million to £194 million and the average maturity of their over-one-year bond books increased from 1.6 years to 3.4 years (Figure 8.3).[51] Holding gilts financed by short-term borrowing would have been very profitable with an upward-sloping and fairly stable yield curve, and the discount

---

[47] As already noted, the Stock Exchange was languishing while gilt turnover was increasing.

[48] Norman, annotation on table showing discount houses' capital resources, 31 December 1942, BOE C47/39. In the same annotation he added that 'the smaller ½ doz concerns ought to increase their capital to or towards £1 mil – not by amalgamation.' Union was the largest discount house.

[49] Bull, 'Discount market – year 1943', 16 February 1944, BOE C47/39.

[50] King (1947, p. 179).

[51] Author's calculations, based on the annual discount market reviews written by the Principal of the Bank of England Discount Office (BOE C47/39 and 40).

houses' total capital increased from £19.3 million to £22.3 million. The Bank of England 'did not expect to be asked to lend against bonds with over five years to run' and required a surplus collateral margin of 5% for loans against under-five-year gilts, but 'without an effective bank rate neither of these requirements has any practical effect in limiting the size or currency [maturity] of their bond books': the houses could borrow on easier terms in the market.[52]

Market liquidity was stressed in December 1943, when the clearing banks appear to have sold gilts heavily in anticipation of the end-year spike in their liquidity needs.[53] The last day of the year was a Friday, so that the banks' needs were augmented by the public's usual increased demand for bank-notes over the weekend. To give an idea of the order of magnitude, between Tuesday 30 November and Friday 31 December, total deposit balances in the Bank of England rose by £121.6 million and the amount of notes outside the Bank of England by £57.6 million. The banks financed at least some of the drain on their liquidity by selling gilts, and their sales of gilts drove all short yields up temporarily. The market yield of 2½% National War Bonds 1951/53 rose above the fixed 2½% available on the current, slightly longer-dated, 1952/54 tap stock, and demand must have been diverted from the tap stock into the secondary market (Figure 6.2). The Issue Department did little: it bought £1 million of National War Bonds 1945/47 but sold £250,000 1949/51s among total net purchases of £15.2 million.

Evidently Norman was concerned that the market had been unable to accommodate the sales more easily. On 6 January 1944, he discussed with the discount market 'pushing all short B^ds (5 years) to [discount] mkt & away from S. Ex. Could they handle <u>all</u> that might come? adjourned till next week.'[54] The following day, Norman held a meeting with the senior partners of the three leading gilt jobbing firms, at their request; they had refused to be accompanied by the Chairman of the Stock Exchange.[55] Norman recorded the meeting tersely:

---

[52] Bull, 'Discount market – year 1944', 29 January 1945, BOE C47/39.

[53] The clearing banks all published weekly statements, but not all on the same day of the week, and each bank held more cash and liquid assets on statement days than other days. The practice was known as 'window-dressing'. They all had to publish end-year and end half-year statements, however, so that the banking system as a whole demanded larger balances in the Bank of England on 30 June and 31 December than on other days (Nevin and Davis 1970 pp. 139–41).

[54] Norman's diary, 6 January 1944, BOE ADM34/33.

[55] The firms were Akroyd and Smithers, Francis and Praed, and Wedd Jefferson and Co. The account of one of the jobbers, G.A. Monkhouse of Francis and Praed, makes it clear that

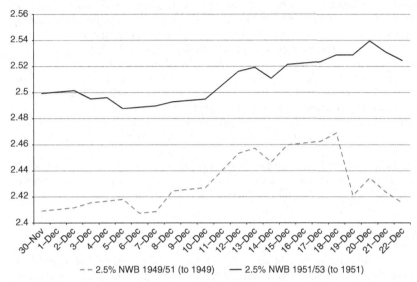

Figure 6.2 National War Bond Yields (Market Offers), December 1943

Agreed results of a long private conversation with Langley Smithers, J.E. Longuet-Higgins and G.A. Monkhouse, which I am to discuss with E.S.C. [Edward Cripps, the Government Broker].

1. Dealings by the Discount Market up to five years are accepted and indeed welcomed as inevitable.
2. These three Jobbers ask that as regards longer stocks they should be free through E.S.C. to send here and swap one long for another, or in times of pressed sales to sell for cash, or under other conditions to buy for cash.

In any case E.S.C. to be satisfied of the need.[56]

Each of the jobbers present made a more extensive record of the meeting, perhaps at the request of the Government Broker, who did not attend the meeting. Taken together, they are much more revealing.

Mr Longuet-Higgins reported:

We told him [Norman] that recently we had found that an increasing amount of business, particularly in shorts, was being done outside the Stock Exchange. The Governor explained that under his direction and guidance the Discount Market

the meeting was held at the jobbers' request: 'J.H. [Longuet-Higgins] thanked him for seeing us . . . ' (Monkhouse, 11 January 1944, BOE C132/1). Norman's diary records that 'they refuse to come with R.B.P. [Pearson]' (7 January 1944, BOE ADM34/33).

[56] Norman, 7 January 1944, BOE C40/422.

had been reorganised and strengthened in order to carry an increasing amount of shorts – less than five years to run. He asked us to say that we welcomed the change, but we could not go further than to say that we felt it was inevitable. . . .

We discussed the difficult period of the closing weeks of 1943 during which we were offered large lines of stock – presumably by Clearing Banks – which we could not take ourselves and for which we could not find even temporary buyers. The Governor explained that this year-end had been exceptionally difficult; the difficulty might arise again but he hoped not more than once.

The Governor asked us what quantity of stock we could altogether carry in the market. We told him that we did not know for none of us knew the capacity of the others.

I did however tell the Governor that I set for my firm a standard of trading which was 15 per cent margin – 5% with the Banks and 10% in the box. I think this is reasonably conservative and the Governor seemed to think so too. I gathered that he considered it too conservative.[57]

Mr Smithers:

John Higgins said he thought we ought to limit our borrowing so that we had 15% cover. That would be the maximum of our books – say 6 times our capital. The Governor thought that was a liberal margin. He said suppose he should lend us some money. We said that was dangerous as we might overtrade on his money but still the risk would be ours. If he shared the risk, it would be different, but we did not suggest he should share it. He said 'I cannot be Joint Account'. We pointed out we had to pay the loss but our profits were heavily taxed.[58]

And coming to the jobbers' main point:

We told the Governor that from time to time we found out that the Bank would do certain kinds of business but not others, and we asked that he would consider the possibility of extending the range of the Bank's market operations to exchanging stock for stock or stock for cash or vice versa. He answered that he would have to be convinced first of the necessity, but would consult Mr. Cripps.[59]

He said he would discuss with Cripps about helping us when we had got enough on our books and were unwilling to buy any more. His difficulty would be to decide a factual as against a psychological situation, meaning that if we bought as much as we would give 15% margin on and then could not buy any more, he would probably help, but that if we felt bearish and were not inclined to put stock on our books, he seemed to infer that he would not be so inclined to help. I pointed out

[57] Longuet-Higgins, 'Note of a meeting held in the Bank of England on 7th January 1944', BOE C132/1. Smithers' account says that the 1943 year-end was particularly difficult because January 1 fell on a Saturday, and that 1944 would also be difficult. In December 1944, the offered yields of the 2½% National War Bonds 1951/53 and 1952/54 rose above 2.5%, but there was no tap stock of similar maturity on offer.

[58] Smithers, 'A memo of a meeting with the Governor on 7th January 1944', BOE C132/1.

[59] Longuet-Higgins, 'Note of a meeting held in the Bank of England on 7th January 1944', BOE C132/1.

that this meant he was only inclined to help when we were nearing the rocks. We were pretty sure to have bought a good deal if the market was weak, we should all be landed before we realised it.[60]

On 11 January, Cripps wrote the following short notes, entitled 'Interview with the Governor following on "A"' ("A" was a copy of Norman's terse note of 7 January):

1. On definite advice of E.S.C.

    Regular Balance Sheets.
    No shorts.
    Swaps readily.
    A general understanding would emerge and become known.

2. No understanding.

    No Balance Sheets.
    When market looks sticky and liable to freeze up E.S.C. would come and suggest a purchase or swap to extent he thought necessary.[61]

Norman's diary records that on Wednesday 12 January, at 2.45pm he saw Eric Ellen, the chairman of the discount market, to discuss the 'limit of Bds (up to 5 yrs) Dis Hses may hold', and at 4pm Cripps and Holland-Martin to discuss '? what facilities for 3 jobbers.'[62] On Friday 14th, Norman recorded, as tersely as before:

Answer to the request of three Jobbers, recorded in the note of January 7th, and agreed with E.S.C.:-
No understanding or agreement. But if at any time E.S.C. considers Market too sticky or liable to freeze, he is free on his own to try to arrange a swap or outside purchase to whatever extent he happens to think necessary.
N.B. Discount Market are not jobbers but holders – to a limited extent.
Discount Market do no business in Bonds over 5 years.[63]

---

[60] Smithers, 'A memo of a meeting with the Governor on 7th January 1944', BOE C132/1.
[61] Cripps, 'Interview with the Governor following on "A"', 11 January 1944, BOE C132/1. 'No shorts' might have any of three meanings: that the Bank would not deal with the jobbers in short-dated gilts, or that the jobbers would not be allowed to sell to the Bank in order to establish short positions (i.e. negative holdings), or that the jobbers would not be allowed to have short positions at all.
[62] BOE ADM 34/33. The Discount Houses Committee became the London Discount Market Association in 1944, adopting a formal constitution in order to satisfy the requirements of the Board of Trade under the Prevention of Fraud (Investments) Act (Bank of England 1967 p. 145; Bull, 'Report for the year ended 30th September 1944', BOE C47/64).
[63] Norman, 14 January 1944, BOE C40/422.

From these documents I infer that, to get a dealing agreement with the Bank, the jobbers would have had to disclose their balance sheets to the Bank, and that they were unwilling to do so. If the jobbers were reluctant because Norman had indicated that he would not buy gilts from them until they were already holding as much as they could, their reluctance is easy to understand. The Bank's dealing records show no sign of any unusual purchases, or any swaps with the market, in the months after January 1944.

On the evening of Friday 14 January, Norman had an accident, 'tripping headlong over a large object behind Moor Place, his brother's country home in Hertfordshire ... '. He reappeared in the Bank the following Monday, but that was the last time. 'By the middle of the next week, Norman was lying at death's door ... ' with pneumococcal meningitis.[64] His life was saved however and he lived on until 1950.

In August 1944, after many months of debate, it was agreed that all gilt dealings on the Stock Exchange should automatically be on a 'plus accrued interest' basis, in which the quoted price did not include accrued interest, when the gilts in question came within five years of their final redemption date. The decision was made in the interests of the discount market, in which day-to-day financing costs were of great importance, but it was inconvenient to others, particularly because the Stock Exchange refused to allow purchasers to deduct income tax from the accrued interest.[65]

The Bank of England appears to have lacked a coherent view of the nature of market-making. Norman gave the jobbers the impression that he thought that they would need help in making markets only when their books were already full. On the other hand, in discussion with the discount market, the Bank 'warned on many occasions that their function is to job and that they cannot do this if they are always running a full Bond book ... '.[66]

[64] Boyle (1967, pp. 1–2, 322–3).
[65] Yeomans, '"Plus accrued" versus "flat"', 24 May 1944, BOE C40/422.
[66] Bull, 'Discount market – year 1946', 4 February 1947, BOE C47/39.

Post-War: 1945–51

7.1 Introduction

The Treasury's National Debt Enquiry of 1945 recommended that the government's debt management policy should continue to set a schedule of interest rates for different maturities and allow the public to determine the maturity structure of the national debt.[1] The tap technique for selling new issues was continued after the end of the war. The Labour government which took office in July 1945 decided to reduce interest rates at all maturities by 0.5%, and monetary and debt management policies were directed at getting interest rates, both long and short-term, down to the new lower levels, namely 0.5% at the short end and 2.5% for very long maturities.[2] The issue in October 1946 of 2½% Treasury 1975 or after (Appendix C) was intended to entrench 2.5% as the prevailing level for very long-term gilt yields.

It was necessary for both the cheap money policy and the management of the UK's precarious external balance sheet that controls over foreign exchange and private capital issues should be maintained after the war. However, the Anglo-American loan agreement, under which the UK borrowed $3.75 billion from the USA, required the UK to liberalise international transactions in various ways, including re-adopting convertibility for current account transactions vis-à-vis the rest of the world, and making non-resident sterling balances which had not been cancelled or blocked convertible for current account transactions, within a year of the effective

---

[1] Howson (1993, pp. 45–54).
[2] Howson (1993, pp. 121–45) describes Labour's cheaper money policy.

date of the agreement, i.e. by the middle of July 1947.[3] In the event, convertibility lasted only a few weeks, owing to an alarming outflow of reserves, and on 20 August the liberalisation of July was reversed (section 7.4).

7.2 Ultra-Cheap Money, the Exhaustion of Market Liquidity and the Strengthening of the Discount Market

Gilt market liquidity was again stressed in late 1945. On 23 October, the Chancellor of the Exchequer, Hugh Dalton, announced and explained to Parliament his plans for intensifying the policy of cheap money:

I should like now to deal with two questions of general financial policy. The first is the question of interest rates . . . There is no sense, or so it seems to me—I hope no high authority will differ from me—in paying more than we must for the loan of money; and I have endeavoured to do my utmost to bring these rates down. I shall say a word in detail in a moment.

The problem differs accordingly as we are dealing with short-term or long-term borrowing, and I have begun by concentrating my attention and my efforts on the short-term rates. On the present volume of the Floating Debt, composed, as the Committee will realise, of Treasury Bills, Treasury Deposit Receipts and Ways and Means Advances, the annual interest charge to the Exchequer is £66,000,000 a year, or was so running till last Friday. A good deal of this represents interest paid on funds held by Government Departments; but none the less there is a net gain to the public finances from any substantial saving on that interest-charge. I have discussed this question with the Governor of the Bank of England, and he has discussed it with the Chairmen of the Clearing Banks; and, as a result, I am glad to say that, as the Committee will already know, adjustments in short-term interest rates have now been made—they were made last week and have been announced—which have reduced the rate on Treasury Bills from about 1 per cent. to about ½ per cent., and the rate on Treasury Deposit Receipts from 1⅛ per cent. to ⅝ per cent.—a reduction of ½ per cent. in each case. This change, which has been made with the co-operation of the Bank of England and the Clearing Banks, and was announced last Friday, will mean a saving to the Exchequer for interest, on the present volume of Floating Debt, of some £32,000,000 a year out of the total of £66,000,000. In other words, we shall nearly cut the charge in half.

After this—as I think—hopeful beginning with short-term rates, I shall now turn my attention, in consultation with my advisers, to the possibility of securing lower middle-term and long-term interest rates; but I shall do nothing here to hinder—indeed, on the contrary, I hope that what I am saying now will assist rather than hinder—the success of the National Savings Thanksgiving Weeks which are being held until the end of November in various parts of the country. Our present tap issues will run on during that time; the terms will not be changed. Thereafter . . . the terms of lending may become less attractive; and this reflection should dispose any

---

[3] Pressnell (1986, pp. 313–16, 322–5, 366–7, 423).

person who is in doubt what to do with his money, with his 'liquid resources' as they are sometimes called . . . to lend these to the Treasury without imprudent delay.

It is perhaps unnecessary for me to add that if the Government should at any time decide to reduce the interest on new issues, such reduction would not affect the terms of existing loans made before the date of the change. That applies not only to the market issues—'tap' issues, as we sometimes call them, again speaking in a financial sense—but to Savings Certificates and to Defence Bonds, and also to deposits in the Post Office Savings Bank.[4]

Dalton also announced the abolition of minimum prices for gilts in his speech – his 'second question'. Notwithstanding the connection which had been made in 1940 between minimum gilt prices and the government's objectives for bond yields (Chapter 6, 6.2), the decision seems to have been uncontentious.[5]

The last two quoted paragraphs of Dalton's statement were an attempt to continue the forward guidance that had been in operation since 1932, with a brief interruption in 1939–40. The statement was followed on 28 November 1945 by the confirmation that the existing long and medium tap issues (3% Savings 1965/75 and 2½% National War Bonds 1954/56) would be closed on 15 December. The guidance had the opposite effect on short gilt yields to what Dalton intended. It incited a rush to subscribe to the existing long and medium-dated taps while they were still available:

The resultant stampede to secure the last of the 3 per cents. produced such huge financing sales of shorter bonds that the discount market's remaining capacity to take in securities was rapidly exhausted. It is estimated that the market absorbed some £40 millions in a week, and one house alone took almost half that sum. But still the selling went on, and with the Lombard Street shock-absorber temporarily seized up, the normal short bond mechanism was thrown completely out of gear. Prices, instead of being dominated by the professional buying, dropped to a yield basis appropriate to private investors, with even the shortest bonds yielding 2½ per cent. – and this at a time when the Chancellor was talking of 2½ per cent. for medium-longs, and faced, within only a few months, heavy short bond maturities.[6]

The Bank managed the Treasury bill issue so as to provide additional liquidity to the banking system; this device succeeded in engendering a sharp fall in short gilt yields (Figure 7.1), presumably by inducing the banks to buy short gilts. In the last four days before they closed on

---

[4] HC Deb. 23 October 1945 vol. 414 cc. 1881–2. Howson (1987 and 1993, esp. p. 149) describes the intellectual and political origins of Dalton's interest rate policy.

[5] HC Deb. 23 October 1945 vol. 414 cc. 1882–3.

[6] King (1947, p. 183). King's account is substantially repeated by Morgan and Thomas (1962, p. 197), Scammell (1968, pp. 229–30) and Fletcher (1976, p. 66). King edited *The Banker* from 1946–66 and was very well-informed.

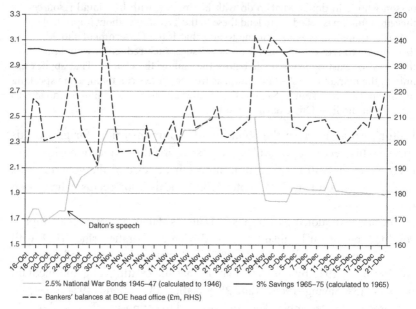

Figure 7.1 Gilt Yields and Bankers' Balances, October–December 1945

15 December, £130 million of the long tap and £27½ million of the medium were sold.[7]

With Treasury bill rates down to 0.5%, the clearing banks reduced their rate for lending to the discount market against bonds to 0.75%. This made 1¾% Exchequer 1950 attractive to banks and discount houses, and the Issue Department was able to sell its large holdings (Chapter 6, 6.2), which were exhausted by April 1946.

The Bank was already concerned about the lack of liquidity in the gilt market (Chapter 6, 6.3). Its Deputy Governor, Cameron Cobbold, proposed to the Treasury that the discount houses be permitted, under the capital issues regulations, to raise new capital in order to act as market-makers in short gilts on a larger scale:

The Discount Market is both by tradition and for reasons of convenience, the channel through which the day to day fluctuations in the volume of money are controlled. With the growth of banking deposits the volume of money employed in the Discount Market by the banks, both domestic and overseas, has expanded.

---

[7] Osborne and Allport (1950, p. 189).

These additional funds have been employed by the market mainly in Treasury Bills, and for the rest in short-term British Government securities.

The Market have for many years dealt in short bonds and have held part of their resources so invested. The supply of such securities has been enormously expanded by the issue of National War Bonds, which appeal mainly to the large investor particularly in the last five years of their currency. The market is, therefore, a narrow one and the individual transactions are large. The capital available to the jobbers in the gilt-edged market on the Stock Exchange is not by itself sufficient to maintain reasonably stable prices in such bonds, and to relieve the position the Discount Market have been given encouragement and facilities to deal in them.[8]

The Treasury agreed to Cobbold's proposal, and several discount houses raised new capital. The capital resources of the discount market went up from £11.8 million early in the war to £16.8 million after capital increases in 1942–44, and to nearly £30 million after the increases in 1946–47 that the Bank's proposal to the Treasury had facilitated.[9]

An interesting aspect of this episode is what the Bank didn't do. It did not act as a market-maker itself, buying short gilts from the market and maintaining short yields at or around the desired level. It could quite well have done so, as the market weakness was quintessentially technical, and it had supported 1¾% Exchequer 1950 heavily while it was on tap. There is no sign in the archives, other than the records of the abortive discussions with the jobbers in January 1944 (Chapter 6, 6.3), that it even considered the idea. The Bank seemed still to be following the hands-off policy enunciated by Holland-Martin in 1939 (Chapter 5, 5.8). In this respect, its post-war policy was different from that of the Federal Reserve, which was willing to buy and sell government securities of all maturities so as to maintain a predetermined pattern of interest rates. The Fed thus acted as a market-maker throughout the entire maturity range; it did, however, change the interest rate pattern that it was maintaining from time to time, beginning in July 1947, the changes being subject to the approval of the US Treasury.[10]

Cobbold's proposal referred to the need for more dealing capacity in the gilt market. In modern practice, dealers are as likely to be short of the asset in question as they are to be long, and the Stock Exchange jobbers had the facility to take short positions. Yet it is clear from the context that Cobbold's intention was that the discount houses, reinforced with new

---

[8] Cobbold–Eady, 30 November 1945, BOE C47/30.
[9] Scammell (1968, p. 231, Table XVI), Bank of England (1967, p. 146).
[10] Bach (1949), Chandler (1949), Walker (1954), Board of Governors of the Federal Reserve System (1948, p. 93).

capital, would be buyers of short-dated gilts on a larger scale than hitherto. For one thing, the Bank's initiative came immediately after a sharp and unwanted fall in short gilt prices. And for another, discount houses had access to cheap financing from the commercial banks: while the clearing banks lent to the discount houses against the collateral of bonds at 0.75%, they charged the Stock Exchange jobbers and money brokers 1.5% for similar loans; thus the discount market had a competitive advantage vis-à-vis the Stock Exchange in running long positions, but not short ones.[11]

The discount houses seem not to have been rigidly restricted to dealing in under-five-year gilts. For example, at the end of 1945, they collectively held £25.7 million of 2½% National War Bonds 1951/53 and 1952/54, whereas their aggregate capital and reserves were £22.3 million. Therefore some of their over-five-year bonds were financed with borrowed money.[12]

7.3 Long-Term Interest Rate Objectives and How They Were Pursued

Developments in the longer end of the market in 1946–47 were dominated by the government's ultimately unsuccessful attempt to get long gilt yields down to 2.5%. In the first few months of 1946, at Dalton's instigation, it was agreed to allow the National Debt Commissioners to use Savings Bank funds, which had hitherto been invested directly with the Exchequer in non-marketable annuities, to buy gilts in the market or from the tap, thereby pushing long yields down.[13] The Treasury included in the Finance Act 1947 a provision that any deficiencies in the Savings Bank funds would be met from the Consolidated Fund.[14]

The Bank opposed intervening to get yields down:

For the next ten years and excluding any new borrowings, H.M.G. will be persistent borrowers in replacement of maturing debt in competition in a greater or less degree with other interests and in the face of active demand for liquidity for reconstruction. In such circumstances it would seem likely that our resources will be strained to the utmost over a period in dealing with the large volume of maturing debt. If ever we found ourselves trying to fight against a definite trend,

---

[11] Committee of London Clearing Bankers, 'The rating structure of clearing banks', 19 October 1945, BOE C42/1. See Scammell (1968, pp. 231–3).

[12] Bull, 'Discount market review – 1945', 31 January 1946, BOE C47/39.

[13] Howson (1987, p. 445), Compton–Bamford, 'A decision to invest Savings Bank funds in the market', 30 January 1948, NA T233/434.

[14] 10 & 11 Geo. 6, ch. 35, Pt VII, s. 72.

the sky would be the limit. We must take the long view in a matter of such vital importance as the credit of H.M.G.[15]

In May, 2½% Savings 1964/67 was issued at par, both for cash and in exchange for 2½% National War Bonds 1946/48, thereby establishing 2.5% as the market level of 20-year yields (Appendix C). The issue was supported by official conversions, and by purchases of long gilts by the NDC.[16] The ultra-cheap money programme culminated in the issue in October 1946 of a 2.5% irredeemable tap stock (2½% Treasury 1975 or after, known as 'Daltons' after their progenitor). The offer was for cash, or reinvestment of the proceeds of the redemption of 3% Local Loans, on which the government had exercised its call option. Wilfred King's devastating analysis of the risks to investors foretold the end of Dalton's debt management policy:

For security of capital they must look solely to Treasury cheap money policies, not simply in the Dalton phase but in years when that has been duly written into the history books along with Goschen's. They are asked to assume that Governments for a generation and more to come will always rely, and rely successfully, upon physical control to maintain equilibrium whenever demand for capital outruns supply. They must assume that whenever, at moments of economic or political stress, public demands for liquidity threaten to push interest rates beyond this modest level, the authorities will ever stand ready to buy back this stock at, or not much under, par. They must assume that the Governments of the future will never return to the classical policies that were abandoned in 1932, but, through good times and bad, will ever eschew the interest rate as an instrument of economic control.[17]

The Issue Department bought £97 million of Local Loans during October–December 1946 and reinvested nearly all of the proceeds into Daltons, but did not subscribe any further money.[18] The National Debt Commissioners reinvested a similar amount, and the public £105 million.[19] In addition, the NDC subscribed £68 million in cash (Appendix C).[20] When the tap was

---

[15] Bank of England, 'Government borrowing', 8 January 1946, NA T233/434.
[16] Howson (1993, p. 137).   [17] King (1946, pp. 67–68).
[18] The announcement of the 2½% irredeemable was accompanied by notice that 3% Local Loans would be called, and by the offer of facilities for holders of Local Loans to reinvest in the 2½% stock if they so wished.
[19] Peppiatt, 'Repayment of Local Loans', 3 December 1946, BOE C40/473.
[20] The combined holdings of the Issue Department and the NDC were £260 million when the tap closed (Compton, 'Stock market transactions by government departments', 25 November 1947, NA T233/143). Each had acquired £96 million by reinvestment and the Issue Department had subscribed nothing in cash, so the NDC must have subscribed £68 million in cash.

closed on 11 January 1947, the issue amounted to £482 million, so that public subscriptions for cash must have been £117 million. By the end of June, the price was down to 92 and the yield up to 2.73%. By 31 October 1947, the NDC held £178.6 million, which implies that it had bought about £14 million of Daltons in the secondary market after the tap was closed.[21] The Issue Department bought none.

Dalton's objective of permanently low long-term interest rates had clearly been lost before the convertibility crisis.[22] The casualties included forward guidance, which was not tried again for several decades.

7.4 The Convertibility Crisis

On 15 July 1947, controls on external transactions were substantially eased, in accordance with the Anglo-American loan agreement, and limited external convertibility of sterling was established (section 7.1). It was unfortunate for the UK that the United States increased its Treasury bill rate from 0.375% to 0.75% at much the same time, taking it above the UK rate. Gilt yields increased by 42 basis points at the short end and 31 at the long end during July and August, and there was an outflow of foreign exchange amounting to $970 million between 1 July and 23 August.[23] Controls were reimposed and convertibility suspended on 20 August.[24] The decision to reimpose controls was made at the latest on Saturday 16 August, when officials were sent to Washington to notify the USA.[25]

A surge of selling of gilts began on 14 July: sales contracted that day would be settled on the 15th, when the sterling proceeds would be convertible. The Bank resisted the fall in prices by buying stock as prices fell (Figure 7.2). It was the first time that the Bank had reacted to falling prices in this way. Initially it bought mainly over-10-year stocks, but after 23 July switched its purchases entirely to shorter maturities, in addition to 3%

---

[21] Compton, 'Investments held by (a) Issue Department and (b) NDC funds', 25 November 1947, NA T233/143. The NDC bought more later: in 1949, the published holdings of certain official funds, not including the Issue Department, were given in answer to a parliamentary question as £255 million. The answer made it clear that there might be other unpublished holdings. HC Deb. 15 November 1949 vol. 469 c. 185W.

[22] Howson (1987, p. 450).

[23] Sir H. Ellis-Rees, 'The convertibility crisis of 1947', December 1962, Treasury Historical Memorandum no. 4, NA T267/3.

[24] The crisis is described by Ellis-Rees (see previous footnote) and by Gardner (1969, ch. XVI), Newton (1974), Cairncross (1985, pp. 121–64), Fforde (1992, pp. 141–64), Cottrell (1995, pp. 117–19), Schenk (2010, pp. 60–8).

[25] Dalton, 'Balance of payments', 16 August 1947, NA CAB 129/20.

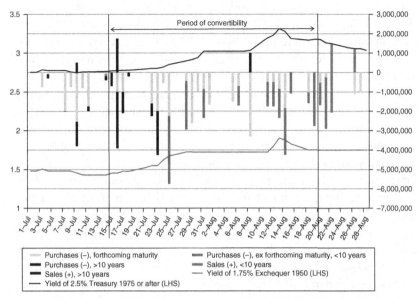

Figure 7.2 Issue Department Operations and Gilt Yields, July–August 1947

Conversion 1948/53, which was to be redeemed on 1 March 1948. Over the period of convertibility, the Issue Department's net purchases were £51.7 million nominal, of which £25.9 million were 1948/53s, £20.5 million were under-10-years to maturity and £5.2 million were over-10-years.[26] In addition, the Banking Department bought £2.0 million of 2½% National War Bonds 1954/56, financed by sales of the same amount of 1948/53s.[27]

The discount houses, who were the main market-makers in short gilts, were also adding to their holdings, and told the Bank that the proportion of bonds to bills in the collateral that they provided to the clearing banks 'might get higher than the Clearing Banks would care for.' It may be inferred that they had been too slow in reducing their prices as the selling orders flowed in. On 14 August: 'After careful consideration the Bank informed the Chairman [of the London Discount Market Association] that they would always purchase Exchequer 1¾s from the market and probably 49/51s', and the prices of those two stocks recovered from that day.[28] The Bank bought £12.7 million of 1¾% Exchequer 1950 between 14 and 31 August, but no 1949/51s.

[26] Source: BOE ADM18/51, author's calculations.   [27] Source: BOE C1/95.
[28] Report of meeting, 15 August 1947, LDMA1/6.

I have found no documents which explain the Bank's policy. A possible interpretation is that the Bank hoped initially to prevent or at least contain a rise in long-term interest rates beyond 2.75% by intervention, but abandoned the objective on 23 July, when the yield of Daltons had risen by 5 basis points since 11 July, to 2.80%, despite official purchases of £6.2 million of longs (Figure 7.2). Thereafter the Bank purchased shorter maturities, but with no more success in restraining yields: the yield of 1¾% Exchequer 1950 rose by 20 basis points net between 23 July and 20 August, to 1.75%, despite net official purchases of £20.4 million of under-10-year stocks (not including the 1948/53s). Long gilts weakened sharply after 23 July, and the yield of Daltons exceeded 3% on 31 July. The undertaking given on 14 August reassured the discount houses that they would be able to sell, but made no commitment as to the price. If the Bank's only concern had been the financing of the houses' gilt holdings, it could have solved the problem in other ways, e.g. by lending to them itself, or by persuading the clearing banks to accept larger proportions of gilts in the houses' collateral. Its purpose may have been to encourage the houses to continue as market-makers in short gilts, despite the losses that they would have sustained.

The Bank's total net gilt purchases between 1 July and 23 August were the equivalent of $262 million. They can only have aggravated the outflow of foreign exchange in some degree, notwithstanding the controls that were still in force. It would, however, be a mistake to imagine that a different gilt-edged policy, or a different short-term interest-rate policy, could have made convertibility sustainable. The government was insolvent, and its debt could be made manageable only by writedowns, which were not acceptable, by implausibly rapid economic growth, or by inflation. Higher interest rates in 1947 might, paradoxically, have accelerated the inevitable inflation.[29]

Thereafter, the Issue Department became less active in the market, despite the heavy flow of new gilts issued as compensation for nationalisations (section 7.5). It underwrote new issues sold by tender for cash (Appendix C).[30] It continued buying stocks which were approaching redemption, of which there had been four in 1946, and would be one in

[29] Sargent and Wallace (1981). Eichengreen (2008, p. 101) describes the decision to restore convertibility in 1947 'the height of recklessness'.
[30] Compton, 'Guaranteed stock issue by the British Electricity Authority', 11 October 1948, NA T233/1348, records the Bank's agreement that the Issue Department would underwrite the first post-war tender issue.

1948, and one in 1950, all of them bar the last having being called before the final possible date. It also bought stocks ahead of conversion offers (as in the case of Local Loans), so that the Issue Department could convert them and have longer-dated stock available to sell later. The Banking Department continued switching into medium and long gilts out of shorts: the total amount was £22 million between August 1947 and March 1948.[31]

7.5 The Nationalisation Programme

Nationalisation of large industries was one of the Labour government's main objectives. The government acquired securities issued by the companies which were nationalised, and issued gilts in exchange. The total amount was £2.2 billion.[32]

The new gilts were issued directly to the holders of the shares of and bonds issued by companies that had been nationalised; they were not sold by tender. The Stock Exchange made a market in them, as it did in other gilts. The Issue Department was initially not much involved. The largest nationalisation was of the transport industries. When these were nationalised, on 1 January 1948, the government compensated the share and bond holders of the affected companies by issuing to them £1,054 million of 3% Transport 1978/88.[33] A long-dated fixed interest bond was no doubt a close substitute for many of the securities that the railway and canal companies had issued, but not for all, and during January, 2½% Consols went up by 8 basis points in yield, and down by 3.1% in price, amid heavy turnover. Despite the fall in prices, the Issue Department did not deal at all in the new issue in January; in February it bought £2.0 million net, of which it sold £1.0 million in August, so that total net purchases in 1948 as a whole were just £1.0 million. However, the Banking Department bought £7.0 million in January–March, as part of its switching programme (section 7.4). The decision not to intervene followed a debate in the Treasury in the last few months of 1947 on the terms of the transport issue, in which the effects on bank deposits and long gilt yields of supporting the market were the main considerations, but in which the liquidity of the gilt market did not feature (section 7.6).[34]

---

[31] Source: BOE C1/95, 96, author's calculations.   [32] Howson (1993, pp. 199–208)
[33] And £13 million of 3% British Transport 1967/72. Source: Howson (1993, table 4.12).
[34] Howson (1993, p. 172). The issues were summarised by Compton, 'Cheap money', 26 November 1947, NA T233/143.

On 1 April 1948, a further £438 million of two new gilts were issued as compensation for nationalisations.[35] The Bank did not deal in either of them until December 1949, when its objectives were concerned with the level of yields in general, rather than the new issues in particular (section 7.7). And after the gas industry was nationalised, on 1 May 1949, the Bank did not deal in the compensation stock until November.[36] The Bank left the market to digest the nationalisation issues by itself.

The Bank's attitude changed. From June 1950 to December 1956, varying amounts of 3½% Treasury 1977/80 were issued at six-month intervals as compensation for the nationalisation of the coal industry (in addition, the iron and steel industries were nationalised in February 1951).[37] The colliery-owners were known to be selling their compensation stock as soon as they received it.[38] The CRND were keen to acquire long-dated gilts, and bought £11 million of the £19 million coal compensation stock sold after the first issue in June 1950. At the second and third issues, the CRND were keen to buy but were temporarily short of cash, and the Bank agreed to buy the stock and transfer it to the CRND in exchange for 2½% Exchequer 1955, which was to be resold to the CRND for cash later.[39] And at each issue date from June 1952 to June 1955, and in June 1956, the Bank bought part of the issue for its own account (see Table 13.1 for further analysis).[40]

7.6 Debt Management and Money Supply

During 1947, Dalton's Parliamentary Private Secretary, Douglas Jay, 'became worried about the inflationary consequences of the monetary expansion during the war and under Dalton's now failed cheaper money experiment.'[41] Gilt sales to the public were seen as a way of absorbing money balances from the public. An issue of £100 million of 3% Electricity

---

[35] £103 million British Transport 1968/73 and £335 million British Electricity 1968/73. See Howson (1993, pp. 204–5)

[36] Compensation took the form of 3% British Gas 1969/72, of which £202 million was initially issued, including £40 million direct to the NDC, followed by a further £15 million up to January 1950.

[37] Howson (1993, table 4.12), Pember and Boyle (1976).

[38] Beale, 'C.R.N.D. stock transactions', 13 December 1950, BOE C40/787.

[39] Beale, 'C.R.N.D. stock transactions', 13 December 1950; Parsons, 'Coal compensation', 12 June 1951, BOE C40/787.

[40] Beale, 14 June 1952, C40/787.

[41] Howson (1993, pp. 223–38). Jay was appointed Economic Secretary to the Treasury in November 1947, when Dalton resigned the Chancellorship.

1974/77 in October 1948, priced at £99½, was allowed to be sold at a yield above 3% because 'the Treasury hold that the paramount need at the present time is to get investors' money out of circulation'.[42] The issue seems to have been acquired entirely by the market.[43]

Late in 1948, when the gilt market had begun to recover after the long rise in yields which had begun early in 1947, the NDC agreed to curtail their purchases of long gilts in the market so as to leave more for the private sector to buy.[44] The Issue Department sold gilts in the secondary market to absorb bank deposits, including the £96 million of Daltons that it had acquired when they were issued.[45] At the same time, the 1943–46 practice was revived whereby the Issue Department acquired long-dated gilts from the CRND for sale in the secondary market.[46] In exchange, the NDC received cash, which they lent to the Exchequer in anticipation of the issue of a non-marketable annuity which would meet their income needs.

7.7 The Bear Squeeze of 1949

The Issue Department went on selling longs until the middle of 1949, when demand dried up. After the pound was devalued in September, yields increased sharply, and during October the Issue Department provided some support, buying, net, £1.9 million of short-mediums (other than the forthcoming maturity) and £4.9 million of longs. This did not stop the rot. On Friday 11 November, some long yields having reached 4% (Figure 7.4 shows a selection of gilt yields), the Bank made a more dramatic intervention. The Deputy Government Broker later testified that he 'did in effect go into the market and say: "I will buy any stock you have to sell"'.[47] The *Financial Times* reported that

---

[42] Compton–Radice, 'B.E.A. issue', 18 October 1948, NA T233/1348.

[43] The evidence for this is that there is no sign in the Bank's monthly returns to the Treasury or in the daily ledger that the Issue Department bought any of it on issue, though it acted as underwriter, and that the CRND 'told Niemeyer [Bank of England] provisionally that I could see no prospect of our being able to handle the proposed Electricity issue by October'. Compton, 'Guaranteed stock issue by the British Electricity Authority', 11 October 1948, NA T233/1348; Pinsent, 'Forthcoming government-sponsored issues', 15 September 1948, NA NDO13/67.

[44] Peppiatt, 'CRND market purchases', 16 November 1948, BOC C40/439.

[45] Part of the sale of 2½% Treasury 1975 or after was to the CRND. Peppiatt, '"Disinflation"/ funding', 2 February 1949, BOE C40/439.

[46] Cobbold–Eady, 18 November 1948, C40/439. The reasons that Cobbold put forward for gilt sales included reducing the floating debt as well as absorbing bank deposits.

[47] Radcliffe Committee (1960b), Q12031.

The appearance of the Government broker in the gilt-edged market soon after mid-day yesterday produced a spectacular recovery in prices. Rises amounted to as much as £3 ... The marked reversal of trend followed bidding for stock by the Government broker in a generally 'short' market. The support had an electrifying effect and brought about large-scale bear covering.[48]

The Bank bought, net, £3.75 million of stock, other than the forthcoming maturity, on Friday and the following Monday and Tuesday, and long gilt prices rose by about 4% over those three days (Figure 7.3). It was a 'bear squeeze'. Jobbers and other traders had short positions which they were forced to close, and the Bank entered the market as a seller on Wednesday 15 November, when it sold £150,000 net, at yields about 15 basis points lower than the closing levels of the previous Thursday.[49] It traded both ways over the rest of the month, and over November as a whole sold more than it bought.

The operation may be judged a success, in the sense that the government was able to issue more than £1 billion of new long-dated gilts in 1950 at yields below 4% (Appendix C). It may nevertheless have weakened the market infrastructure by causing further losses to the already-struggling jobbers (see below). As an admittedly extreme illustration, a hypothetical jobber which had gone short of long gilts at the low point on 9 November by six times its capital and closed the position on 2 December might have lost 40–50% of its capital.[50] The losses could have been yet more serious for jobbers whose capital was partly in the form of loans (Chapter 8, 8.4).

For the first time since 1932, the Bank operated so as to bring down long yields. There is remarkably little material referring to the 1949 operation in either the Bank of England archives or in the National Archives, and Fforde's official history of the Bank (1992) curiously does not mention it, but none of that detracts from its significance: it was the beginning of a long period of much greater interventionism.[51]

[48] Financial Times, 12 November 1949.
[49] Although I have been able to find very little contemporary material in the archives, a report of a discussion with the Prudential in 1953 about gilt lending refers to 'the excessively large bear positions which had been built up in 1949.' O'Brien, 'Stocks loaned to the Market', 11 August 1953, BOE C40/968.
[50] Six times capital was roughly the maximum exposure limit that Wedd Jefferson had mentioned to Norman in 1944 (Chapter 6, 6.3).
[51] A powerful, if arcane, indicator of its significance, telling for *aficionados* of bureaucratic practice, is the fact that within the Bank of England, the detailed weekly reports of official gilt transactions, which had hitherto been incorporated within a report of general domestic financial developments, were, after the intervention took place, circulated on a separate sheet of paper, obviously so that they could be withheld from those not deemed to need to know. BOE C11/1.

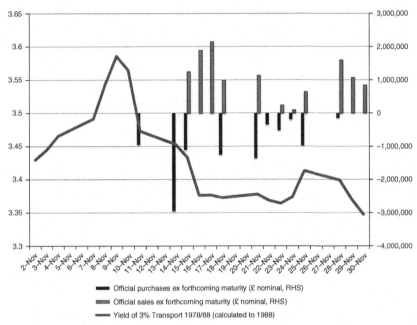

Figure 7.3 Issue Department Operations and Long Gilt Yields, November 1949

Official purchases were resumed in December, when £21 million net of gilts maturing in 1975 or after were bought (partly offset by sales of shorter stocks), largely in the week beginning 2 December, after a week in which gilt prices had recovered strongly. They may have represented a vain attempt to push the recovery further, or to prevent a relapse.

7.8 The Condition of the Market-Makers

The Bank of England had, beginning in around 1942, and without any announcement, established a dual-capacity dealer market in short gilts, in which the discount houses were the main market-makers. It thrived during and immediately after the war. The yield curve was upward-sloping, and short yields, though not steady, had no upward trend, while Treasury bill rates were pegged at 0.5% (Figure 7.4). It was profitable to run a long position in gilts maturing in the early 1950s, of which there were plenty, financed by cheap short-term borrowing. Discount houses prospered in the gilt market, except when they ventured into longer maturities, and between the end of 1945 and the end of 1951, the discount market's capital and

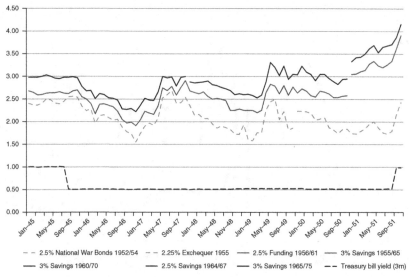

- - 2.5% National War Bonds 1952/54   - - 2.25% Exchequer 1955   —— 2.5% Funding 1956/61   —— 3% Savings 1955/65

—— 3% Savings 1960/70   —— 2.5% Savings 1964/67   —— 3% Savings 1965/75   - - Treasury bill yield (3m)

Figure 7.4 Gilt Yields, 1945–51

reserves went up from £22.3 million to £41.5 million. Out of the increase of £19.2 million, £10.6 million represented new capital raised from investors in 1946–47; the rest must have represented retained profits.[52] The discount houses' gilt holdings increased from £194 million at the end of 1945 to £345 million at the end of 1950, but the average maturity of their over-one-year bond books fell from 3.4 years to 2.9 years (Figure 8.3).[53] Early in 1951, the Bank of England told the discount houses that they should cut their bond books: by the end of the year they were down to £314 million and the average maturity had fallen very sharply to only 1.6 years.[54]

By contrast, all was not well in the Stock Exchange. For one thing, the government had taken away the pre-war tax concession under which jobbers were allowed to average profits over a three-year period for tax purposes.[55] And in his Budget speech in Parliament in April 1947, Dalton referred to 'a momentary loss of nerve in the gilt-edged market and particularly among the jobbers', which he held responsible for the rise in

[52] Sources: Discount market annual reviews, BOE C47/39, King (1947, table III).
[53] King (1947, p. 185), author's calculations based on data in annual discount market reviews in BOE C47/39 and 40.
[54] Johns, 13 January 1951, BOE C47/39, author's calculation.
[55] Wincott, 'The problem of the jobbers – II', 8 January 1952, FTHA.

yields after the tap for the 2½% 1975 or after was closed.[56] By early 1949, the jobbers were complaining about falling levels of business.[57] If they had been tempted by the upward-sloping yield curve and the government's cheap-money propaganda to run long positions in long-dated gilts, they would have lost money as long yields rose. However, as already noted, by the time of the November 1949 intervention, they were short of long gilts, so they would have lost money then as a result of the price reaction to the operation.

In the late 1940s Francis and Praed, hitherto the biggest of the gilt jobbers, were overtaken by Wedd Jefferson.[58] It was the beginning of a long decline: Angus Ashton, who joined Francis and Praed in the mid-1950s, described the firm as 'geriatric'.[59] The small gilt jobber Gibbs and Tatham failed, and the Official Assignee of the Stock Exchange reported in April 1950 that

they had been relying for some time on the fact that some of their cheques would not be cleared on the day of issue ... It is evident that this sort of thing had been going on for at least a year, as their cash book during this time shows a daily debit balance of between £5,000 and £10,000 ... Going back further, it will be found that up to the end of 1947 their daily bank position showed on the credit side, but from the beginning of 1948 debit balances often appear, small at first but increasing as time went on until at about the end of 1949 the position worsened very considerably, and it is very probable that many times during this period they were relying to carry on, on the bank not clearing their smaller cheques.[60]

Gibbs & Tatham had been exploiting the banks' practice of not clearing Stock Exchange cheques for less than £5,000 on the same day. The Bank of England, concerned to prevent further failures, tried to get the pre-war practice of same-day clearing of all Stock Exchange cheques reinstated, but could not do so immediately because of staff and premises difficulties at the banks and the clearing house.[61]

In July 1950, John Booth, the senior partner of the gilt jobbing firm Booth and Partridge wrote to the Deputy Government Broker that the firm had lost money in 1947, 1948 and 1949, and that they expected a loss for

---

[56] HC Deb. 15 April 1947 vol. 436 c. 60.
[57] In a memorandum handed to Cobbold, January 1949, BOE C40/968.
[58] Interview with Brian Peppiatt, CMH. I am extremely grateful to Mr Peppiatt for allowing me to quote from his interview.
[59] Interview with Angus Ashton, CMH.
[60] 'Notes regarding the bank position of Messrs. Gibbs & Tatham', Official assignees' office, 24 April, 1950, BOE C40/969.
[61] 'Jobbing facilities', 25 May 1950, BOE C40/968.

1950. After describing the firm's access to capital resources, he said that 'we've got until 1954 to recoup the worst of our losses.'[62]

I have found no independent evidence to support the contention, but the Bank's actions between 1945 and 1951 suggest that it was more concerned about liquidity in under-five-year gilts than in longer maturities. It made special arrangements to enable the discount houses to make markets in under-five-year gilts, but it did nothing to soften the impact of nationalisation compensation issues on the long market. It used the long market to try to restrain bank deposits, and its price support operation in November 1949, which was aimed at altering long yields, imposed incidental losses on the jobbers. In the language of Benos and Wetherilt (2012), it supplied liquidity at the short end and consumed it at the long end. Probably not coincidentally, its intervention in the 1950s and 1960s was concentrated on short maturities.

[62] 18 July 1950, BOE C132/1.

8

The Gilt Market from the Reactivation of Monetary Policy until 1960

8.1 The Reactivation of Monetary Policy

Immediately after the general election of 1951, the new Conservative government tightened monetary policy, for the first time since 1931.[1] First, the Bank of England ended its practice of pegging Treasury bill rates at 0.5%, and Bank rate was increased from 2% to 2.5%. Second, the banks were urged to restrain credit more tightly. Third, the government issued £1 billion of short-dated (one, two and three-year) gilts – the so-called Serial Funding stocks. The clearing banks were compelled to buy £500 million of them, to absorb some of their liquid assets, and the discount market took £40 million.[2]

The effective increase in short-term interest rates was from the previous pegged rate of 0.5% to something under 2%, because there was a special rate of 2% at which the Bank would buy Treasury bills; however, the Bank undertook open-market operations in Treasury bills and the 2% rate became operative only when the operations left the market short of funds. Bank rate was increased again, in March 1952, from 2.5% to 4%, and this imposed losses on the holders of the Serial Funding and other stocks (see section 8.3).[3]

8.2 Bank of England Policy towards the Gilt-Edged Market

The reactivation of monetary policy caused further problems for the gilt-edged jobbers. The journalist Harold Wincott noted in the *Financial Times*

---

[1] Leaving aside the quickly reversed Bank rate increase of August 1939 (Chapter 5, 5.10).
[2] Fforde (1992, pp. 398–412), Allen (2014, ch. 3).
[3] For fuller accounts, see Howson (1993) and Allen (2014).

on 1 January 1952 that the gilt market's 'reaction to Mr Butler's new monetary policy was far more violent than anyone expected. The gilt-edged market, of the utmost importance to everyone in the country, became at times virtually nominal.' Wincott attributed the problems largely to taxation, and in a second article, suggested some possible remedies.[4]

The same day, Peppiatt circulated a note in the Bank of England, to which he attached Wincott's article. He warned against greater interventionism by the Bank, and instead advocated strengthening the jobbers in the Stock Exchange. The note is worth quoting in full:

The suggestion has been made from time to time that in order to prevent wide fluctuations in prices we should operate in the Gilt-Edged Market far more freely than we do at present – in fact that we should 'job'.

Broadly speaking, the existing practice is to confine our activities to the following:-

a. to buying the next maturing stock in order to facilitate conversion/redemption; and to selling, over a period, stocks left with us as a result of such operations:

b. to acting as involuntary 'underwriters' of cash issues to the public by H.M.G. and/or by nationalised industries; and to selling stocks thus left with us:

c. to assuring a market (short term) at the time of issue of compensation stocks (e.g. Coal) by purchases and subsequent sale as opportunity offers:

d. to smoothing out any relatively small technical troubles which may at any particular time be embarrassing the Market:

e. most exceptionally, to making a demonstration such as we made in November 1949 when clearly stocks had fallen to an unduly low level: also, very occasionally, to giving some moderate end-year support for balance sheet purposes:

f. to assisting funding, in a general way, by a willingness always to sell longs in exchange for shorter Government securities.

Such activities are, in my opinion, both necessary and proper.

As the Central Bank we have a duty to control the volume of credit. But we have, I should maintain, no such duty to control the price of Government securities – even if we could (cf U.S.A.). In fact, it would be difficult, if not impossible, to achieve both these objectives at the same time; because, when we are restricting credit, securities tend to fall and if we are to seek to reverse this movement it would involve pumping large sums of money into the market, this defeating our primary purpose.

---

[4] H. Wincott, 'The problem of the jobbers I and II', FTHA, 1 and 8 January 1952.

Moreover, if we were to job actively, we should tend to amass a large portfolio of securities, usually at unfavourable prices on a falling market (we could not act on the 'bear tack') and my belief is that had we so acted during the recent fall we might have found ourselves with a further £50/100 million stocks at prices most of which would now look absurdly high. We should become the target for criticism and pressure by both Whitehall and the public. And, above all, we should soon create a situation where we were in fact THE jobber and should thus destroy the very market which we were trying to maintain.

The Gilt-Edged Market at present functions on the whole satisfactorily though the enormous volume of securities now dealt in and the difficulty experienced by the jobbers of accumulating capital certainly raise problems (see attached article in to-day's "Financial Times"). But the answer to any problem which may arise is, in my opinion, to be found in consultation between ourselves and the Chairman of the Stock Exchange with a view to strengthening the position of the jobbers, as may from time to time become necessary, by the following means:-

1) by encouraging a greater flow of capital in their direction, e.g. from Insurance Companies, Investment Trusts:
2) by fiscal remedies:
3) by persuading the Banks to give favourable terms to gilt-edged jobbers for carrying stock –

or by a mixture of all three. In short, we should, if and when the need arises, take such action as would tend to support and strengthen the machinery of the market and not to destroy it.[5]

As a result of Peppiatt's note, Cobbold, who had become Governor in 1949, spoke to the Chairman of the Stock Exchange asking whether jobbers might be permitted to acquire capital from outside investors. The reply, according to Cobbold, was that he had 'from time to time thrown a fly over jobbers but gets no hint that they feel short of capital. I said it was their business, but I wanted him to know that we were interested if he ever felt inclined to pursue.' Peppiatt commented that 'the problem, though at present dormant, will inevitably become active as the years (and the Partners!) pass.'[6] I have found no record of the Stock Exchange ever following up Cobbold's invitation.

Ironically, Peppiatt's note coincided with the beginning of the upward trend in the Issue Department's involvement in the secondary market

---

[5] Peppiatt, 'Gilt-Edged Market', 1 January 1952, BOE C42/12. Cobbold and Beale both noted their agreement with Peppiatt. The origin of the suggestion that the Bank should become a jobber is not clear.
[6] Cobbold, ms note, 15 January 1952, and annotation by Peppiatt, BOE C42/12.

in gilts, which was to grow in the 1950s and 1960s, until it was curtailed in 1971 (Figure 1.1). There is no record of any discussion of the change in policy, and the very existence of the upward trend was barely acknowledged for a long time.

One manifestation of greater interventionism was the Bank's reaction to issues of gilts as compensation for nationalisation operations (Chapter 7, 7.5). In 1948 it had been content for the market to absorb £1½ billion of compensation issues without official help or support. By 1952, it felt the need to provide support even for relatively small amounts. What caused the change of attitude? It might have been the concern about yield levels that had provoked the bear squeeze of November 1949 (Chapter 7, 7.7); it might have been indications of increasingly inadequate market liquidity; or it might have been signs of distress among the jobbers. I have found no records which provide an answer. Another, later, indication of greater interventionism is the marked increase from 1957 onwards in the estimated sensitivity of the Issue Department's net sales to changes in market yields (Table 13.1).

The Bank described its functions in the gilt-edged market in its evidence to the Radcliffe Committee in 1957–59, but it did not make clear that they had recently undergone radical change. Cobbold's evidence, given in 1957, defined them as follows:

The general objective of the Issue Department is to maintain an orderly market in gilt-edged securities, sometimes by providing a market or meeting a demand for a particular stock, and sometimes by ironing out what seems an unreasonable fluctuation. Occasionally, when some new development takes place which might cause uncertainty or fluctuation, the Issue Department intervenes temporarily in the market to give a lead or to steady the market, but it is no part of general Issue Department policy to resist a definite trend of markets in one direction or the other.

Superimposed on this general function has been the part which the Issue Department has played for many years, and especially during the war, in the Government's borrowing and refinancing operations . . . .

The Issue Department is therefore, and is known to be, normally a seller of stock of various dates when the market is receptive but a buyer of the next maturities, when they are on offer.[7]

The Bank was a natural seller of gilts, but its purchases amounted to 85% of its secondary market sales in 1951–59. An analysis of its turnover in 1951–59 (Appendix D) reveals the following main points:

[7]   Radcliffe Committee (1960b), Q1762.

a. Purchases of stocks approaching maturity, defined for present purposes as within nine months of maturity, were fairly steady from year to year but with fluctuations according to the incidence of maturities.
b. The Issue Department's turnover in shorts, including forthcoming maturities (up to five years), and mediums (5–15 years), relative to the amounts outstanding, increased from 15% to 47% and from 6% to 11% respectively, between 1951 and 1959.
c. However, its turnover in longs (more than 15 years) rose only slightly, from 3% to 4% of the amount outstanding, though there was a hump in 1957 and 1958.

I have found no documentary evidence explaining the Bank's increased interventionism in short and medium gilts, and surmise that it reflected more active market-making by the Bank motivated by the desire to maintain market liquidity, particularly after September 1957, when the commercial market-makers lost money and perhaps retrenched.

Beginning no later than January 1958, the Bank was willing to buy gilts from the jobbers just before tenders for new issues, in exchange for guaranteed applications by the jobbers for the new issue. The terms of the deals were negotiated between the Government Broker and the jobbers.[8]

Witnesses to the Radcliffe Committee gave their impressions of the Bank's operations:

Q7822 [Chairman] ... Your impression is that there is official support in general? – [Mr Althaus] When the pressure gets very severe. One would suppose that the authorities concerned have a special interest in the maintenance of some semblance of order in the market, and when it is a question of someone not being able to sell £5 or £10 millions of stock, there is generally speaking only one buyer with the resources and the courage needed to do that.'[9]

Q7834 [Chairman]: I think it follows from what you said in an answer just now, and I think also from paragraph 21, that the possibility of official intervention in support of the market when it is reasonable is not unwelcome to you at the Stock Exchange? You would like to see it on a larger scale than you think you have seen it? – [Mr Althaus] Not necessarily, no. We should like to go on our own feet as long as we can, but occasionally the pressure is large, when these lots of £10, £15 or £20 million come along, as they do from time to time, and that is rather a large undertaking in an uncertain outlook.

Q11927 [Mr Mullens] ... whenever the market wanted to buy a particular stock which they had not got on their own books, they would go immediately to my partner and ask and then it would be for me with the agreement of the Chief

---

[8] For example, the Bank was ready to buy gilts against guaranteed applications for 5½% Exchequer 1966. O'Brien, '5½% Exchequer Stock 1966', 10 January 1958, BOE C40/450.
[9] Mr F.R. Althaus was a prominent stockbroker. See cast of characters.

Cashier to see if we were able, or if it was in the Government's interest, to find that stock for them.[10]

Q11941 [Professor Cairncross]: Have you any idea in what proportion of cases or over what proportion of sales a jobber would come to you in order to obtain stock, compared with the total dealings in which he was engaged? – [Mr Mullens] If it was a stock which had been recently issued, 90 per cent. of the time he would come to me. If it was a stock that had settled itself in the market, he would as often get that stock from an insurance company or a bank through a broker as through me.'

Q11942 Chairman: When we are talking about the sales on behalf of the Government how much of this is to be regarded as switching, in which you are exchanging one kind of stock you want to get rid of for another you are taking in against it, and how much is direct sales for cash? – [Mr Mullens] Without looking into detail it would be difficult for me to answer your question specifically, but I might put it this way. When the market is really firm and is expecting lower interest rates, nearly all of the business we do on behalf of the Bank would be selling. On the other hand, when markets are inclined to be quieter or indeed perhaps even going down, we are then prepared, in consultation with the Chief Cashier, to sell one stock of which we have a lot and buy another of which we may have none or anyway very little. But nearly always it would be a security of shorter date, so that we are in effect stepping back all the time.

Another clue as to what was going on is provided by an internal note, written for himself and his deputy only, by the Government Broker in 1958, which includes the clause 'one was prepared on occasion to do things disadvantageous [to the Bank and the government] in order to get the market out of a muddle and in fact had frequently done so in the past.'[11]

The Bank did not heed Peppiatt's 1952 warning. Cobbold's rather anodyne description to the Radcliffe Committee of the aims of the Issue Department, quoted above, revealed very little about the very large expansion of the Bank's role in the gilt market in the 1950s.

8.3 Market Support Operations and Monetary Policy

At times of market weakness, the Bank of England had to decide how to behave in the market. It needed to sell gilts to refinance maturing stocks, and to finance the budget deficit (if any). If prices were falling, should it press on with its selling programme regardless, should it pause, or should it

---

[10] Mr Derrick Mullens was the Government Broker.

[11] Note dated 15 October 1958, BOE C132/76. The context of the comment was that the Government Broker was anxious to ensure that a transaction being proposed at the time would not benefit his partners on the commercial side of Mullens and Co.; if it had done, he would have declined it.

support the market by buying gilts, as a commercial dealer might do? Pressing on regardless would risk precipitating heavy price falls and imposing losses on traders, including the jobbers and discount houses who made the market, and perhaps causing them to withdraw from the market, with consequent damage to future market liquidity. Pausing or providing support meant accepting a setback to the selling programme, and facilitating monetary expansion at a time when contraction might have been more desirable.

In November 1949, the Bank had supported the market because it judged that yields had become too high. Yields were increasing most of the time after 1951, so that the question became very pertinent. The Bank provided moderate support to the gilt market in two periods in late 1954 and early 1955, and in late 1955.[12] And there was a deliberate slowdown of official sales in 1959.

What motivated the gilt market decisions of the 1950s? The decision to provide only limited support in 1952 was an important one, consistent with the reactivation of monetary policy that had begun in November 1951, and the Bank was not deterred by the very heavy falls in gilt prices that year. Nevertheless, it bailed out the jobbers after the March Budget, in which Bank rate was raised from 2.5% to 4%, by purchasing £11.4 million of gilts, some at generous prices involving a subsidy of about £35,000 (Appendix A). It seems likely that the Bank's motivation was to protect the jobbers' solvency, and to lighten their books. However, in March as a whole, net official purchases of gilts were just £4.6 million, so that on other days there were net sales on balance. Some witnesses to the Radcliffe Committee suggested, when they gave evidence in 1958, that the Bank had supported the market in 1952.[13] They were not explicit, and it may be that they were referring to the bailing-out of the jobbers, but there was no general and protracted market support (Figure 8.1).

There followed an interlude of falling yields in 1953 and 1954. A major easing of exchange controls in March 1954, which amounted in substance to reintroduction of convertibility of external sterling, did not provoke any adverse reaction in the gilt market, in contrast to the 1947 experience.[14] Late in 1954, however, yields began to rise. The economy was overheating and, even before the unwisely expansionary Budget of April 1955, the Bank had been considering ways of restraining bank credit. Nevertheless, for

---

[12] During these episodes, the Bank sold gilts approaching maturity to the market, contrary to its usual policy.

[13] See the evidence of Mr F.R. Althaus, especially his answers to Q7817 and Q7821–2. Radcliffe Committee (1960b).

[14] Schenk (2010, pp. 110–11), Fforde (1992, pp. 492–505).

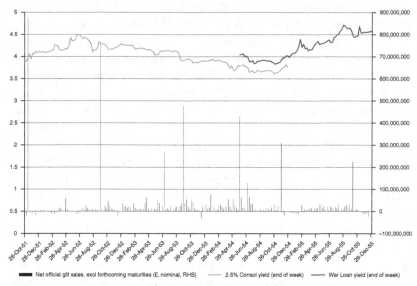

Figure 8.1 Net Official Gilt Sales and Long Yields, October 1951–December 1955, Weekly

a period, the Bank supported a weakening gilt market, and thereby helped the banks expand credit by providing them with the liquid assets that they needed to maintain their liquidity ratios at the minimum required level of 30%.[15] Why did the Bank make these purchases?

Cobbold was slow to recognise that economy was overheating, and had been convinced for a long time that the weakness of financial markets, including the foreign exchange market as well as the gilt market, was part of what he called a 'technical crisis', which could be cured by resolute intervention. The Bank purchased, net, £65 million of gilts, mainly shorts, between 3 December 1954 and 17 February 1955 (Figure 8.1). During that period, Bank rate was increased once, on 27 January, by 0.5% to 3.5%. The support was withdrawn shortly before a second increase, to 4.5%, on 24 February, and the withdrawal was part of that tightening of monetary policy.

Later in 1955, the Bank still believed that gilt yields were unjustifiably high. In September 1955, contemplating the upcoming maturity of 3% Serial Funding 1955, the Chief Cashier, Leslie O'Brien, remarked that 'With rates at their present level, we would not wish to issue anything but the shortest possible stock in exchange for this maturity and for cash.'[16]

---

[15] Allen (2014, ch. 8).   [16] O'Brien, 'Credit policy', 1 September 1955, BOE C42/3.

With this mindset, it perhaps seemed natural to buy gilts when prices fell again in November and December (Figure 8.1), and the Bank bought £58 million, weighted towards the long end, in December.

Thus there were arguments based on fundamentals which, even if they were mistaken, were used to justify supporting the gilt market in 1954 and 1955; it is not the case that support was provided partly or wholly in order to protect the market-making structure. And the absence of substantial support in 1952 and during the Suez crisis of 1956, and after the Bank rate rise of September 1957, when the Stock Exchange jobbers were 'nearly ruined' and the discount houses also took losses, show that the Bank was not then willing to provide general market support at the expense of monetary policy purely to help the market-makers (Figure 8.2).[17]

The Bank, however, remained willing to provide capital support to keep the market-makers in business. Immediately after the 1957 rate rise it bought from them £8.7 million of gilts – the amount almost certainly being related to their own holdings just before the rate rise – at above post-rate rise market prices, as it had done in 1952. In doing so, the Issue Department incurred a loss of about £100,000, which represented a subsidy to the market-makers.[18] Perhaps this is why the jobbers were only 'nearly' ruined. And, as already noted, the Bank became a more active participant in the market for short and medium gilts after 1957.

The deliberate slowing-down of gilt sales in 1959 took place on the instructions of the Prime Minister, Harold Macmillan, who was advised by the economist Roy Harrod. The purpose was to stimulate growth by getting long-term interest rates down.[19]

8.4 Market Microstructure in the 1950s

What was happening to the structure of the gilt market? The Stock Exchange was 'drifting towards oblivion' in the 1950s.[20] One reason was the jobbers' lack of capital:

---

[17] The Bank made moderate net purchases of gilts as yields rose in the few weeks before the September 1957 Bank rate rise: it bought £18.7 million (excluding forthcoming maturities) between 9 August and 12 September (Figure 8.1). The market was confused by these purchases about the Bank's attitude to interest rates, as the jobber Hugh Merriman explained to the Parker Tribunal (Parker Tribunal, 1958, Q 2165).
[18] See Appendix A for evidence.   [19] Allen (2014, ch. 12).
[20] This is the title of chapter 9 of Michie (1999), which deals with the 1950s.

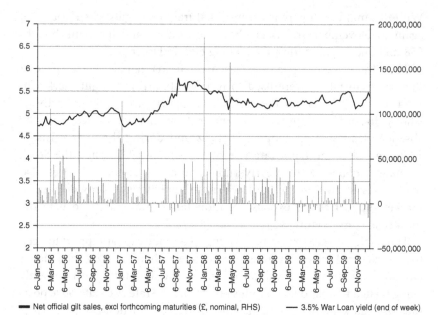

Figure 8.2 Net Official Gilt Sales and Long Yields, January 1956–December 1959, Weekly

In the past members, out of their current earnings, could accumulate capital for the business and provide savings for their retirement. For some appreciable time this has not been possible owing to the high rates of taxation and the incidence of the previous year basis of assessment, which does not permit the averaging of good years with bad.[21]

Harold Wincott explained:

A jobbing partnership these days finds it virtually impossible to build up capital. The lion's share of its profits go to the Government; its losses have to be met from its capital. What capital there is belongs almost exclusively to the older generation. This generation may at best leave its funds, or some of them, with a partnership on retirement. But that, in view of the eventual weight of death duties, is merely a postponement of the ultimate loss to the system.[22]

The Bank of England had failed in 1952 to persuade the Stock Exchange that the jobbers were short of capital (section 8.2). The number of partners in jobbing firms (in all securities, not just gilts) fell from 801 in 1950 to 539

---

[21] London Stock Exchange Council document, 22 January 1951, quoted by Michie (1999, p. 391).

[22] 'Jobbers' capital', *Financial Times*, 6 December 1955, FTHA.

in 1960, and the number of firms fell from 191 to 100.[23] Firms became larger on average. In the gilt market, the Bank was concerned that the decline of Francis and Praed, which had been the largest of the jobbers, was weakening the force of competition, and in 1956 it was happy to allow Akroyd and Smithers to have their overdraft facility enlarged, despite the restrictions on bank credit in force at the time, to enable Akroyds to 'keep Wedd Jefferson on their toes.'[24] Akroyd and Smithers' capital in the late 1950s was £100,000 of equity, supported by the unlimited liability of the partners; in addition, the firm had an undisclosed amount of loan capital provided by some of the older partners.[25] In the 1930s, Montagu Norman had enforced a minimum of £300,000 for discount houses (Chapter 6, 6.3).

The Radcliffe Committee asked the Government Broker about the size of the jobbers' books:

Q11948 Professor Cairncross: Are you able to give us any idea of the size of the jobbers' books? What is the magnitude of the resources they bring into this market? – [Mr Mullens] The amount of stock that they would carry on their books would vary according to their view of what was going to happen, but I suppose it would not be unusual for the bigger firms to hold a position of somewhere between £5mn. and £10mn. worth of stock.

Radcliffe also asked about the jobbers' resilience, and got a revealing answer:

Q12015 Chairman: What would happen to the jobbers if you made sharp overnight adjustments of the kind we are talking about [sharp price reductions so as to stimulate official sales]? – [Mr Mullens] For anything of the nature we have been discussing we should have to take them into our confidence, or we should ruin them. They were nearly ruined over the 7 per cent. Bank rate.
Q12017 What would you do? Would not taking them into your confidence mean giving them advance warning of a Government move that is equivalent in its importance to a change of Bank Rate? – Mr. O'Brien: Possibly a better alternative, would be to clear their books for them without loss, after the change.
Q12018 To give them an indemnity, in fact? – [Mr O'Brien] Yes.

This evidence was given in November 1958, after the bailing-out of the jobbers following the Bank rate increase of September 1957, which was not disclosed to the Radcliffe Committee.

Information from the Government Broker seems not always to have been disseminated even-handedly to the market, as the following note written by the Government Broker, Derrick Mullens, for Mullens' files, shows:

---

[23] Table dated 14 July 1965 in BOE C40/1053.   [24] O'Brien, 17 May 1956, BOE C40/968.
[25] Interview (CMH) and private correspondence with Brian Peppiatt.

O'Brien told me this morning that at 10 o'clock last night the Chancellor had at last agreed to our proposals, and he proposes to go ahead this afternoon [with a new issue], and a copy of the hand-out is attached.

The market had been rather dull all day, and I did tell Dick Wilkins of Wedd Jefferson [one of the big jobbers] not to have too much stock on his book. He told me that he had got about £5 million Stock, and I promised to take some off him, but I made it quite clear that this was a personal matter between him and me at that stage.

When I later told Lord Glendyne [a broker] the terms of the new issue at 2.45 p.m., he told me that he had heard that I had warned the market to cut down their books. This of course was not true as I had only spoken to Dick Wilkins, and I was very upset that this had got around. I immediately spoke to Dick Wilkins about it, and he told me that he had spoken to nobody except Jimmy Priestley [also of Wedd Jefferson], and after some discussion it appears that Jimmy Priestley had formed his own idea about the market, as RN & Co [R. Nivison and Co, Lord Glendyne's firm] were sellers of £1 million Savings 3% 1965–75 which I was reluctant to take off them, and he may inadvertently have given the impression that I was a reluctant dealer.

P.A.D. [Peter Daniell, the Deputy Government Broker] tried to find out what had actually happened and seemed satisfied that nobody in Wedd Jefferson had in effect passed on such information to Lord Glendyne, and I am prepared to let the matter drop.[26]

It was alleged that the decision to increase Bank rate in September 1957 had been leaked by members of the Bank of England Court, who knew about it in advance, to their firms, which had used it for commercial advantage by selling gilts before the announcement. The government announced a tribunal of inquiry, chaired by Lord Justice Parker, to investigate the allegation, and the evidence provided to the tribunal is a valuable supplement to the Radcliffe evidence on the gilt market at the time.[27]

The Stock Exchange did not measure gilt turnover regularly until 1964, but the Parker Tribunal was given an estimate of £50 million a day, or £13 billion a year.[28] The Issue Department's turnover in 1957 was £2.8 billion. Although some of it was outside the Stock Exchange, with Union Discount Company (see below), the Issue Department might have accounted for roughly 22% of the gilt turnover on the Stock Exchange that year. In interpreting this figure, it is useful to consider a hypothetical extreme case in which every customer order received by a stockbroker and

---

[26] Mullens, 11 February 1958, BOE C132/76. It is not certain that the Bank of England would have known of this incident; Mullens' files, in which the note was placed, were transferred to the Bank only after Big Bang in 1986.

[27] Kynaston (2002, pp. 87–92), Capie (2010, pp. 96–99).

[28] Radcliffe Committee (1960b), Q11951. This estimate probably does not include transactions conducted outside the Stock Exchange, e.g. by the discount houses.

satisfied by a jobber was immediately matched by a transaction between the jobber and the Government Brokers acting on behalf of the Issue Department. In that hypothetical extreme case, in which the jobbers are mere cyphers, the Issue Department's share of recorded turnover would be 50%. So the estimated figure of 22% suggests that the backstop provided by the Issue Department was, in 1957–58, a very important feature of the market-making apparatus of the Stock Exchange.

The discount market, which had done well out of the gilt market in the cheap money era, continued to prosper for the most part after the reactivation of monetary policy. Having shortened their books after the Bank of England's warning in early 1951, they did not sustain serious losses when monetary policy was reactivated in November that year, and the losses they made when Bank rate was increased again in March 1952 were made good in the remainder of the year. The houses prospered as interest rates fell in 1953 and 1954, and were no doubt infected by the prevailing economic euphoria. At the end of 1954 their over-one-year bond books were up to £350 million (7.3 times their capital), with an average maturity of 3.5 years (Figure 8.3).

Serious problems emerged in early 1955, when Bank rate was increased to 4.5% and several houses suffered heavy losses. During the year, the discount market's capital resources fell from £48.0 million to £29.9 million. Alexanders Discount Company asked for, and was given, a six-month unsecured loan facility by the Bank of England for £500,000. The Bank also reduced from 5% to 2% the margin of excess collateral that it required for loans of money against Treasury bills and very short gilts.[29]

The discount market did much better in 1957, when there was another big increase in Bank rate. The houses had made good profits in the first half of the year, but they cut their over-one-year bond books, perhaps because the Bank warned them in May that they would have to make a special return at the end of June.[30] They became uneasy about the economic outlook in August, and no doubt shortened their positions further.[31] Cobbold and Mynors told them at their regular weekly meetings during August that sterling was under pressure but the minutes record no Bank rate warning.[32] Over the year as a whole, the houses' capital resources increased moderately.

The larger discount houses were the dominant market-makers in up-to-five-year gilts and collectively held a much larger book than the

[29] Clarke, 'Discount market 1955', 23 January 1956, BOE C47/39.
[30] 17 May, 1957, BOE LDMA1/10.   [31] Clarke, 'Discount market – 1957', BOE C47/40.
[32] Notes dated 16 August–13 September 1957, BOE LDMA1/10.

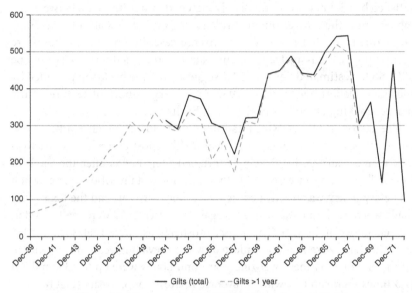

Figure 8.3 Discount Market Gilt Holdings (£m), 1939–72

Stock Exchange jobbers, even though the jobbers were not confined to short maturities.[33] The smaller houses treated their gilt holdings more or less as investment portfolios.[34] Between 1951 and 1959, the discount houses' holdings (Figure 8.3) represented roughly 5–15% of the total of under-five-year gilts. Their turnover in bonds from 1950 to 1956 is shown in Table 8.1. In 1956, it was a little over £10 million a day, compared to the £50 million a day estimated for the Stock Exchange in 1957.

Among the discount houses, Union Discount Company was by far the largest and most active; its capital base was £14.25 million at the end of June 1957.[35] Its manager was Arthur Trinder, who once said that 'I am the market in certain short bonds'.[36] Despite his and others' efforts, the Bank became worried in June 1957 that liquidity in short gilts was insufficient to attract investors who might want to sell quickly. Daniell therefore approached Trinder and agreed to support his market-making activities

---

[33] O'Brien described the discount market as 'the principal dealers in short gilt-edged securities' in 1956. O'Brien–Mullens, 'Bond-washing', 31 July 1956, BOE C132/79.

[34] Radcliffe Committee (1960a, vol. 2 p. 24 para. 22).

[35] The financial journalist Wilfred King remarked in a lecture (1962, p. 13) that 'one big house may operate as a true jobber' in short gilts. Undoubtedly he meant Union.

[36] Parker Tribunal (1958), 18 December 1957, Q 8979.

Table 8.1 *Discount Market Turnover in Bonds, 1950–56 (£m)*

Year	Turnover.	Amount of short gilts outstanding, outside NDC, as at 31 March.	Turnover as % of amount outstanding.
1950	1,839.3	2,340.6	79
1951	1,505.5	1,781.8	84
1952	1,653.5	3,141.2	53
1953	3,184.7	3,379.9	94
1954	4,802.4	3,201.3	150
1955	2,607.2	3,219.0	81
1956	2,733.1	3,735.8	73

Sources: Radcliffe Committee (1960a, vol. 2, p. 25), Pember and Boyle (1976), author's calculations.

'on the basis that if he gets into a muddle the Bank will bail him out.'[37] In this context 'bailing him out' would have meant buying gilts from him at the market price, not at an artificial price. A little later, it was agreed that 'The position is that if on any day it is inconvenient for the Bank to take stock off the Union Discount because of the money position, etc. he [Trinder] would always take Funding 2¼% against it provided that the Bank would take this back at a time more suitable to themselves. We also checked that should he wish to sell us stock at the end of the day, this would go direct into W.J.M.'s name [i.e. the Government Broker's name] and of course not go near the market [i.e. the jobbers].'[38] The agreement with Trinder was not intended to be permanent: the Government Broker commented on 14th June that 'Hawker gave me the impression that the Governor was anxious to contract out the moment the market was working again. I said I appreciated this and in fact we would all like to do so, but it was terribly important not to do so too soon. We must see the initial stage through, and then could tell Trinder that we were no longer there and hoped that things would stand on their own feet.'[39] And on 28 June, the Government Broker recorded that

---

[37] 11 June 1957, BOE C132/2. Daniell added that we (i.e. he and Trinder) 'both foresee that the real danger is the rest of the Discount Market taking this as an opportunity of getting out and staying out.'

[38] 12 June 1957, BOE C132/2. 'Funding 2¼%' must mean 2¼% Serial Funding 1957, which matured on 14 November.

[39] 14 June 1957, BOE C132/2. Sir Cyril Hawker was an executive director of the Bank of England.

I saw Trinder today and thanked him for all he had done to help us as far as the short market was concerned, and there is no doubt that this all worked out very satisfactorily.

I told him that we would no longer want his services, but if at this stage he wished to sell us any stock we would be perfectly happy to take it from him. He said, however, that his book was of quite reasonable size and that he could go on taking stock if it was offered in any reasonable size. If, however, he was asked to make a bid for any large amount of stock he would of course let us know.[40]

Over the period 7–27 June, the Issue Department bought £9.7 million net of under-five-year gilts. The net total includes the sale in the week beginning 14 June of £4.5 million of 2¼% Serial Funding 1957, which had five months to run, presumably to Union, and the purchase of the same amount of the same stock the following week.

Trinder disclosed quite a lot about Union's gilt business in evidence to the Parker Tribunal, in December 1957. He said that his turnover was £31.5 million a week (Q 8954), and that 'we are the biggest dealers. I cannot always do what I want to. I make the market. If the Union Discount suddenly appears to sell £5,000,000 or £10,000,000 worth of stock, generally I cannot deal, because nobody is buying from me. So you have to sit reasonably quiet and hope for the best at certain times' (Q 8995). Then he added that, 'I had a short-dated investment book of about £80,000,000 to £85,000,000 at that time [just before the Bank rate rise in September 1957], but to do anything worth while you have really to think about selling £10,000,000 or £15,000,000, and that was not possible' (Q 8997).[41]

The figures that Trinder disclosed suggest that Union's book alone (mainly in shorts) was larger than that of all the Stock Exchange jobbers combined, but that his turnover was of the order of a tenth of that on the Stock Exchange. So Union's business was based much more on position-taking and carry (i.e. the difference between the yield on gilts and the cost of financing them), and much less on turnover, than that of the jobbers. Discount houses could borrow money cheaply: in January 1959, they could borrow against gilts at 2.375%, whereas the large jobbers were paying 3.5%.[42] Union was able and willing to quote dealing prices in larger amounts than the jobbers could accommodate, and thus reduced the amount of business that the Bank of England had to do to absorb large

---

[40] 28 June 1957, BOE C132/2. At the end of June, Union had £21.9 million of over-one-year bonds (Clarke, 'Discount market – 1957', BOE C47/40).

[41] Parker Tribunal (1958). It seems likely that much of Trinder's £80–85 million had less than a year to maturity, for example 4% Conversion 1957/58, which was redeemed on 15 June 1958.

[42] Mullens, 27 January 1959, BOE C132/2.

orders as a backstop for market liquidity. Union dealt both directly with investors and, via brokers, with the Stock Exchange jobbers.[43] Later, in 1964, Jasper Hollom, the Chief Cashier of the Bank of England, commented that

the market would certainly benefit substantially from the presence of a skilled dealer in command of a substantial block of resources. This is just what our jobbers fail nowadays to provide – and what, to some extent, Trinder did provide in the short market in his heyday.[44]

Trinder himself, however, fell out with the board of Union, who thought his gilt book was too large, and he retired in 1958.[45] Nevertheless, his retirement was not followed by any large fall in the discount market's gilt holdings, as Figure 8.3 shows.

In 1960, two medium-sized discount houses, Cater Brightwen and Co and Ryders Discount Company, merged. It was hoped that the creation of another large discount house would make for a better bond market.[46] The merged firm prospered, but there is no evidence as to whether the hope was fulfilled.

The impression of the gilt market in the late 1950s that emerges from the evidence is of a market-making structure consisting of the jobbers on the Stock Exchange, having only limited capacity and unable to handle large orders, the discount houses, having perennial but fluctuating long positions in short gilts financed by fairly cheap borrowing and (at least in the case of Union) able and willing to quote prices in relatively large amounts, and the Bank of England Issue Department acting as the backstop market-maker. And the Issue Department was occasionally a backstop provider not just of market liquidity, but also of capital (section 8.3).

8.5 The Radcliffe Report

The Radcliffe Committee on the working of the monetary system was set up in 1957 in response to dissatisfaction and confusion about the role of monetary policy in macroeconomic management. Its report, published in 1959, paid close attention to public debt management. It took copious

---

[43] In Allen (2014, p. 175), I stated erroneously that discount houses were obliged to use the infrastructure of the Stock Exchange when dealing in gilts. They were not.

[44] Hollom, 'The gilt-edged market – Sir George Bolton's suggestion', 12 August 1964, BOE C42/14.

[45] Cleaver and Cleaver (1985, p. 90). Trinder died in 1959.

[46] Clarke, 'Discount market 1959', 4 February 1960, BOE C47/40.

evidence from the Treasury, the Bank of England, leading figures in the Stock Exchange and overseas central bankers.[47] However it was not satisfied with the policies of the Bank of England and the Treasury in the gilt-edged market, nor was it convinced by their explanations. Like other critics of official policy in the 1950s and later, it was impatient with a policy which left the timing of gilt sales, and therefore the certainty that they would be achieved, largely to the market:

551 ... the authorities have not been prepared to force interest rates on the longer bonds upwards in order to tempt holders of short bonds to switch to long bonds.[48]

The committee could not understand the authorities' desire to moderate price movements, and wanted the authorities to act so as to get prices more quickly to levels at which there was demand for gilts and official sales could take place:

562. The task of debt management is therefore to push the rate of interest to a level that is high enough to attract sufficient firm holders for the debt and yet is consistent with a balance between demand in the public sector, demand in the private sector, and the available resources of the economy ... The debt manager's task looks straightforward enough, once he is over that awkward preliminary, the diagnosis of economic trends. He has only to lower interest rates and allow the debt to become more liquid, or to raise them and make it less liquid by selling more long bonds.

563. Unfortunately this straightforwardness is illusory. It depends on an assumption that the demand for illiquid securities becomes greater as their prices fall, and *vice versa*, and that this characteristic of the demand is stable enough to be of use for operational purposes. Witnesses from the Bank of England and the Treasury strongly contested this view of the demand for securities. The basis of their criticism – and this has coloured their debt policy throughout the period – is that, because a transaction in marketable long-term securities can be easily reversed (at market prices) at any time during their lifetime, and because deferment of a purchase today leaves the owner of money the option of making a purchase tomorrow or next week, the market in long-term securities is dominated by expectations of future prices and is therefore seriously liable to react perversely to a movement of prices. The importance of expectations in influencing the structure of interest rates and the level of interest rates has been stressed in economic literature, and the arguments commonly developed there afford some support for the monetary authorities in their stress on expectations. Our view is that expectations have been overrated as independent market forces, and that at times the influence of the authorities themselves on those expectations has been correspondingly underrated.[49]

---

[47] Radcliffe Committee (1960a and b).   [48] Radcliffe Committee (1959).
[49] Radcliffe Committee (1959).

The report echoed the Macmillan Report of 1931 (Chapter 5, 5.1) and the National Debt Enquiry of 1945 (Chapter 7, 7.1) in its conclusion about debt management:

982. Thirdly, monetary policy must take its influence upon the structure of interest rates as its proper method of affecting financial conditions and eventually, through them, the level of demand. There is no doubt that it has, and can, exert this influence through the management of the National Debt which, if burdensome to the financial authorities in other respects, affords in this respect an instrument of singular potency. In our view debt management has become the fundamental domestic task of the central bank. It is not open to the monetary authorities to be neutral in their handling of this task. They must have and must consciously exercise a positive policy about interest rates, long as well as short, and about the relationship between them.[50]

In the United States, the Federal Reserve reached precisely the opposite conclusion (see Box 8.1).

Unfortunately, the committee had been given incomplete evidence. It was not told that the jobbers had been rescued in 1952 and 1957; nor did the evidence make clear to what extent the Bank of England become a market-maker in gilts, standing behind the Stock Exchange jobbers, who were increasingly becoming a façade. Cobbold had asked Radcliffe to be allowed to give evidence in secret – 'I should find it very awkward to give evidence with complete freedom for a 100% published record about Issue Department operations and policy'[51] – but the committee had demurred.[52] This was a pity. It meant that the committee was not told how fragile the market structure was, and perhaps that the Bank felt able to ignore the debt management aspects of its report.

What exactly were the authorities, and in particular the Bank of England, worried about? What did they think would happen if they allowed gilt prices to move more suddenly?

First, market-makers adjust prices gradually in response to fluctuations in supply and demand, and the Bank was the main market-maker. It would have been rational for the market to interpret a fall in gilt prices as an initial official reaction to a wave of offerings of gilts, and to infer that the Bank had also bought some of the gilts on offer, so that it would need to sell more

---

[50] Radcliffe Committee (1959). See also Cristiano and Paesani (2017).
[51] Cobbold–Radcliffe, 13 May 1957, BOE G1/131.
[52] Radcliffe Committee (1960b, Q223, p. 12; Q750, p. 44, and ensuing statement from Lord Radcliffe). I am very grateful to Lord Armstrong of Ilminster, who was the secretary of the Radcliffe Committee, for confirming that the committee was not told of the rescues in secret.

later. Indeed, in the late 1960s, such an interpretation would have been entirely realistic (Chapter 11).

Second, it may be assumed that the rescue operations of 1952 and 1957 (section 7.3), and those that were to follow in the 1960s, together with the tacit assurance that capital support would be available in case of dire need, were necessary to keep the jobbers in business. To have allowed price movements to be more violent would have risked either more, and more expensive, rescues, or the disappearance of the commercial market-making structure. Market liquidity was meant to be one of the main attractions of gilts, and its impairment could have made it difficult or impossible to refinance maturing gilts except perhaps at very short maturities and led to the gradual monetisation of the stock of gilts.[53]

Nobody can know whether fuller disclosure by the Bank of England might have affected the Radcliffe Committee's thinking. The report does not, in my judgment, pay adequate attention to market microstructure issues, and this inadequacy seriously weakens the force of its analysis of gilt market operations. However, there is no reason to think that its conclusion that the authorities should have a positive policy about interest rates at all maturities would have been any different. And to say that the authorities' intervention policies in the gilt market had a secure rationale is not to say that they were wisely implemented.

There is another possible explanation of extrapolative market expectations and behaviour, about which the Radcliffe Report was sceptical, not directly related to the microstructure explanation, but not inconsistent with it. Theories of efficient markets developed since the Radcliffe Report assert that all information relevant to asset pricing is instantaneously incorporated into the price, and that if new information arrives randomly, then price movements will likewise be random. Extrapolative behaviour would be irrational. These theories however assume that all relevant information is made available to all market participants at the same time. This was clearly not the case in the gilt-edged market. Rather little information about the public finances was published, at least until the Bank of England and the Treasury disclosed information in evidence to the Radcliffe Committee, and such macroeconomic information as was published was available to the Treasury and the Bank of England before it was disclosed to private investors. The discretionary nature of the Issue

---

[53] Foucault, Pagano and Roell (2013, ch. 9) explain that there are powerful reasons to expect security yields to be very sensitive to market liquidity. The theory had not been developed in the 1950s.

Department's operations enabled the Bank to use non-public information in its market operations.[54] Investors knew that the authorities had a great deal of information relevant to the valuation of gilts to which they were not privy. In those circumstances, they might reasonably have interpreted any price movement as the result of a change in economic fundamentals which had not been disclosed to the public and which had either influenced the behaviour of the authorities in the gilt market, or which had leaked to other private investors and influenced their behaviour. In those circumstances, it could have been rational to extrapolate: to sell on a fall in price or buy on a rise. The Radcliffe Report did not explore this possibility.

BOX 8.1 'Bills-only' in the United States

The Federal Reserve reactivated monetary policy in the United States in 1951, several months before the Bank of England, when it reached its Accord with the US Treasury. From 1942, the Fed had supported the prices of US government securities of all maturities at levels determined by the Treasury.[55] The Accord withdrew the price supports, and incidentally also withdrew the market liquidity which the price supports had implied.[56]

The Federal Reserve had acknowledged, after the war, 'responsibilities for maintaining an orderly and stable market for Government debt'.[57] After extensive debate and despite internal disagreement, it adopted in 1953 a 'bills-only' policy which confined its operations in Treasury securities 'to the short end of the market (not including correction of disorderly markets).'[58] The Fed's policy was thus the polar opposite of the Bank of England's.

---

[54] Fforde's account of the Issue Department's operations in May–July 1968, quoted in Box 11.1, shows how the Bank used information not available to the market.

[55] Mehrling (2011, ch. 3) points out that the Fed had set out to 'maintain orderly markets' in government securities in 1937; this consisted of augmenting market liquidity by acting as a dealer within limits determined by the Federal Open Market Committee.

[56] Binder and Spindel (2017, ch. 5) give a convincing account of the genesis of the Accord.

[57] Thomas and Young (1947, p. 100), quoted by Garbade (2012, p. 345).

[58] Federal Reserve (1954, p. 88), Konstas (1966, ch. III), Sproul (1980, pp. 105–11), Meulendyke (1998, pp. 35–9), Bremner (2004, pp. 99–103), Wood (2005, pp. 247–56), Meltzer (2009, pp. 59–69). Conti-Brown (2016, pp. 44–6) presents the debate as a power struggle between the Federal Reserve Board and the Federal Reserve Bank of New York, which the former won.

BOX 8.1 (cont.)

The Fed Chairman, William McChesney Martin, in explaining his policy, said that:

As investors continue to operate in a free market for Government securities I am confident that they will develop a fuller understanding of the minimum role to be played by the [Federal Reserve] System in such a market. They will then feel freer to express their own judgments about market values and will thus develop a market with greater depth, breadth and resiliency.[59]

The post-Accord market in US government securities appears to have been very liquid at the short end, but less so at longer maturities, according to a study carried out for the Joint Economic Committee of the US Congress:

In the case of short-term securities most large dealers describe themselves as willing to 'stand on their market' for almost any amount the customer offers. But, in the event that a customer desires to sell a relatively large amount of a long- or medium-term issue, e.g. $5 million, a large dealer will normally buy some proportion of the offer, say $½ million or $1 million. He will then try to dispose of the remaining amount through interdealer trading or after inquiry, among those customers who are likely to have a need for the particular issue or maturity range. The dealer will not normally take the remaining $4 million or $4½ million into position until he is able to arrange the sale of these securities to a customer. On occasion an infrequently traded issue is offered. Even the largest dealers indicate an unwillingness to take such 'thin' issues into position until an offsetting sale has been arranged.[60]

Moreover:

Most dealers now recognize the weakness or 'thinness' of the long-term market for Government bonds . . . Failure of the market to become more active and the closely related failure of dealers to take larger positions in bonds result from . . . the failure of the 'bills only' policy to restore the now famous trinity – depth, breadth, and resiliency – to the long-term market.[61]

8.6 Bond Washing

Bond washing was a species of transaction in gilts intended to exploit differences in the tax treatment of different kinds of return on gilts

---

[59] Martin (1953, p. 12).   [60] Meltzer and von der Linde (1960, p. 15).
[61] Meltzer and von der Linde (1960, p. 47).

(dividends and capital gains), and/or different kinds of investors in gilts. For example, for some investors, some of the time, capital gains were taxed in the same way as dividends, while for others, they were taxed either not at all or less heavily. Dividend income migrated towards those investors in whose hands it was relatively less heavily taxed.

Because of the time it took to prepare dividend warrants manually, gilts were traded ex-dividend – i.e. without the right to receive the next dividend – for a period before each dividend date. Bond washing was facilitated by the fact that, for a period before each stock went ex-dividend, it was possible to deal in it either cum-dividend or ex-dividend – that is, with or without the right to receive the next dividend. If A sold to B cum-dividend, and simultaneously purchased from B ex-dividend, A would in effect simply have sold the dividend to B without affecting his risk exposure.

The Inland Revenue had long been aware of bond washing. In January 1935, presumably at the Revenue's behest, the Bank procured from the dealers in the gilt market an undertaking not to deal in 3½% War Loan – the biggest stock in the market – at ex-dividend prices prior to the closing of the books for the dividend. This was evidently not the first such undertaking that they had been induced to give: 'As a result of a request made many years ago, the Dealers in the Consol Market agreed not to deal in War Loan 5% at an ex-dividend price previous to the closing of the books for the dividend.' A similar undertaking was extracted from the discount houses.[64]

The Inland Revenue and the Bank had periodically persuaded the Stock Exchange to introduce new rules aimed at preventing the new variants of bond washing which periodically appeared. As Mullens put it in commenting on

---

[62] E.g. Konstas (1966, ch. III) reviews the issues.

[63] Radcliffe Committee (1960b, Qns 9498–9504, 9735–9819). See also Sayers (1957, pp. 142–5).

[64] 10 January 1935, BOE C40/958; Harvey–Campbell, 30 January 1935, BOE C40/958.

a new anti-washing rule introduced in 1956, 'The general attitude seems to be Oh well, we must find a way round this'.[65] Michie (1999, p. 373) complains that the Inland Revenue responded to new manifestations of bond washing by causing the Stock Exchange to impose new rules on its members, but did nothing about bond washing outside the Stock Exchange, e.g. by the discount market. However the Inland Revenue was well aware of the discount houses' role in the gilt market, and the Bank of England was careful to accompany each tightening of the anti-bond washing rules of the Stock Exchange with a parallel injunction to the discount market. One example from 1935 was mentioned above; and in 1956 the Bank induced the discount market to observe rules about delivery of gilts traded on and just before their ex-dividend dates, which had also been imposed on the Stock Exchange.[66]

Some forms of bond washing amounted to outright fraud. Cum-dividend sales to jobbers combined with ex-dividend purchases created tax claims for the jobbers which in some cases were unrelated to any tax that the Inland Revenue had received.

This is not the place for an extensive discussion of bond washing.[67] Bond washing contributed virtually nothing directly to market liquidity, since it involved the exchange of one (or more) bonds for others that were identical or very similar. It perhaps contributed indirectly to market liquidity by providing the jobbers with a source of income which helped them maintain their market-making activity, but at considerable risk to their reputation. Francis and Praed, which had been the largest gilt jobber before and immediately after the Second World War, was censured in the 1960s for participating in bond washing; this was a milestone in the long decline of the firm, which eventually went out of business in 1973.

---

[65] Mullens, 14 August 1956, BOE C132/79.
[66] O'Brien, 'Bond washing', 31 July 1956, BOE C132/79.
[67] Wormell (1985, pp. 138–9) provides further information.

Gilt Market Liquidity in the 1960s

9.1 Monetary Policy and the Problem of Market Liquidity

The conflicts created by inadequate bond market liquidity were vividly exposed in February 1960, when the Bank of England was forced to act as a price-setter. Since 1958, the clearing banks had been selling large amounts of gilts to finance increased commercial lending. Until 1959, the authorities had accommodated their sales, acting as a buyer in case of need, in the interests of economic growth. Early in 1960, they became concerned, belatedly, about inflation and the exchange rate, and on 21 January increased Bank rate from 4% to 5%.[1] The Bank now had no monetary policy reason to help the clearing banks acquire additional liquidity. Moreover, the previous week the Treasury had suggested to the Bank 'that there was a growing feeling that the long-term rate was not high enough'.[2]

During February, Lloyds Bank was a persistent seller of gilts in the 1965/69 bracket, and by Friday 19th the jobbers had grown restive. Having ascertained that Lloyds wanted to sell a further £9 million (money value), they asked the Government Broker for a bid. The Bank, in its market-making capacity, bid 0.125% below the prevailing market price and acquired £10 million nominal of stock.

On the following Tuesday, 23 February, Barclays Bank appeared as a seller of £20 million and the jobbers immediately approached the Government Broker:

---

[1] Allen (2014, ch. 12).
[2] 'Economic situation' (minutes of meeting between Amory, Cobbold and others), 16 February 1960, BOE C42/13.

We bought £14 mn. nominal in the 1965/69 bracket at 5/8% below the market, and £6 mn. nominal, short-dated at 1/8% below the market. This special deal (which was not 'marked') was arranged at just about the close of business on the Tuesday, so that on that day no change was made, as a result of this transaction, in the price at which official dealings in stock were made.[3]

While yields, as calculated from prices recorded in the press, had risen by only about 4 basis points at short and long maturities on Friday, Monday and Tuesday, net official purchases were £25.6 million (excluding the £6 million special deal).[4] This was very heavy support by the standards of the time: it was equivalent to a coefficient of about £650 million on the 'rise in yields' variable in part B of Table 13.1.

Early on Wednesday 24 September, the Bank decided that a downward adjustment in market prices was needed.

It was therefore agreed that the Government Broker should let it be known that he was a seller of stock in the 1965/69 bracket at $^3/_8$% below the previous market price. Before this decision was implemented, it was learned that Midland [Bank] wished to sell stock to the value of £25 mn.

It was then felt that a distinctly sharper reduction in market prices was warranted.[5]

The Bank bid 1% below the prevailing market level for the Midland stock. According to the *ex post facto* interpretation of the Bank's economic adviser, Maurice Allen, the decision was based on macroeconomic considerations:

... one action in giving effect to a change in general outlook, and so in credit policy, which had begun some time earlier, and not as a piece of routine management of the gilt-edged market.

As to the details:

This [1%] was an unprecedentedly large 'penalty'. But the bid was decided not in terms of the size of the penalty but in terms of the reduction in market prices felt the practical one to select.

---

[3] W.M. Allen, 'Committee on internal statistics. Gilt-edged market: 19th February 1960 onwards', 3 March 1960, BOE C42/13. In this context, I think that 'official dealings' means dealings recorded by the Stock Exchange, not dealings conducted by the Issue Department. The Bank of England thus arranged for the publication of misleading information about the prices at which transactions had been done. It is interesting that the Bank knew the identity of the sellers, and I surmise that the arrangements under which the clearing banks approached the Government Broker directly when they wanted to sell, which were in operation in 1968 (see quotation in Chapter 11, 11.1.3) were also in operation in 1960.
[4] Source: BOE ADM18/64, TDA, author's calculations.
[5] W.M. Allen, 'Committee on internal statistics. Gilt-edged market: 19th February 1960 onwards', 3 March 1960, BOE C42/13.

Midland did not accept this bid until nearly 3 o'clock on Wednesday, when they sold £29¾ mn., nominal, in the 1967/69 bracket. Though the Bank were unaware of it at the time, it is now believed that Midland also sold £10 mn. of short-dated stock to Union Discount at ½% below the market price. Meanwhile the Government broker had purchased, at broadly opening prices, £5 mn., nominal, medium-dated and £2½ mn., nominal, short-dated stock to enable jobbers to square their books before price [*sic*] to be established for the Midland sale was allowed to have its full impact on the market. Correspondingly, jobbers were aware that some price movement was under way and were not taking stock on their books. The Government broker avoided deals – apart from those just mentioned. Prices widened and weakened throughout the day; by close of business prices had fallen to the range where the Government broker was prepared again to deal.[6]

The Bank's purchases from the jobbers at 'broadly opening prices' could be regarded as a kind of rescue, though a relatively small one: the mark-to-market cost, according to my calculations, was about £44,000 (Appendix A).

Over the day, yields rose by up to 20 basis points at the short end and about 5 basis points at the long end.[7] The following day (Thursday 25 February), there were small net official sales of gilts.

The episode provoked questions in Parliament from Labour members asking whether the government had been aiming to tighten credit, to which the Chancellor, Derick Heathcoat Amory, replied as follows:

It was in line with the Bank's normal practice, except that the amount of stock offered, on top of what the Bank had already bought, was quite exceptional and unusual and, therefore, the [price] differential was larger than usual. It is that rather than any sharp change in policy.[8]

The episode also provoked a protest from the jobbers, who had been little more than spectators after 19 February. Akroyd and Smithers produced a 'memorandum on co-operation between the authorities and the gilt-edged market', which assumed

that the authorities would agree with us that it is desirable that the present jobbing system in the gilt-edged market should continue and be improved upon. We feel that it would be most undesirable from every point of view that the system should be reduced to that of an agency and that such a development would be most unwelcome in the City generally[9]

---

[6] W.M. Allen, 'Committee on internal statistics. Gilt-edged market: 19th February 1960 onwards', 3 March 1960, BOE C42/13.

[7] Sources for this and preceding paragraph: BOE ADM18/64, TDA (closing prices and 'Gilt prices to find their own level', 25 February 1960), author's calculations and interpretation.

[8] HC Deb. 15 March 1960 vol. 619 c. 1118.   [9] March 1960, BOE C42/13.

The memorandum complained of 'how difficult it is for jobbers to assess the day to day policy of the authorities from the sparse information available', and claimed that there was

no reason why jobbing operations, when related to the volume of business over the last few years and to the type of market in existence over that period, should not become sufficiently profitable, providing that the authorities conduct their open market operations on a more flexible and co-operative basis.

  If the present jobbing system is to be maintained, a greater degree of practical understanding of the difficulties by the authorities than ever before would appear to be essential.

The jobbers asked for:

  a. more information about government policy, comparing their position unfavourably with that of the discount market, which had regular weekly meetings with the Bank Governor;
  b. more generous terms on the sale of tap stocks;
  c. an undertaking that 'where policy regarding any particular operation changes . . . the authorities . . . allow jobbers to try to make their book accordingly, before the change is implemented, having regard to their responsibility to keep the market going': in other words, the jobbers wanted exclusive advance information about policy changes;
  d. an undertaking by the Bank to make a bid for large blocks of stock offered for sale by investors;
  e. purchases of stock to stabilise the market to be conducted earlier in the day;
  f. 'rescue operations', when 'the jobber, through a misreading of the market, finds himself with too much stock', to continue: 'On such occasions it has been a normal, but in no way guaranteed, practice for the authorities to help them out at, say, ¼ below the market price'; and
  g. lower interest charges for borrowing money from the commercial banks.

Some of these requests were for formalisation of existing practices. In any case, they were all comprehensively rejected by the Bank. In an internal Bank of England note, O'Brien dismissed the comparison with the discount market, and noted that the big jobbers already had information about official operations: any additional information would have to be released to the public at large. As regards more generous terms on tap sales, he pointed out that the Bank's duty was to operate to the government's best advantage, and that it was up to the jobbers themselves to negotiate their 'turn' on tap sales. As regards policy changes, O'Brien said that 'where a major change in official policy is concerned, the authorities have in the past given appropriate notice to the market and they will be prepared to do the same in like circumstances in the future; but they must remain the judges of what is a sufficiently substantial change to justify action of this sort.' The Bank had 'tacitly accepted for a considerable time' the obligation to make a bid for large offerings of stock, and that would continue. O'Brien rejected the idea of making support purchases earlier in the day, as it would mean 'a more artificial market and one which might come to depend more and more on official support.' 'Rescue operations' could continue at the Bank's discretion, and the cost of borrowing was for negotiation between the jobbers and the lenders.[10]

O'Brien's reply was conveyed to the jobbers on 18 May 1960 by the Government Broker.[11] The fact that the Bank communicated through an intermediary perhaps bore out part of the jobbers' complaint.

Relations between the authorities and the jobbers remained testy at times. In July 1964, after a week in which the Bank had made heavy purchases, the jobbers complained to the Government Broker about the terms on which the purchases had been made. In the ensuing discussion, as recorded by the latter, Hugh Merriman, the senior partner of Akroyd and Smithers, said 'that he considered that the Bank taking the Market out [i.e. buying unwanted stock from the jobbers] was a right, as far as the market was concerned, rather than a privilege.' This was one of the issues that had been raised in 1960, and the Government Broker refused to concede it.[12]

The malaise of the jobbers Francis and Praed continued. In January 1960, Cobbold was visited by the senior partner, Jack Jarrett. Cobbold recorded that: 'Most of the money in the business belongs to two people in their middle 70's. The death of either of them would present a formidable problem and the death of both would practically force them out of the market.' Jarrett wanted help in finding new recruits to the firm, which Cobbold agreed to provide. Cobbold obviously thought that was enough: 'Mr Jarrett tried to introduce one or two other subjects but I stopped him.'[13]

---

[10] O'Brien, 6 April 1960, C42/13.   [11] 18 May 1960, BOE C132/2.
[12] Gore-Browne, 'Market management', 21 July 1964, BOE C132/6.
[13] Cobbold, 27 January 1960, BOE G3/123.

9.2 The Gilt Market and the Money Market

The rupture between the money market and the gilt market that took place in 1914 was perhaps not fully repaired until the advent of a repo market in 1996 (Chapter 4). It was partly responsible for the lack of liquidity in the gilt market in the period discussed in this book. The discount houses had ready access to short-term loans at relatively low cost, because their liabilities were regarded as liquid assets for the banks, but the jobbers had no such advantage. They needed to borrow money from the banks to finance their long gilt positions, and to borrow gilts from investors so as to be able to deliver stocks that they had shorted. These transactions, which were collateralised, constituted a continuing link between the gilt market and the money market.

The Stock Exchange money brokers, which were departments of stock-broking firms, acted as intermediaries, both in the financing of the jobbers and in stock borrowing. They were able to find the stocks that the jobbers needed to borrow, and to arrange loans of money to the jobbers to finance their long stock positions. The two activities fitted neatly together. The ultimate lenders of stock – typically large investors – required collateral, which took the form either of bank deposits or money market instruments (which might be owned by the money brokers or might have been pledged as collateral to them by the jobbers), or of stock which the jobbers had pledged to the money brokers as collateral for money borrowed to finance their long positions. The ultimate lenders of money, the banks, also required collateral, which took the form of the stock of which the jobbers were long.[14] The loans of both money and of stock were overnight, or at call, so that the jobbers could repay loans of money when they ran down their long positions and repay loans of stock when they bought back the stocks that they were short of. Likewise, the lenders of stock could recall the loan if they wanted to sell the stock that they had lent. Before the war there had been 20–30 money broking firms, but from 1945 until 1972, there were only three.[15]

Discount houses could borrow money against gilt collateral more cheaply than the jobbers (see Chapter 7, 7.2 and Chapter 8, 8.4). They were no doubt able to borrow gilts as well, but appear to have had long positions most or all of the time.[16]

---

[14] Alford (1959) describes the money brokers' functions.   [15] Wills (2006).
[16] The Bank of England Discount Office's internal annual reviews of the discount market provide information on each discount house's holding of each gilt-edged stock with

Michie has criticised the Bank of England for unnecessarily constraining the range of business that the Stock Exchange could conduct:

> The failure, for example, to permit forward trading, or trading for the account, in government stock, made it difficult to conduct risk-free sale and buy-back operations on the Stock Exchange, and so the business was arranged elsewhere. Here the blame lay with the Bank of England, rather than the Stock Exchange in the 1960s. The Bank of England did not want its existing arrangements with the discount houses exposed to competition and so it stopped the Stock Exchange from introducing a facility that would have permitted that.[17]

The Stock Exchange had indeed approached the Bank about forward dealing in gilts at the end of 1959 after a deal done in good faith with Union Discount Company had been cancelled because it infringed the rule against forward dealing. It was suggested that forward dealing would 'make for a freer market', that the restriction had little practical value, and that there was quite a lot of forward dealing anyway.[18] The Bank dismissed the approach on the grounds that forward dealing 'could only encourage speculative business.'[19]

The Bank's objection to forward dealing in gilts seems unpersuasive. The Bank itself had many times issued new gilts in partly paid form, thereby in effect selling forward and hoping to attract speculative buyers (see e.g. Chapter 5). Forward dealing might have created complications with exchange control, and perhaps with bond washing, but they could probably have been overcome. All that said, however, it seems most unlikely that a more liberal attitude to forward dealing would have enabled the Stock Exchange to compete much more effectively with the banks and discount houses as an outlet for short-term funds. The crucial obstacles were that Stock Exchange member firms were partnerships whose financial resources were not known to their counterparties, and that they did not have access to the Bank of England as a lender of last resort.

A more pertinent question, therefore, is why the Bank did not lend directly to the gilt jobbers, and to the money brokers, until 1971.[20] It is true that Norman had hinted at a loan facility in 1944, and that the jobbers had

---

between one and five years to maturity, on the last day of each year from 1939 to 1968 (BOE C47/39 and 40). Not a single short position is to be found.

[17] Michie (1999, p. 475).

[18] Priestley–Secretary of the Council of the Stock Exchange, 30 December 1959, BOE C40/969.

[19] Hollom, 30 December 1959, BOE C40/969.

[20] Michie (1999, p. 409) mistakenly asserts that in 1957 the Bank of England began charging jobbers a higher interest rate than it charged discount houses for lending against gilt collateral. The Bank did not lend to jobbers at all in 1957.

responded negatively (Chapter 6, 6.3), but there had been many subsequent occasions on which the jobbers would have welcomed such a facility.
Traditionally, the Bank had provided funds to the money market through
the discount houses; but the gilt market had become much more important
after two wars, and could offer good collateral. It is hard to see that any
issue of principle was involved, and in 1971 the proposal to establish a loan
facility for the jobbers aroused little comment and no objection of principle
within the Bank (Chapter 12, 12.2).

9.3 The Bolton Plans

The lack of commercially provided liquidity in the gilt market had been
exercising the mind of Sir George Bolton[21], and in August 1964, he visited
O'Brien to discuss it:

> He [Bolton] returned to his favourite theme of the 'paralysis' which seizes this [gilt-
> edged] market from time to time, and wondered whether it might be helpful if he
> could organize some of the overseas banks into assembling a fund of gilt-edged
> securities which could be managed with due regard to their shareholders' interests
> but also in a way as helpful to the authorities as possible, with full information
> being provided to the authorities, through Mullens, of the operations of this group
> at all times.
>   I said I would think about this and come back to him.

O'Brien mentioned that the fund might be of 'about £100 million
revolving'.[22]

Hollom was unclear whether the fund was intended to underwrite new
issues, or be a dealing fund. He saw little benefit in an underwriting fund:

> But would it even so be wise to bring on new issues when the market was not really
> receptively inclined? If there was any prospect of the bad patch being prolonged, on
> what basis could one fix the issue terms? And would it not be the case that, if the
> market was anywhere near 'paralysed' and the fund had to realise securities (or
> bills) to enable it to intervene, we should find ourselves acting as the counterparty

---

[21] Bolton, who had joined the Bank of England in 1933, and had become an executive
director in 1948, became Chairman of the Bank of London and South America in 1957
but remained a non-executive director of the Bank of England until 1968. According to
Fforde (1992, p 196), his judgment was 'at times erratic and over-influenced by his
personal opinions'. In 1961, he had circulated to a wide range of influential people
a paper deploring the state of the gilt market and proposing that the Issue Department
accept a responsibility for making a market in all interest-bearing securities in which
Trustees were legally able to invest. It appears to have achieved nothing except to annoy
O'Brien.
[22] O'Brien, 6 August 1964, BOE C42/15.

and putting the necessary cash into the market for the fund to use? There seems only limited benefit in that.'

As to a dealing fund:

... the argument about the supply of cash seems again to apply to some extent. If we have, indirectly, to put up the cash for the dealings, we might as well do the transactions ourselves, except for the point that the support might be more effective if seen to be coming from elsewhere.

Moreover:

A more serious consideration would arise from any knowledge of a connection. Sir George suggests that the fund should keep close to Mullens in its operations, providing them with full information. But such a flow of information, however carefully handled, could hardly be wholly a one-way street – and would not be thought to be one. If it were to be believed at any time that a group of banks were receiving inside information from Mullens about official operations or intentions that could be turned to their own advantage, the position would at once become intolerable. This is a risk we should never run.

He therefore recommended replying to Bolton that 'virtually equal benefit could be derived from a fund operated wholly at arm's length from the authorities and seeking simply to serve its shareholders' interests.' He also expressed concern that such a fund might by-pass the Stock Exchange by dealing directly with large gilt investors, thus weakening the jobbers further, but thought that it was 'not a risk that we can effectively guard against.'[23] In the event, no such fund was ever established.[24]

Hollom had a further hopeful thought about the Bolton plan:

... if such a fund were to be established and operated successfully its lead might be followed, especially perhaps among the Clearing Banks. I cannot see, however, that if the banks were to manage their gilt-edged portfolios more actively this would have undesirable consequences from our point of view.[25]

Bolton returned to the subject in 1966, when the Stock Exchange had agreed to limited partnerships (section 9.5). According to Hollom's account:

[23] Hollom, 'The gilt-edged market: Sir George Bolton's suggestion', 12 August 1964, BOE C42/14.

[24] Bolton claimed to have had some expressions of interest: Hollom, 'Sir George Bolton's scheme', 20 August 1964, BOE C42/14.

[25] Hollom, 'The gilt-edged market – Sir George Bolton's suggestion', 12 August 1964, BOE C42/14.

Whereas on the previous occasion there had been talk of forming a syndicate of banks, the intention now was that they [Bank of London and South America] should operate alone with one jobber, up to a maximum of £5 million each ... The technique would be for the jobber to approach B.O.L.S.A. whenever he felt it appropriate, inviting them to take a 50% interest in a particular position. If they agreed, they would finalise the transaction through one of two firms of brokers who would be privy to the underlying arrangement.[26]

It is not clear whether this latter arrangement was ever implemented.

9.4 Capital Gains Tax

Capital gains tax was high on the agenda of the Labour government elected in 1964. The Bank of England unsuccessfully resisted its application to gilts, though superannuation funds were exempted. Its introduction was announced in the Budget of April 1965. The Chancellor, James Callaghan, made clear that it would be applied to gilts, and told the House of Commons that the introduction of the tax would not affect the 'fluidity' of the gilt-edged market.[27] His assertion was counter-intuitive: markets are more liquid if there is a body of traders willing to buy and sell in response to small price movements; taxing capital gains means that traders keep only part of any profits but bear the entirety of any losses, so that the activity is made less attractive. It is true that many traders were unaffected by CGT, as their capital gains were already taxed as income, but the investors that were affected accounted for £6,300 million of the £14,400 million of gilts in the hands of the market in January 1965.[28] Callaghan's assertion appears to have been based on the report of a working party which had included the following remarks:

22. It has also been argued that taxing gilts would impair management of the market by the authorities. This depends very much upon the effect of the tax on switching operations ... The effect upon holders affected by the tax would be to inhibit them from selling, lest they incur liability to tax; this would tend to reduce the volume of their dealings. The main effect on debt management would be to make it more difficult for the Issue Department to 'peddle out' stocks in the market, and to buy in next maturities; these operations depend on a consecutive chain of dealings whereby particular stocks change hands as their length to maturity declines and they become suited to different investment purposes. The tax would tend to inhibit this sequence of dealings. The tax might also have

---

[26] Hollom, 'B.O.L.S.A.', 5 May, 1966, BOE 6A385/1.

[27] HC Deb. 06 April 1965 vol. 710 c. 248.

[28] Treasury working group on gilt-edged and capital gains, Note of a meeting held at the Treasury on 11 January 1965, 15 January 1965, NA T326/413.

a certain de-stabilising effect on general price movements in the market. (In the United States a market rise tends to be accentuated by the reluctance of holders to realise capital gains.) On the other hand, it would seem that the general level of dealings (or activity) in the market is less important in making for general stability of prices than the ability of the authorities, in their capacity as 'underlying jobbers' to the market, to prevent persistent anomalies in the structure of rates, and to give an effective lead to prices when it is required.

23. The tax would no doubt tend to impede 'smoothing' operations, but the market is of very great size, the maturity structure is very well spread, and the general volume of transactions is very large in comparison with that of any capital market other than the United States market. Switching between holders unaffected by the tax and those affected could bring additional business to the market. The effect of the tax upon management of the debt can therefore easily be exaggerated. The difficulty of market management over the past decade has been due mainly to the long secular rise in interest rates, punctuated by sharp setbacks resulting mainly from recurrent balance of payments crises. The prime causes of difficulty have been and are likely to remain, economic, rather than technical.[29]

It was realised that it would be unreasonable to impose capital gains tax on the increase in value of a stock between the price at which it was issued, if that was below £100, and the redemption price of £100: to do so would be to impose a levy on a real or hypothetical investor who bought the stock on issue and held it to maturity. A little later, on 26 May, the government announced that

. . . as regards stocks issued before Budget day, capital gains tax would not apply to price movements within the range between the lowest price at which a stock had been issued and the redemption price. This altered the pattern of relative yields, because it increased the attraction of stocks issued at a discount for investors whose funds are subject to tax. Accordingly, although dealings were suspended for a time on the 27th while the implications for prices were being worked out, when business began again a certain amount of switching took place.[30]

Thus each stock had a 'neutral zone' of prices, and CGT was not charged on capital gains arising from price movements within the neutral zone.

CGT made gilt dealing much more complicated. It was charged on the totality of capital gains, net of losses, on all assets subject to the tax.[31] Losses on gilts could be offset against gains on equities, and decisions about gilt sales were therefore influenced by the investor's capital gains position. A phenomenon of 'locking in' thus occurred, whereby investors were deterred from undertaking gilt transactions which would either increase

---

[29] Working group on capital gains and gilt-edged, Draft submission to the Chancellor, 30 January 1965, NA T277/1646.
[30] BEQB Commentary (1965, pp. 221–2).   [31] Finance Act 1965, s. 20 (4).

their liability to CGT in the current tax year or deny them the opportunity to offset capital gains on other assets and thereby reduce their CGT liability in future years. In particular, CGT inhibited switching in reaction to price anomalies in the market by selling stocks that looked relatively expensive, and buying those that looked relatively cheap. Switching created liquidity in the market; the introduction of CGT therefore damaged market liquidity.[32]

In September 1965, when proposing a new long tap stock, Hollom complained that:

1. The development of the market over recent years owes a good deal to the increasing readiness of the Issue Department to act, where it can do so advantageously, as jobber of last resort and to the regular existence of a series of 'tap' stocks which the jobbers know they can draw on as a basis for their trading. In recent months turnover in the Stock Exchange has been greatly diminished by a number of factors, in particular the Capital Gains Tax, and the breadth and capacity of the market have been much reduced thereby. To leave the market for long without a 'tap' stock except in the short and medium range must sharpen these difficulties and add to the frustration and depression of dealers. This in turn could lead to contraction in the number of jobbing firms, which could permanently damage the market's structure.

2. It was demonstrated recently when a short-lived burst of institutional demand for long and undated stock occurred that, against this background, any sizeable buying interest can lead to exaggerated price movements and markedly wider quotations. Even sharply increased prices failed to bring out offers of stock (partly no doubt because holders with potential capital losses are reluctant to sell until these have been worked off). The buying interest soon evaporated so that substantial difficulties did not occur; but when eventually expectations of a considerable fall in long-term interest rates do develop it is not inconceivable that, in the absence of a long-date 'tap' issue, dealings could be brought to a halt.[33]

By 1968, the Bank was asking the Treasury to exempt long-term capital gains on gilts from tax. Deputy Governor Maurice Parsons wrote that:

The imposition of long-term gains tax on gilt-edged, as the law now stands, has produced the phenomenon of 'locking in'. This has greatly restricted worthwhile

---

[32] See, for example, 'Capital gains taxes ossify gilt-edged market', *The Times*, 1 September 1966, TDA.

[33] Hollom, 'The case for a new long-dated government issue', 3 September 1965, BOE 5A44/40.

switching operations in gilt-edged operations which have nothing to do with tax avoidance, and has reduced activity in the market below what it would otherwise have been. One of the principal attractions of gilt-edged, in particular to large institutional investors, is the opportunity offered for active management through large-scale switching operations that seek to gain advantage from anomalies in the yield structure. 'Locking in' has, in our opinion, damaged the market. The effect, which I agree cannot be quantified, is that less money is attracted to the market and that the cost of Government borrowing therefore becomes marginally higher.[34]

The government listened to the Bank's representations, and gilts were exempted from long-term capital gains tax in the 1969 Budget: the Chancellor, Roy Jenkins, said that 'This measure should make gilt-edged more attractive to investors and will encourage a more active market in gilts—a necessary condition for a successful selling policy.'[35]

It was not possible to quantify the effect of CGT on the gilt market at the time, and it is not possible now. It cannot be excluded that the imposition of CGT on gilts was indirectly responsible for the very high share of the Issue Department in market turnover in the second half of the 1960s, because heavier official intervention was needed to sustain adequate market liquidity; nor can it be excluded that the 1969 exemption was a necessary condition for the success of the retreat from heavy intervention that began at the end of 1968.

9.5 The Stock Exchange and the Jobbers' Capital

By the mid-1960s, the Stock Exchange had become concerned about the sustainability of the jobbing system, noting that the number of jobbing firms had fallen from 191 in 1950 to 59 in 1965, and the number of jobbing partners and associates from 1,014 to 613.[36] It recognised that the jobbing system needed additional capital resources. In 1961, a special committee recommended allowing jobbing firms to accept capital funds from people who were not full partners in the firm, and described various ways in which it could be done.[37] Another committee, which reported in January 1966, commissioned a report from the accountants Spicer and Pegler, who made

---

[34] Parsons–W. Armstrong, 'Capital gains tax and gilt-edged', 28 February 1968, BOE G41/2.

[35] Finance Act 1969, s. 41; HC Deb. 15 April 1969 vol. 781 c. 1009.

[36] Table dated 14 July 1965 in BOE C40/1053. The figures include equity as well as gilt jobbers.

[37] 'Report of special committee on jobbers' capital', 17 November 1961, BOE C40/1052.

financial inquiries among jobbing firms. However, Spicer and Pegler's report did not contain any reference to the gilt-edged market, probably because only five of the 11 gilt jobbers then operating provided their accounts to the inquiry.[38]

The obstacles to the accumulation of capital by the jobbers were at the root of the liquidity problem:

An even more powerful restraint on the growth of large firms [than the ban on advertising] was the insistence that all partners had to be members [of the Stock Exchange] and that they could have no other occupation apart from broking and jobbing. This, effectively, deprived Stock Exchange firms of the ability to obtain additional capital, in exchange for a share of the profits, or the opportunity to establish close alliances with others providing financial services.[39]

The Bank of England agreed. Hollom blamed 'Stock Exchange rules against the bringing in of outside capital combined with the difficulty (due substantially no doubt to taxation) for young men coming into a firm of finding the necessary capital.' He went on to say that:

It should be noted here that the gilt-edged jobbers have in a sense had the benefit of outside capital (and perhaps rather cheap capital at that) to a growing extent in that over the years they have had increasing support from the operations of the Issue Department. This has given them in effect the option of calling, at a price, on a much bigger book than they can themselves afford to maintain; or, put another way, to accommodate and encourage a larger volume of business than their own capital could have sustained. I believe that nothing in this review suggests that it would be in the interests of the authorities to curtail the Issue Department's activities.

And, he added:

It is also worth noting here that the attempt which I believe we consciously made to bring in the Discount Houses to supplement the jobbing system in the short bond field and to make up in this field for the jobbers' lack of capital has been an almost complete failure. The Discount Houses (with the notable exception of the Union under Trinder's management and, to a lesser extent, of Gerrard and Reid under Whitaker) have preferred to act as institutional investors rather than as jobbers and so have added to rather than alleviated the jobbers' problems.[40]

---

[38] Spicer and Pegler, 'Report to the jobbers committee', August 1966, BOE 6A385/1.
[39] Michie (1999, pp. 433–4).
[40] Hollom, 'The jobbing system', 30 September 1965, BOE C40/1053.

Hollom did not mention that Trinder, for whom he felt so nostalgic, had left the market because Union's board had been unwilling to go on accepting the risks he had been taking in gilts.[41] The discount houses generally seem to have become less effective over time as market-makers: 'when it came down to it, they didn't have the source of outlets, or they didn't have the range of outlets that the larger brokers had and so they weren't able ever to achieve what they might have liked to have done in that area.'[42] However, Hollom noted that despite the discount houses' retreat:

Competition from outside sources for big blocks of institutional business is also of great importance. The jobbers often find that much of a major deal has been done outside the market (generally through a merchant bank) on the basis of the prices the jobbers make, the jobbers being left with the task of handling the balance for which it has already proved difficult to find takers.

Hollom concluded that:

. . . our aims should be –

  i. to encourage the Stock Exchange to press on with arrangements, preferably flexible in form, for the introduction of outside capital,
 ii. to explore the possibility of a tax concession under which jobbers might be assessed on a triennial basis, and
iii. to encourage the formation of larger and stronger groupings among jobbing firms, particularly by the merging of gilt-edged and industrial jobbing.[43]

However, for a long time all efforts to solve the problem proved fruitless:

One solution to the shortage of capital was to allow firms to recruit partners who would provide capital in return for a share of the profits or losses, but not participate in the actual business. Simple as this remedy was it created numerous complications, which long delayed its implementation. There were those who were afraid that if outside capital was introduced it would allow the creation of a few very large broking and jobbing firms. These would then be able to drive the smaller firms out of business. Brokers were also worried that if there were only a few large jobbers then they could dictate prices in the markets. Jobbers feared that large broking firms could match more sales and purchases internally, so bypassing them completely. Consequently, for a variety of reasons there was considerable opposition to the idea of outside capital. Nevertheless, the need to find some solution to

---

[41] Cleaver and Cleaver (1985, p. 90).
[42] Interview with the former broker George Birks, CMH.
[43] Hollom, 'The jobbing system', 30 September 1965, BOE C40/1053.

the problem remained, forcing the Stock Exchange to consider the idea of limited partnerships in 1964, as capital drained away through retirement.[44]

The jobbers continued to look for capital. The job description that Akroyd and Smithers supplied to the Oxford University Careers Board in 1966, when they were keen to recruit a graduate trainee for their gilt-edged book, tells its own story. The prospect of 'something to come', i.e. an inheritance, was highlighted as a 'significant advantage' to an aspiring candidate. Nonetheless, the successful applicant was accepted without it.[45]

In 1966, the Stock Exchange allowed member firms to accept limited partners, and approached the clearing banks and the accepting houses about providing capital. The Bank of England was supportive:

> While it would certainly be wrong to press the [clearing] banks to participate against their better judgment, I think we might do well to ask them to think carefully before standing aside. The well-being of the jobbing system should be a matter of real concern to them.[46]

Nothing came of it, however.

While the Stock Exchange authorities and the Bank of England were ruminating, something more important was happening in the market, possibly unknown to them. The way in which the jobbers ran their businesses changed during the 1960s, so that it came to depend more on position-taking and less on turnover:

> ... we [Akroyd and Smithers], in the sixties, started taking much more positive positions in the gilt-edged market. And I think we were joined by others ... Again, we used to run this so-called back book suspense account. Also I suspect ... we used to job very much on the bear tack, being short of stock, which of course you could do in those days because you could borrow the stock and there was a very real money advantage in doing that ... So as I say the position-taking became very, very much more important than the jobbing side of it ... [47]

The discount market had relied on positioning rather than turnover as a means of making money in the gilt market; they were hampered by the narrowness of their distribution channels. The jobbers had ample distribution capacity, albeit through the brokers; now they were exploiting their capacity to make profits through position-taking – and in the later 1960s, with yields generally rising, position-taking was potentially lucrative.

---

[44] Michie (1999, p. 435), footnotes omitted.
[45] I am very grateful to Rodney Offer for this information.
[46] Hollom, 'Jobbers' capital', 1 February 1966, BOE 6A385/1.
[47] Interview with Brian Peppiatt, CMH.

The jobbers themselves had recognised that they needed more capital, and did something about it:

Well, the firm [Akroyd and Smithers] developed tremendously in that the gilt-edged market came to the fore, very much in the '60s. Some of the old family firms in the Stock Exchange in the equity market were finding it very difficult to continue through lack of capital in that the senior members who wanted to retire were basically taking their capital out. And as I say the capitals of firms made a tremendous difference to the firm and there was no way that any of the younger members could provide that capital, so it was quite a problem then. But that did equally give some of us who were doing reasonably well in the '60s [a chance] to expand through taking in some of these firms that covered other markets.[48]

Mergers economised on capital:

[You can] understand that when Akroyd and Blackwell, for instance, came together, you did achieve a degree of flexibility in the allocation of capital. If the gilt-edged market was running, it was unlikely that the oil market . . . was running at the same time. You could therefore, if you were properly organised and had the proper co-operation between partners, reallocate the capital that was set aside to be used in the equity market towards the gilt-edged market because that was the market that was running.[49]

The larger jobbers took responsibility for the solvency of the smaller ones. In January 1965, a small jobbing form, Alexander Thomson & Co, was 'thought to be insolvent; but . . . the large firms in the market would have joined together in a rescue operation to ensure that Thomsons were not hammered.'[50] They would thereby have ensured that Thomson's clients did not lose any money.

In June 1969, the Stock Exchange made a breakthrough:

. . . it was agreed that not only could brokers and jobbers incorporate themselves as limited liability firms but they could accept shareholdings from institutions.[51]

In the Stock Exchange as a whole, the number of jobbing firms fell from 59 in 1965 to 31 in 1970.[52] Akroyd and Smithers 'did take the route of placing, I think it was 25% of our capital and became a limited company in 1972.'[53]

Although partnerships were obstructed in building up their capital by the requirement to distribute all their profits, which were taxed as personal income, some alleviation was provided by the combination of the

---

[48] Interview with Brian Peppiatt, CMH.   [49] Interview with David Leroy-Lewis, CMH.

[50] Thornton, 4 January 1965, BOE C40/1053. 'Hammering' a Stock Exchange firm meant declaring it insolvent.

[51] Michie (1999, p. 437).   [52] Interview with David Leroy-Lewis, CMH.

[53] Interview with Brian Peppiatt, CMH.

preceding-year basis of tax assessment then in general use and the Partnership Change Provisions, which 'enabled, in certain circumstances, with a certain pattern of profits, a particular year to fall out of assessment for tax.'[54]

Thus in 1972, the Government Broker, though he was concerned about the general condition of the gilt-edged market, told the Bank of England that Akroyd and Smithers was 'a very large Firm, now a public limited company, with a good capital backing', and that the other large gilt jobber, Wedd Durlacher, was the 'biggest Firm in the Stock Exchange, now a public company with plenty of capital.'[55] Wedd Durlacher Mordaunt and Co, which had been formed by the merger in 1968, after several years' discussion, of the large gilt jobber Wedd Jefferson with the equity jobber Durlacher Oldham Mordaunt Godson and Co., was the eventual product of the mergers of 34 jobbing partnerships.[56] Durlachers' motive for the merger was that they had substantial surplus capital which they wanted to employ in the gilt market.[57]

---

[54] Interview with David Leroy-Lewis, CMH.   [55] Daniell–Page, 24 July 1972, BOE 3A92/1.
[56] 'Jobbing giant now registered', 13 April 1968, TDA; interview with Richard Durlacher, Robert Wilson-Stephens and Don Bailey, CMH.
[57] Hollom, 'The jobbing system', 30 September 1965, BOE C40/1053.

10

The High Tide of Intervention: 1960–66

10.1 The Pursuit of Economic Growth

From late 1957 onwards, the Prime Minister Harold Macmillan made economic growth his main economic priority. His initial concern was the 1959 general election, but growth remained the objective after the election had been won, and Macmillan chose his Chancellors with it in mind. His technique, influenced by the version of Keynesian macroeconomics that was dominant at the time, and by his private adviser Roy Harrod, was to stimulate demand by expansionary monetary and fiscal policies, in the expectation that output would respond. Inflation was to be contained by the maintenance of the Bretton Woods exchange rate parity, supplemented by incomes policies, a variety of which were tried out. The growth objective influenced debt management, as it did all other aspects of macroeconomic policy.

10.2 The Support Operation of 1961

During the Bretton Woods era, the UK was committed to maintaining the exchange rate parity of sterling against the dollar, which had been fixed at £1 = $2.80 after the devaluation of September 1949. Short-term interest rates were generally kept at the lowest level thought to be compatible with maintaining the parity, while exchange controls remained in force, and were intensified in the 1960s.

The Bank supported the gilt market during two periods in 1961 (Figure 10.1). The first period began in February amid pressure for a revaluation of the Deutsche Mark and accompanying outflows from sterling. A revaluation by 5% duly occurred on 4 March, but was widely

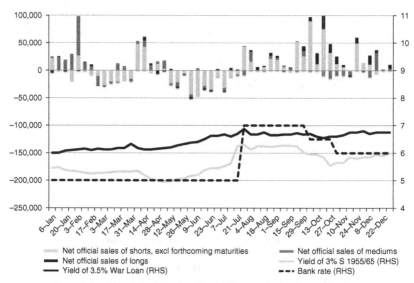

Figure 10.1 Net Official Gilt Sales (£000s) and Yields, 1961, Weekly

regarded as inadequate and therefore likely to be followed by another revaluation. The UK's gold and foreign exchange reserves fell by £80 million in February and March, and the Bank resisted rising yields with net gilt purchases of £120 million between late February and early April (Table 10.1). Yields fell back in April and early May, and the Bank made net gilt sales of £151 million. But a steeper rise in yields then began, and gold and foreign exchange continued to flow out. The Bank supported both the exchange rate and the gilt market: the gold and foreign exchange reserves fell by a further £177 million in May–July and the Bank bought £294 million (net) of gilts (Table 10.1) between mid-May and late July. Market intervention, super-sterilised by gilt purchases, failed to stop the rot: something more fundamental was needed.

On 25 July the Chancellor, Selwyn Lloyd, announced a package of measures intended to restrain domestic demand, including some fiscal tightening, an increase in Bank rate from 5% to 7%, a call for further Special Deposits from the banks, a tightening of exchange controls, and a request to the banks and insurance companies to be more restrictive in lending. He also announced that the UK would draw from the International Monetary Fund.

I have found no record of the Bank's reasons for supporting the gilt market. The *Bank of England Quarterly Bulletin*, which had been

Table 10.1 *Support Operations in 1961 (£m, Nominal, Sales +/Purchases -)*

Period	Forthcoming maturities (< 9 m)	Other shorts (< 5y)	Mediums (5–15 y)	Longs (> 15y)	Total (excl forthcoming maturities)	% of M3
24/02–06/04/1961	−76.1	−110.9	−7.4	−1.4	−119.6	1.0
12/05–27/07/1961	0	−263.4	−26.5	−3.6	−293.5	2.3

Sources: BOE C11/19–20, Bank of England Statistical Abstract (1970), author's calculations.

inaugurated in 1960 so that the Bank could explain what it was doing, merely noted that 'During March, sales by the banks and the absence of overseas buying tended to depress both short and medium-dated stocks: the market in these stocks was steadied by official purchases', and, as regards April–June, that 'Net purchases by the authorities of £260 million of stocks over the quarter as a whole were heavily concentrated at the short end of the market: they included the redemption of 2½% Funding Loan 1956/61 in April.'[1]

The only relevant document I have found in the archives is a one-page note written on 12 June by L.P. Thompson-McCausland, which makes a cogent argument against the policy:

Doubtless others will also be urging extreme caution in laying out money to support gilt-edged in present circumstances. This is to add my voice to theirs.

Our own underlying balance of payments will probably not be exerting much pressure until the late summer. The immediate threat is 'speculative' operations, leads and lags, and short selling. All these must be financed somewhere. The best immediate defence against them is a very tight rein on money here. With only a strictly limited part of our reserves and borrowing power remaining spendable (the most part being needed to see us through the correction of our own balance of payments), we cannot afford to give much ease to the market by purchases of gilt-edged.

The choice between a crack in gilt-edged and a crack in the exchange rate is unpleasant. But a crack in gilt-edged is reversible and, properly presented will be remembered as a move in the defence of sterling. A crack in the exchange rate is irreversible and will rightly be remembered as the mark of failure.[2]

There are two annotations on Thompson-McCausland's note: Sir Cyril Hawker, the executive director of the Bank responsible for domestic finance, wrote that: 'I am quite sure the policy agreed at Books the

---

[1] BEQB (1961 Q2, p. 4 and 1961 Q3 p. 12).
[2] Thompson-McCausland, 12 June 1961, BOE C42/5.

other day is the right one'. Books was a daily meeting of the top officials of the Bank. There do not seem to have been any minutes in 1961. Hawker's comment suggests that gilt policy was decided orally at Books. Thompson-McCausland was obviously aware of what the Bank was doing in the gilt market, but was equally obviously not a member of the small circle which decided policy. The other annotation came from Sir Humphrey Mynors, the Deputy Governor, who wrote that 'I agree that it [the choice between a crack in gilt-edged and a crack in the exchange rate] would be a very awkward choice, if it were to present itself.' It did present itself, soon afterwards.

There was no immediate recovery of the gilt-edged market after the July measures (Figure 10.1). The *Bank of England Quarterly Bulletin* commented that:

As a result of the measures announced by the Chancellor of the Exchequer on the 25th July, and in anticipation of the Trustee Investments Bill which received the Royal Assent on the 3rd August, prices in the gilt-edged market fell sharply. On the 2nd August rumours began to circulate to the effect that the authorities intended to withdraw their support. The Bank therefore reminded the market that it was not the practice of the authorities to support the gilt-edged market in the sense of pegging it at any particular price level; that the authorities would continue to be concerned to ensure orderly market dealings so that dealings at a price could continue; and that prices would continue to depend upon general market conditions.[3]

The Trustee Investments Act 1961 widened the investment powers of trustees, and was thought likely to lead to sales of gilts. It was a bit rich for the Bank to say that prices would 'continue to depend on general market conditions', after several months of doing its utmost to prevent prices from depending on general market conditions.

10.3 The Attempt to Manage Long-Term Interest Rates, 1962–64

As interest rates and bond yields fell back gradually from their 1961 peaks, the authorities, and especially the Bank of England, made it an objective to encourage the fall. This was in the interests of promoting economic growth, which, as already noted, was the Prime Minister's main economic preoccupation. It was also consistent with one of the Radcliffe Committee's recommendations, namely that the authorities 'must have and must

---

[3] BEQB (1961Q3, p. 12).

consciously exercise a positive policy about interest rates, long as well as short, and about the relationship between them.'[4]

It was in 1962 that the interventionism which the Bank had practised in short and medium gilts since the 1950s was extended to the long gilt market (Appendix D). The programme was an unacknowledged echo of Operation Twist, which was carried out in the United States in 1961 with similar intentions.[5] The techniques that the Bank of England used included making unusually attractive bids for gilts, notably including long-dated ones, that it was willing to buy in exchange for sales of the current long tap stock. In addition, the tender prices of new issues were set at above current market levels, in order to make it clear that the authorities would not obstruct falling yields: this meant that an unusually high proportion of official sales took place in the secondary market. By those means, the authorities intended to get long-term interest rates lower than they might otherwise have been; they also shortened the maturity of outstanding government debt.

It is not possible to identify the effects of the programme separately from those of the other influences on long-term interest rates. The implementation of the programme was notable for misunderstandings between the Bank of England and the Treasury about what operations had been undertaken and what objectives had been agreed between them, and, within the Treasury in 1963, between an expansion-minded Chancellor (Reginald Maudling) and his more cautious officials. The programme did not survive the change of government in October 1964. It had the incidental effect of further increasing the scale of the Bank of England's activity as the main market-maker in gilts.

10.4 The Support Operation of November–December 1964

The Labour government elected in October 1964 inherited a situation of excess demand, which was being manifested in a current account balance of payments deficit, an unsustainable growth rate of wages, and reserve losses. The government announced a temporary import surcharge on 26 October, and the new Chancellor, James Callaghan, increased income and excise taxes in a special Budget on 11 November. He also announced that he intended in the spring to extend the scope of capital gains tax (Chapter 9, 9.4).

---

[4] Radcliffe Committee (1959, para. 982). See Allen (2016) for a fuller account of the episode.
[5] See Swanson (2011) for more on Operation Twist.

These measures failed to stop the outflow of reserves, and Bank rate was increased from 5% to 7% on Monday 23 November. Gilt prices fell sharply and the Bank bailed out the jobbers by buying from them £19.6 million of gilts, mostly at above post-rate hike prices, taking an immediate mark-to-market loss of about £230,000.[6] The Government Broker recorded that 'We then sent the Dealers round the Market to clear all the Jobbers' books, dealing at our middle closing price for Friday.'[7]

The Bank rate rise, like the Budget, failed to stop the drain of reserves and the Bank of England arranged a loan of $3 billion from 11 central banks, plus the Bank for International Settlements and the Export-Import Bank of the United States. In addition, the UK drew $1 billion from the IMF on 2 December. These official loans were supplemented by official purchases of forward sterling in the market during December.

The gilt market was unsettled by the possibility that CGT would be levied on gilts, and prices fell after Callaghan had failed to exclude that possibility in a statement about CGT on 8 December (Figure 10.2). The Bank supported the market by net purchases each week from 27 November until Christmas (Table 10.2). Indeed, according to *The Economist*:

The dramatic action on Thursday of last week [17 December] by the Government broker in virtually taking over the London gilt-edged market has achieved its immediate purpose; market nerves have been soothed, order has been restored, and business has this week sunk to a low ebb. But on a wider view this official intervention marks an awkward conflict for official monetary policy. What happened last Thursday morning was that the normal mechanism of the gilt-edged market virtually ceased to exist. A steady stream of sales particularly by banks and discount houses, which was itself attributable simply to the general pressure on liquidity, caused disproportionate disarray because the uncertainties left by the proposed capital gains tax deterred buyers who would normally have stepped in. The upshot was that the market was entirely one way.

Jobbers were caught with increasing quantities of stocks on their books, and widened their prices; so that the normal switching operations between the different stocks, which is the particular pride of the market in British Government Securities, were virtually at a halt. In this situation, the Government broker, who acts as the ultimate jobber of the gilt-edged market and was himself taking increasing quantities of stock, took unusual action to restore market flexibility. He intimated not only that he was prepared to take in every stock on the list at existing (but not fixed) market prices, but that he would act as a seller of these

---

[6] See Appendix A for details. There were also £20.25 million of official gilt sales on 23 November, at close to post-rate hike prices.
[7] 23 November 1964, BOE C132/6.

Table 10.2 *Issue Department Net Gilt Sales (+)/Purchases (-),*
November–December 1964 (£m, Nominal)

Week beginning Friday	Forthcoming maturities (<9 m)	Other shorts (< 5y)	Mediums (5–15y)	Longs (> 15y)	Yield changes (basis points)		
					3½% Conversion 1969	5¼% Conversion 1974	3½% War Loan
20/11/1964	−0.5	107.1	6.7	11.0	+37.5	+17.5	+10.0
27/11/1964	−32.1	−8.8	2.9	2.0	+2.5	+5.0	+2.5
04/12/1964	−11.3	−11.0	−3.7	0.6	+27.5	+12.5	+5.0
11/12/1964	−6.2	−11.8	−7.0	−0.4	+12.5	+15.0	+5.0
17/12/1964	−31.0	−8.4	−0.2	−6.5	+7.5	+2.5	0

Sources: BOE C11/26, FTHA, author's calculations.

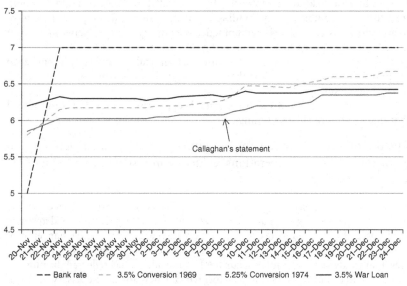

Figure 10.2 Gilt Yields (%), November–December 1964

stocks too. The result, as intended, was to move dealing prices closer together, and to restore an orderly market mechanism.[8]

[8] 'Support versus squeeze', *The Economist*, 26 December 1964, EHA.

Peter Daniell, who was now the Government Broker, described his actions in a note which was internal to Mullens and Co. as follows:

The Gilt-Edged Market, which has been weak for several days and has been aggravated by the fact that whenever we were offered stock we knocked larger amounts than usual off our bid prices, became really demoralised this morning. Prices fell ½% in the first half hour and although selling was not heavy people were prepared to take any price provided they could get out of the stock.

As a result, T.A.G.B. [his deputy, Thomas Gore-Browne] and I had a consultation with J.M.S. [John Stevens, an executive director of the Bank of England] and the Chief Cashier and decided we should intervene to steady the market. We then saw the three leading jobbers with Dobby [Mullens' dealing partner] and discussed how best to deal with the matter. We got them to agree among themselves to the middle price of most stocks and said that for the time being we would be prepared to buy stock at these prices.

We dealt with the short market slightly differently because the Bank are most anxious that the yields of these stocks should not fall. Consequently I said we would treat them in the normal way, bidding probably 1/16 below the price if we were offered stock. As a result we bought practically nothing, spending between two and three million, of which £1¾ million is the next two maturities.

How long we shall be able to go on with this is difficult to say as buyers appear to be unlikely until they know how they are going to be taxed but we have got some form of breathing space.

We told the Bank that this would inevitably appear in the Press but we all agreed that this was not really a bad thing.[9]

The Bank Governor, Lord Cromer, sent the Treasury on 23 December an account of the Bank's operations, evidently in response to a request. He said:

The most recent phase of weakness in the Gilt-edged market started on the 9th December. The proximate cause was the market's inability to determine the impact of capital gains tax on fixed interest securities from the Chancellor of the Exchequer's statement on future taxation. At the same time it was the Bank's view that yields on Government securities had not adequately reflected the move to a 7% Bank Rate and the underlying factors which had made this necessary; and that it was desirable to see some rise in those yields in order to ensure that interest rate should provide full support to other measures of economic policy.

Accordingly the Bank's operations in the market in the week ending 12th December were calculated to ensure that when they were forced to act as buyer of last resort the price should reflect their reluctance to support the market at ruling levels; prices accordingly fell, on modest supporting operations, by ¼ to 11/16 for short-dated stocks and by ¼ to ½ for longer-dated and irredeemable stocks.

---

[9] Note by Government Broker, 17 December 1964, BOE C132/6.

The market was selling particularly the stocks with low interest coupons which are most vulnerable to a capital gains tax; and the prices of those stocks fell most.

The weakness of the market persisted at the start of last week; turnover dropped off and prices tended to fall more markedly. The Bank again did not intervene to any great extent, except to steady a sharp fall in prices of short-dated stocks caused by some substantial selling in advance of the Clearing Banks' make-up date. But on Wednesday the publication of the adverse trade figures for November sparked off a general fall in the market. This gathered pace on Thursday morning (17th December) when a sign of incipient dismay in the market was the widening by the leading jobbers of the normal spread between their buying and selling prices, a move designed to fend off substantial selling. The Bank therefore instructed the Government Broker to steady the market, if possible without any great expenditure on purchases. He therefore told the three leading jobbers in confidence that he was ready to consider offers of stock at around the prices then ruling.

The leading jobbers reacted to this information by bringing the margin between their prices back to normal. This both steadied the market and provided others with a clue to the action which had been taken. That no direct information on the Government Broker's action had been passed on is evidenced by the fact that the smaller gilt-edged jobbers first learned of it in the Press.

The action taken by the Bank, although it received an undue degree of misleading publicity, has had the desired effect. Since last Thursday the market has been quiet and steady; and prices have been a little higher than those ruling at first on Thursday of last week. The Government Broker has been able to disengage himself somewhat. Nevertheless the market remains sensitive and conditions seem unlikely (in the absence of a decision to exempt gilt-edged from the capital gains tax) to improve appreciably before the turn of the year and then probably not until the economy and the exchanges look more settled and the market is better able to assess the impact of future taxation.[10]

Treasury officials were not satisfied with Cromer's account. One of them, I. de L. Radice, complained that the Chief Cashier had not told him, in an earlier discussion, that the Bank thought that yields had not risen sufficiently to reflect the increase in Bank rate to 7%. He thought that the Bank was exaggerating the effect of uncertainty about capital gains tax on the market, and that the pressure on sterling and the balance of payments were more important.[11] Samuel Goldman agreed with Radice, but the Treasury decided that no action was called for.[12]

Callaghan, too, was dissatisfied: according to his private secretary, he was 'much concerned by the policy which the Bank adopted in the week

---

[10] 'Gilt-edged market support', attached to letter from Cromer to W. Armstrong, 23 December 1964, NA T 326/574.

[11] Radice, 'Gilt-edged market', 30 December 1964, NA T326/574.

[12] Goldman, 'Gilt-edged market', 31 December 1964, including annotations by Rickett and W. Armstrong, NA T326/574.

ending 12th December, and by the fact that we were not told of it. He feels that, if the price of gilt-edged is taken by the foreigner to reflect the credit standing of the British Government, then the action which the Bank took worked in the direction of depreciating that standing.'[13] William Armstrong told O'Brien on 4 January that Callaghan was annoyed that gilt prices had been allowed to drop in the week ending 12 December; O'Brien commented that 'if banking credit is being squeezed, it makes no sense to give general support to gilt-edged prices at the same time and to that extent offset the effect of the squeeze.' O'Brien also 'explained the position to the Chancellor this evening [7 January]. He appeared to be satisfied.'[14]

The operation provided liquidity to the gilt market at a time when it would otherwise have been lacking, but in other respects it must be judged a failure: gilt yields continued to increase in the first half of 1965, probably partly because capital gains tax was levied on gilts in the 1965 Budget (Chapter 9, 9.4).

10.5 The Jobbers' Jobber

The Issue Department's turnover continued to increase between 1959 and 1966, though it did little more than keep pace with the increasing amount of gilts outstanding (Appendix D). The following points stand out from an analysis of its purchases:

a. Purchases of stocks approaching maturity were fairly steady from year to year, but with a hump in 1965, when there were heavy maturities.
b. Between 1959 and 1966, the Issue Department's turnover in short gilts, including forthcoming maturities, was little changed relative to the amount outstanding. It was 48% in 1966.
c. Its turnover in mediums and longs (5–15 years) increased from 11% and 4% to 16% and 15%, respectively, of the amounts outstanding. There was a hump in 1962, when the figures reached 29% and 22%, respectively. The hump was caused by the authorities' attempt to manage long-term interest rates (section 10.3 and Table 13.1, part B).

---

[13] Bancroft–Walker, 'Gilt-edged market', 4 January 1965, NA T326/574.
[14] O'Brien, 5 January 1964, BOE C42/14, and annotation.

    d. Official turnover increased sharply in 1965: the imposition of CGT on gilts that year probably led the Bank to intervene more heavily in the market to maintain liquidity (Chapter 9, 9.4).

The jobbers' jobber had become very busy. From March 1968, the Bank of England itself published statistics, beginning in 1966, both of market turnover in gilts, and of the turnover of official accounts (Figures 12.1 and 12.2). In 1966–70, the official share of total market turnover averaged 23% in under-five-year gilts and 27% in over-five-years. As explained in Chapter 8, 8.4, this implies that the Issue Department was the ultimate counterparty to about half of the market's transactions; and in the third quarter of 1966, the fraction reached three-quarters. Moreover, it seems reasonable to surmise that much of the market turnover represented switching between stocks of similar maturity so as to exploit yield differentials (or for bond-washing purposes), and that a smaller proportion of this business was passed through to the Issue Department than in the case of outright transactions or switches between stocks of widely differing maturities.[15] It seems clear that the gilt-edged market was still heavily dependent on the Issue Department standing behind the jobbers.

    The Bank of England evidently became uneasy about its own prominence after the mid-1960s. In 1968 it encouraged the jobbers to make wider prices in gilt-edged, in the hope that they would find it attractive to retain more of the positions they took in trading on their own books, but this did not seem to have much effect (Figures 12.1 and 12.2).[16]

10.6 The Jobbers' Jobber's Job

The Bank's concerns about market liquidity were perhaps the reason for the curious formulation of its debt management objectives which it published in an exposition of its gilt-edged operations in 1966. Instead of saying that its main objective was to meet the government's financing needs, or to restrain monetary or credit growth, it said that the 'chief purpose of debt management ... is to maintain market conditions that will maximise, both now and in the future, the desire of investors at home and abroad to hold British government debt.'[17] It was implicit that maintaining such market conditions was an essential precondition for meeting the government's financing needs, and that it thus had a higher short-term

[15] Chapter 8, 8.6.
[16] Fforde, 'Gilt-edged market: Friday September 27th', 27 September 1968, BOE 3A92/16.
[17] Bank of England (1966, p. 142).

priority. The article stressed the importance of the liquidity of gilts, and was quite explicit about the Bank's role:

The aggregate of the resources that the jobbers in gilt-edged stocks are able to commit, however, is small in relation to the volume of trading; unsupported, they might not be able, even with the help of wide swings in prices, to absorb the kind of pressures that build up when sentiment in the market veers sharply one way or the other. It has therefore become a prime consideration in official dealings to keep the pressures on the jobbers within supportable limits, and so contain the risk that a holder of government debt might find it impossible to deal either way in the market for whatever amount of stock he wished – subject only, if he is a buyer, to the particular stock he wants being available . . . .

   In normal official dealings . . . the Bank leave it to the jobbers in the market to take the initiative; the Bank offer stock – when they have it to offer – in response to bids made by the jobbers to the Government Broker, and bid for stock, if conditions justify doing so, when it is offered by the jobbers to the Government Broker. In this way they stand behind the jobbers in the gilt-edged market – acting as the jobbers' jobber, or a jobber of last resort.[18]

The article did not identify the discount houses as market-makers in gilts, but merely included them among the various categories of gilt-edged investors.

   In fact, the Bank's jobbing activities were not always 'last resort'. In discussing possible new issues in July 1960, O'Brien noted that 'We have £8 million War Loan, of which we are buyers at 60 and sellers at 60¼'.[19] The Bank's yield spread was thus 2½ basis points. The price spread quoted in the next day's *Financial Times* was 60 to 60½. It seems that the Bank was a keen jobber rather than a reluctant one. Likewise, in 1963, the Deputy Government Broker recorded that the National Debt Commissioners were willing to 'sell Conversion [presumably 3½% Conversion 1961 or after] and buy War Loan at a gain of 2/- [10 basis points] in the yield. The terms on which they will sell War Loan and buy Conversion are for a loss of not more than 1/- [5 basis points] in the yield.'[20]

   The position that the Bank occupied in the gilt-edged market was a complicated one. It stood behind the jobbers in the Stock Exchange, who provided what was on some occasions little more than a façade. It might have tried to replace or supplement the jobbers with more effective market-makers, as it had done in 1942. However, it is not clear how it could

---

[18] Bank of England (1966, pp. 142–3) façade
[19] O'Brien, 'Government loan operations', 6 July 1960, BOE C40/457.
[20] Gore-Browne, 'National Debt Commissioners', 14 August 1963, BOE C132/5.

have done so in the 1960s. Post-Trinder, the discount houses had been less effective as market-makers, and the failure of the Bolton plan suggests that there were no other potential market-makers on the horizon.

The Bank could in principle have made itself the exclusive market-maker in gilts, cutting out the gilt jobbers in the Stock Exchange, though it never considered it. To do so would have had serious disadvantages: although the Bank was doing much of the market's business, it was not by any means doing it all; and it would have had to take on a very large volume of small transactions for which it had neither the facilities nor the inclination. And it would have eliminated the possibility of the revival of the jobbers, which fairly soon took place. More generally, it would have threatened the continued existence of the Stock Exchange, something for which the Bank had no mandate.

11

The Conflict with Monetary Policy Recognised and Addressed: 1967–70

The Bank's involvement in the secondary market for gilts peaked in the mid-late 1960s (Figures 12.1 and 12.2 and Appendix D). The experience of those years demonstrated the truth of what Sir Kenneth Peppiatt had said in 1952 about the inherent conflict between controlling credit and controlling the price of government securities. The conflict had to be addressed, and it was.

11.1 Support Operations 1967–70: Narrative

Long-term bond yields were rising most of the time between 1967 and 1970 (Figure 11.1), and the pound was devalued in November 1967. Short bond yields rose in parallel with long yields until 1969, but then fell back, so that when long yields began to increase in spring 1970, the yield curve steepened. The Bank of England supported the gilt market periodically, and there were several periods when support was sustained over a few weeks (Figure 11.1, Table 11.1).

11.1.1 May–August 1967

Very large support was provided to the gilt market between May and July 1967. Moreover, it was more heavily weighted to longer maturities than in most other support operations (Table 11.1, Figure 11.2). The operation was better documented than the 1961 episode, partly because of the conscientiousness of John Fforde, the Chief Cashier at the time, who recorded the reasons for the initiation of the support operation, and partly because it became entangled with the renationalisation of the steel industry and therefore a subject of discussion with the Treasury.[1] Its monetary

---

[1] Fforde, 'Support in the gilt-edged market: 15th May, 1967', 15 May 1967, BOE C42/14.

Table 11.1 *Support Operations, 1961–70 (£m, Nominal, Sales +/Purchases -)*

Period	Forthcoming maturities (< 9 m)	Other shorts (< 5y)	Mediums (5–15 y)	Longs (> 15y)	Total (excl forthcoming maturities)	% of money supply (M3)
24/02–06/04/1961	−76.1	−110.9	−7.4	−1.4	−119.6	1.0
12/05–27/07/1961	0	−263.4	−26.5	−3.6	−293.5	2.3
27/11/1964–24/12/ 1964	−80.6	−40.0	−8.0	−4.3	−52.3	0.3
12/05–06/07/1967	−69.0	−226.6	−161.5	−287.1	−675.2	3.4
05/04–30/05/1968	−107.6	−324.3	−29.6	−56.5	−410.4	1.9
08/11/1968–16/01/ 1969	−146.3	−271.6	−30.8	−109.0	−411.4	1.9
21/02–20/03/1969	−57.0	−238.2	−17.9	−8.9	−265.0	1.4
17/04–30/04/1970	0.0	−121.5	−93.6	−155.9	−371.0	1.9

Sources: BOE C11/19–20, 26, 33–4, 36–7, 39–40, 44–5; Bank of England Statistical Abstracts 1970 and 1975.

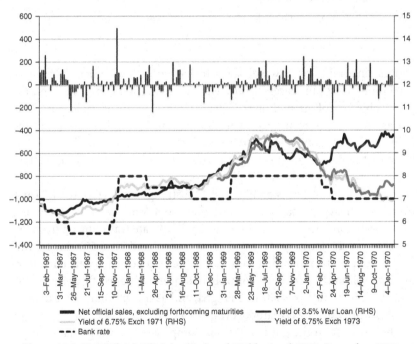

Figure 11.1 Net Official Gilt Sales (£m) and Yields, April 1967–December 1970, Weekly

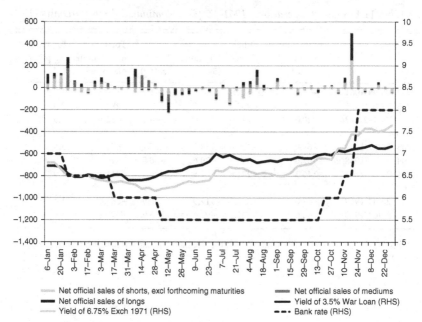

Figure 11.2 Net Official Gilt Sales (£m) and Yields, April–December 1967, Weekly

consequences do not however seem to have provoked much discussion, even though gilt purchases in 1967 were *prima facie* inconsistent with the policy objective of maintaining the exchange rate parity of sterling at $2.80. It was only after sterling had been devalued in November 1967, and the IMF had been drawn into British monetary policy, that the conflicts between the Bank's role in the gilt market and the objectives of monetary policy were acknowledged and discussed.

In the first few months of 1967, sterling strengthened (Figure 11.3) and there were heavy gilt sales: from 6 January to 4 May, net sales, excluding forthcoming maturities, were £1.2 billion. Bank rate was reduced from 7% to 6.5% on 26 January, to 6% on 16 March and to 5.5% on 4 May. Restrictions on bank lending were eased. Sterling however weakened during May, although exchange controls had been tightened further in 1965 and 1966. Bank rate was left unchanged, and as the gilt market weakened, the Bank provided heavy support (Figure 11.2).

The situation in the gilt market was complicated by the re-nationalisation of the steel industry, which was completed in August. The government had announced that holders of steel company securities would be

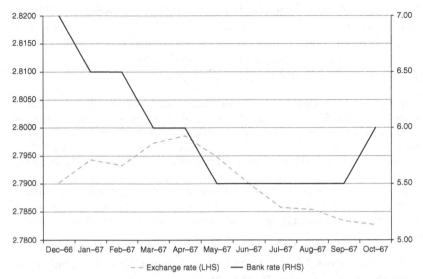

Figure 11.3 £/$ Exchange Rate and Bank Rate, December 1966–October1967 (End Months)

compensated with newly issued gilts, though they did not specify until 28 July that a new stock, 6½% Treasury 1971, would be issued for the purpose. For some gilt investors, there were tax advantages to buying steel shares and holding them until the re-nationalisation took effect.[2] Therefore it was uncertain whether the weakening of the gilt market reflected merely temporary switching into steel shares, in which case official purchases of gilts would clearly be warranted, or something more fundamental. The fact that steel shares were also falling in price was acknowledged at the time as an indication that the latter explanation was the correct one, but nevertheless the support operation continued, and after 17 July came to include purchases of steel shares.[3] In total, £485.7 million of 6½% Treasury 1971 were issued as compensation for steel shares. The Bank had spent £328.1 million on steel shares and on 6½% Treasury 1971 for forward delivery, so only £157.6 million of gilts were newly issued to the public.

On 15 May, prices fell sharply in the morning and the Bank bought £20 million of gilts. In the afternoon the market weakened further and the Bank

---

[2] R.T. Armstrong, 9 May 1967, NA T326/649.
[3] Cairncross, 'The gilt-edged market', 17 May 1967; R.T. Armstrong, 'The gilt-edged market, 22 May 1967, NA T326/649.

bid for three stocks – 3½% War Loan and the two current tap stocks, 6¼% Exchequer Loan 1972 and 6½% Funding Loan 1985/87 – at one-eighth of a point above the market. It acquired just more than £½ million, and bid again at a further one-eighth of a point higher. This time it got no stock.[4] Fforde explained the motivation for providing support:

in our view, the various news items, etc., [bad trade figures, rise in administered electricity prices which, it was feared, would undermine the government's incomes policy] did not warrant a further and appreciable upward movement in U.K. long-term interest rates. These rates had already risen by over $1/_8$% since the Budget, in response to widespread selling by speculative holders and perhaps also by those (often the same people) who were taking advantage of the very attractive opportunities in Steel equities. There were therefore some grounds here for an official 'demonstration'. The more so if, as seemed to be the case, the market was becoming somewhat disorderly and the pressure of selling was spreading to the short end.[5]

On 16 May, despite the demonstration, the Bank bought around £100 million more stock.[6] The demonstration continued for a while, but yields went on rising until July (Figure 11.2).

Fforde's explanation suggests that the Bank had clear views about the appropriate level of long-term interest rates, as in 1962–64, but makes no reference to the possible effect on the foreign exchange market of supporting the gilt market. It is clear that this intervention was not motivated by concern about market liquidity. Nor was it inconsistent with other aspects of monetary policy, none of which seemed to be directed towards maintaining the exchange rate parity: in addition to the reductions in Bank rate and the easing of bank lending restrictions noted above, hire purchase restrictions were eased in June and August. At the central bank governors' meeting in Basle in September, two months before the pound was actually devalued, O'Brien, who had become Governor in 1966, 'was informally taking soundings of the maximum sterling devaluation that was possible without others following'.[7] He knew the game was up.[8] Cairncross and Eichengreen comment delicately that 'The government was not particularly conscious, however, of its dependence on monetary weapons to counter external pressure or of the risks of dispensing with them when public expenditure was rising fast.'[9]

---

[4] Fforde, 'Support in the gilt-edged market: 15th May 1967', 15 May 1967, BOE C42/14.
[5] Fforde, 'Support in the gilt-edged market: 15th May 1967', 15 May 1967, BOE C42/14.
[6] Government Broker, 16 May 1967, BOE C132/9.   [7] Schenk (2010, p. 190).
[8] Capie (2010, pp. 235–51) suggests that the game was already up in July 1966. Coombs (1976, p. 147) thinks that the British government was considering devaluation in August 1967.
[9] Cairncross and Eichengreen (1983, p. 186).

11.1.2 Rescuing the Jobbers after Devaluation

When the pound was devalued over the weekend of 19–20 November 1967, Bank rate was increased from 6½% to 8%. Consequently gilt prices were much lower on Monday morning than on Friday evening, but they strengthened sharply from the new lower levels. As the Government Broker recorded, the Bank agreed

to take out the Jobbers from their position of Friday at Friday night's prices, although I pointed out that our attitude in the market had been such last week that I did not think this was really a necessity. However, the Bank were anxious to be as helpful as possible.[10]

The operation cost the Issue Department around £230,000 (Appendix A).

11.1.3 Support Operations in 1968

The early response of the economy to devaluation was disappointing, above all in that the balance of payments failed to improve significantly until 1969. The exchange rate continued to need support, and market participants came to fear another devaluation.[11] The gilt market was weak, and the support operations continued. There were two periods of support in 1968: April–June and November–December.

In March, before the first support episode, the Bank bought gilts from the clearing banks, which needed to sell to meet their minimum liquidity requirement at a time of seasonal pressure:

The clearing banks sold some £20 million gilt-edged last week, in anticipation of liquidity ratio requirements this month. The existing arrangements, under which they directly approach the Government Broker, continue to work satisfactorily.

Before the week-end, and again since, Mr. Wilde [General Manager of Barclays Bank] has told me that we must expect some further bank selling of gilt-edged. I told him that we would be very prepared to do these deals tomorrow (Wednesday) for cash tomorrow; and I have suggested to him that it would be much better if the banks waited until the Budget news had been announced before making any further approaches to us. He has agreed.[12]

---

[10] Government Broker, 'Devaluation – 1967', 21 November 1967, BOE C132/9. See also interview with Angus Ashton, CMH.

[11] See Needham (2014, ch. 1), Oliver and Hamilton (2007).

[12] Fforde, 'Clearing banks: March make-up day, Wednesday the 20th', 19 March 1968, BOE 3A92/16. Note that Fforde took it for granted that the Bank of England would be the clearing banks' counterparty.

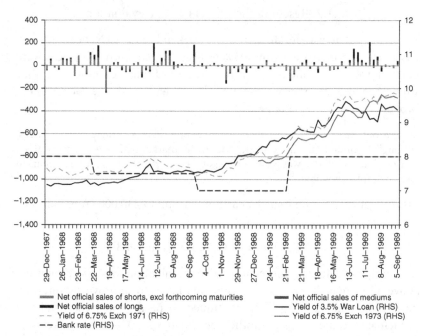

Figure 11.4 Net Official Gilt Sales (£m) and Yields, January 1968–August 1969, Weekly

In April 1968, the Bank of England was concerned that the discount houses were holding far too many gilts, largely financed by borrowing from the Bank, and expressed its 'strong disapproval'.[13] The Government Broker recorded that:

We were asked by the Bank to carry out a fantastic operation today as the Discount Market had far too many Bonds which were being financed almost entirely by the Bank of England.

As a result it was suggested to the Discount houses that they should sell their Bonds to us, if they felt it reasonable to do so, and the Bank would be quite happy to take anything they offered . . .

We actually bought approximately £206 million Bonds.[14]

This operation thus accounted for a large part of the purchases recorded for that period in Table 11.1. The Bank's willingness to buy the whole amount sold by the discount houses directly from the jobbers ensured that the houses had a ready buyer and may be regarded as an act of charity on

[13] 'The discount market 1968', BOE C47/40.
[14] Government Broker, Thursday 11 April 1968, BOE C132/10.

the Bank's part, bearing in mind that the houses seem no longer to have been significant market-makers in gilts. Moreover, it created some moral hazard. In July, the Bank bought a further £25 million from National Discount Company, which had been performing badly and was about to produce 'very depressing half-yearly figures'; the transaction was not put through the jobbers, for fear that it should become known about in the market.[15] The effect of these purchases on broad money and domestic credit will have been negligible, as the gilts that the Bank bought all came from the banking sector.

Support operations from May onwards, and the thought processes of those responsible for them, were described in remarkable detail by Fforde in a paper written for the seminar with the IMF in October 1968 (section 11.2), which is reproduced at length in Box 11.1. It contains many interesting features:

- It begins on 24 May, but there had been purchases of £96 million, excluding forthcoming maturities, in the preceding fortnight. Nor does it mention the July purchase of £25 million of gilts from National Discount Company, described above.
- The setting of a target for long-term yields, in this case 7.75%. While it is claimed that the authorities had a policy objective for long-term interest rates, the figure of 7.75% is not supported by any substantial analysis. It had become clear that 7.25% was no longer sustainable, and the imperative was to find a new level of yields at which official sales could be made. The choice of a target is therefore better interpreted as an attempt at price discovery made by the 'jobber of last resort'.
- The Bank was willing to buy gilts in moderate amounts before the yield adjustment that it had in mind was complete; this was consistent with its practice of being willing to bid for gilts on request.
- Fforde used the word 'disorder' to describe a hypothetical situation in which a rise in yields to or above 8% coincided with 'large-scale unloading'. In such a situation, the existence of a market-maker able to buy substantial amounts of gilts might reassure investors about future market liquidity, and thereby forestall an abrupt reduction in the market's willingness to hold gilts at any particular yield level.
- The Bank was willing to use as-yet-unpublished information to inform its dealing tactics, which aimed to 'discomfort certain speculators', and informed the Stock Exchange jobbers about its own likely future behaviour so as to enable them to protect themselves.

---

[15] Government Broker (Gore-Browne), 'National Discount Company Ltd', 2 July 1968, BOE C132/10.

After the April–May operation was over, the Bank sold £620 million of gilts, net, before a second support operation, which ran from November 1968 to January 1969. On 12 November, Fforde told the Treasury that ' . . . it is beginning to look as if 7¾% is no longer a valid yield, in the sense of being a yield at which stock can readily be sold to the public.'[16] Fforde could see no reason why market sentiment should improve in the near term, and concluded 'that our best policy would be to "wait and see", while being prepared to re-sell non-tap stock to the market fairly readily if the demand should arise, though this latter tactic would depend on our agreeing among ourselves that for the time being we do not want to encourage a return to 7¾%.'[17]

Bad trade figures were released on Wednesday 13 November, about which Fforde would have known in advance. On Friday, he reported that:

The long tap stock now yields just over £7:19:- [7.95%] . . . At the short end yields range typically from 7⁹⁄₁₆% to 7⅝%. Market performance at the long end gives some grounds for the belief that 8% is a resistance point. There have been one or two other buyers besides us. Not much was offered this morning and we did not get all we bid for. At the short end (where we bought some £110 million yesterday) the selling has abated considerably and it may be that the Discount Houses have thinned out their books enough for the time being.

Tactically, we have been trying to steady the long end at just under 8%. At the short end we have also been avoiding an abrupt further retreat.[18]

The following Monday morning (18 November):

the market resumed in a highly nervous and sensitive condition . . .

In response, we have to-day been playing with the straightest of possible bats. We have responded to offerings of short-dated stock by bidding 1/32 below the middle market price while being prepared to take in a fairly large quantity before dropping our price further. We have adopted similar tactics at the long end, but bidding¹⁄₁₆ below the market price instead of the more usual ¹/₈.

We had taken in just under £48 million (cash) by lunch time, of which £41 million nominal of shorts and £10½ million nominal of longs. At the short end prices at lunch time were³⁄₃₂ below Friday's close. The market is steadier at the lower levels but remains highly uneasy. The highest yields at the long end are just over 8%. Shorts are yielding 7⅝% plus.[19]

---

[16]   Fforde–Figgures, 'Gilt-edged market: prospects for long-term interest rates in the U.K.', 12 November 1968, BOE 3A92/16.

[17]   Fforde–Figgures, 'Gilt-edged market: prospects for long-term interest rates in the U.K.', 12 November 1968, BOE 3A92/16.

[18]   Fforde, 'Gilt-edged market', 15 November 1968, BOE 3A92/16.

[19]   Fforde, 'The gilt-edged market up to lunch time to-day, 18th November', 18 November 1968, BOE 3A92/16.

Meanwhile the Treasury, preoccupied by money supply and domestic credit, 'expressed concern that an 8% yield at the long end of the market should not be regarded by us as a Rubicon' and did not want 'to see a large amount of money spent by us in the gilt-edged market without the Treasury having an opportunity to comment and discuss.'[20]

Prices continued to fall and on 19 December, with War Loan yielding 8.05%, Fforde saw no reason why things should get better and accordingly proposed a new tactic of 'allowing the market to fall of its own accord while being prepared to take in at the lower prices any resulting stock offered to us.'[21] Long yields reached 9.625% in June 1969, but market purchases were largely confined to the short end (section 11.1.4).

Net purchases of mediums and longs from 27 December 1968 to 12 June 1969 were just £45 million, for an increase in long yields of about 1.5% (see next section), compared with the £111 million (net) bought between 8 November and 26 December 1968 as long yields had gone up by less than 0.5%. This more economical performance, discussed further in section 11.1.4 and documented in Table 13.1, resulted from the application of Fforde's new tactics, which constituted a major but unannounced change: after December 1968, the Bank's bids for gilts were much less attractive than hitherto.[22]

11.1.4 1969

The Issue Department bought £322 million of gilts between 21 February and 20 March. They included £57 million of forthcoming maturities, and of the remaining £265 million, £224 million were 1970–72 maturities. Net purchases of mediums and longs were small, despite their falling prices, reflecting the Bank's changed dealing tactics. The purchases of short gilts were one convenient way of using the exceptionally large seasonal central government cash surplus of £1.5 billion in the first quarter of 1969.[23]

The clearing bank returns show a reduction of £135 million in the London clearing banks' gilt holdings between 19 February and 19 March, plus another £9 million from Scottish and Northern Irish banks; while the

[20] Hollom, 'Conversation with Mr Figgures and Mr Goldman, 25th November 1968', 26 November 1968, BOE 3A92/16.
[21] Fforde, 'The gilt-edged market', 19 December 1968, BOE 3A92/16.
[22] Government Broker, 'Memorandum: market management', 9 September 1970, BOE C132/12.
[23] Gilts and Treasury bills in the market fell by about £0.5 billion each. Bank of England Statistical Abstract no. 2, 1975.

discount market's total gilt holdings fell by £52 million in the first quarter of 1969. The latter included a special deal done outside the Stock Exchange:

The Union Discount find that they have got rather a large Bond book and have been discussing this with the Bank. It was eventually decided that they could sell up to about £30 million stock to the Bank ... [24]

The Issue Department's purchases of short gilts of February–March 1969 did not undermine the objectives of monetary policy because, being largely from the banking system and being paid for by a budget surplus, they caused domestic credit to contract.[25] They were of the nature of a money market operation, relieving a shortage of cash by repaying government debt to the banking system.

11.1.5 1970

By late 1969, the long-awaited post-devaluation economic adjustment was at last taking place; above all, the balance of payments was improving, helped by the deteriorating external position of the United States. Between 28 November 1969 and 16 April 1970, net official gilt sales, excluding forthcoming maturities, were nearly £1.2 billion.

The pre-election Budget, delivered on 14 April 1970, was accompanied by a cut in Bank rate from 7.5% to 7%. After a pause of a few days, the gilt market weakened very sharply. In the week beginning 20 April, yields rose at all maturities: by 43 basis points at the short end (five years) and 48 basis points for War Loan.

The Bank bought large amounts of gilts as prices fell (Table 11.1, Figure 11.5). According to the *Bank of England Quarterly Bulletin*, 'the authorities allowed prices to fall unusually quickly'.[26] However, the estimated equations reported in Table 13.1 suggest that the Bank was more responsive to increases in gilt yields in 1970 than it had been in 1969, and not much less responsive than in 1968, before it had changed its dealing tactics. There was a change of policy, but it was an unplanned one: nobody at the time compared the scale of official operations to the change in yields after the fashion of Chapter 13.

---

[24] Government Broker, 'Union Discount', 25 February 1969, BOE C132/11.

[25] Money supply was defined as bank deposits held by the domestic non-bank private sector with banks, and domestic credit as lending by banks to the public and domestic non-bank private sectors. They contracted by £301 million and £550 million respectively in the first quarter of 1969.

[26] BEQB (1970 Q2, p. 133).

The scale of purchases in April led to considerable heart-searching after the event. O'Brien was away while they were taking place, and there is some circumstantial evidence that he considered them excessive. For example, in late May, just before the election, he responded to a question from Jenkins about whether a modification of gilt-edged policy (i.e. more support) was called for, by saying that 'In any case, since the Budget we had modified our policy and had bought over £300 million of stock.'[27]

The Chancellor was content with the purchases and

said he was unhappy over the possibility that the market might continue to go down, and wondered what the behaviour of the market over the past week would have been if we had been following our old policy of support. Sir Douglas Allen said that he did not see how we could give more support to the market because this would mean that we would give the impression of abandoning our present monetary policy.[28]

John Page, who had been installed as Chief Cashier on 1 March, analysed events as follows:

First, a brief retrospect of events since the Budget. The immediate and very short-lived reaction was a strengthening of the market on the grounds that anxieties about an inappropriately large relaxation had proved unfounded. But within a few days two different factors became dominant. First, those who had acquired gilt-edged, both long and short, during the preceding six months in the expectation of short-term capital gain decided that a further rise in prices was not in prospect and to take such profits as they had. Secondly, it became apparent to many that the Budget had not contributed (as it could hardly have been expected to do) to curbing the accelerating rate of growth of domestic inflation; expectations of rapid inflation thus became more firmly held; and the Budget Speech pointed to a domestic monetary policy which, in the face of domestic inflation, might well lead to a rise rather than merely no fall in medium and long-term interest rates.

As a consequence there was a sharp bout of selling which, despite rapid reductions in the prices at which we responded to offers, led to us buying well over £300 million of stock; and yields rose by nearly ½% on shorts to around 8¼% and by rather over ½% to 9⅜% or more on mediums and longs, from which levels they have since fallen only very little.

No detailed analysis of the source of the selling is practicable at this stage but a simple analysis suggests that it was widespread, coming from both the banking system – including the Discount Market but excluding the Clearing Banks– and from longer-term holders, such as insurance companies and pension funds. This tends to confirm that the selling had more general causes than the liquidation of short-term bull positions.[29]

[27] Ryrie, 'The equity and gilt-edged markets', 27 May 1970, 3A92/17.
[28] Ryrie, 'The Gilt-Edged Market', 29 April 1970, BOE 3A92/17. Sir Douglas Allen was the Permanent Secretary of the Treasury.
[29] Page, 'The gilt-edged market', 7 May 1970, BOE 3A92/17.

The *Financial Times* and the *Bank of England Quarterly Bulletin* also attributed the price fall to an increase in inflationary expectations.[30] O'Brien commented a little later that 'with the benefit of hind-sight it would have been preferable not to make the second move in Bank Rate at the time of the Budget'.[31]

Yields fell after the unexpected Conservative victory in the general election on 18 June. Official gilt sales resumed and amounted to £670 million, net, excluding forthcoming maturities, between 12 June and 6 August. Thereafter, yields began to rise again (Figure 11.5) and the Bank provided periodic support to the market, including purchases of £120 million in each of the weeks beginning 7 August and 23 October. On 3 September the Bank told Mullens that they were 'slightly worried' about two large purchases in the last two days.[32] And the October episode provoked tension between the Treasury and the Bank, and an explanation from Sir Douglas Allen, as recorded by Hollom, that:

> The situation was simply that the Chancellor was being assailed by Ministers, both above and below him, who believed that we ought to stop spending money in this market. In general the Chancellor was more relaxed on this question than other Ministers and Allen had little doubt that he could be persuaded that our right course was to continue along the lines we were currently pursuing.[33]

And indeed, at a meeting in October the new Chancellor, Anthony Barber, 'thought it was a pity that it was not possible to do more [to restrain money supply] by adjusting gilt-edged management.'[34] At a later meeting, it was concluded that tactics in the gilt market 'should be to continue to retreat reasonably fast, but circumspectly if stock was offered in substantial quantities.'[35] Lacking quantification, this was an insubstantial conclusion.

11.2 Perceiving the Conflict with Monetary Policy

The large-scale support operations of 1967 were undertaken at a time when the United Kingdom was attempting to avoid devaluing its currency; they,

[30] 'Reappraisal of gilt-edged', 23 April 1970, FTHA, BEQB (1970 Q2, p. 133).

[31] Hollom, 'Note of the Governor's conversations with the Chancellor and Sir Douglas Allen', 29 April 1970, BOE G3/271.

[32] Gore-Browne, Thursday 3 September 1970, BOE C132/12.

[33] Hollom, 'The gilt-edged market', 30 October 1970, BOE 3A92/17. The Chancellor was Anthony Barber, who took office on 25 July after the sudden death after only a month in office of the previous incumbent, Iain Macleod.

[34] Ryrie, 'Record of a meeting held in the Chancellor of the Exchequer's room on Tuesday 20th October 1970', 20 October 1970, BOE 3A/8.

[35] Ryrie, 'Note of a meeting held in the Chancellor of the Exchequer's room at 11.45 am on 2nd November', 4 November 1970, BOE 3A/9.

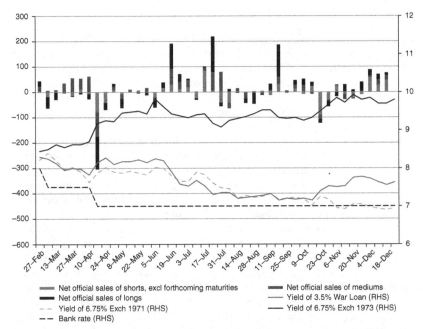

Figure 11.5 Net Official Gilt Sales (£m) and Yields, March–December 1970, Weekly

---

BOX 11.1 The Support Operations of Summer 1968

The following is a long extract from a note written by Fforde in October 1968 for the seminar with the IMF (section 11.2). It is the fullest written account I have come across of any of the Bank's interventions in the gilt market.

The paragraphs which follow describe the conduct of official operations in the gilt-edged market over the upward adjustment of long-term interest rates, from 7¼% to 7¾%, that occurred early last summer. The reader should be warned that this episode was unusually 'clear cut' and ought not to be regarded as one that is readily repeatable in all similar circumstances. An axiom of market management is that all situations are different.

The gilt-edged market became pronouncedly weak following the intensification of credit restrictions on the 24th May. These measures implied a growth in private sector borrowing on the capital market – a growth which was already becoming very apparent to the authorities (who marshal the timing of such issues in order to avoid pointless collisions on particular days). As a matter of policy, we were looking for a rise in long-term rates; while, as a matter of

BOX 11.1 (cont.)

expectation market forces were working in the same direction. Our objective, therefore, was to secure this upward adjustment with the minimum of disorder; and subsequently to establish a new and sustainable level of market prices at which official sales of stock could be resumed. It was not possible to judge with accuracy, in advance, how high the long-term rate would go. Tentatively, however, we had 7¾% in mind – implying a rate of 8¼% and more for first-class industrial and commercial borrowers.

Between the 24th May and the 18th June yields drifted up from rather over 7¼% to around 7⅝%. Official operations in medium and long-dated stocks were not large, but we purchased a total of £17 million over this period, steadying the market when this seemed appropriate. After 18th June the upward movement became much sharper and it is here that a description of official objectives becomes interesting – in the light of the above objective.

The trade figures for May were adverse and the market judged them to be gravely disappointing. Jobbers responded by a sharp marking down of prices. This did not deter sellers and, in accordance with normal practice, the Bank were asked to make bids for substantial amounts of stock. In view of our own judgment of the situation, and our objectives, we responded by making bids at prices ¼ below the then market prices which were themselves⅜ below the closing prices of the previous day. In terms of current market experience, these bids were distinctly unattractive. ¼ of a point on long-dated stocks is about 6d. in the yield [2½ basis points]; and a fall of a full point in a day (nearly ⅛% in the yield) is unusually large. Notwithstanding our unattractive bids, we acquired some £11 million of stock on the 18th June. Similar tactics were adopted on the 19th June, when the market continued very weak, and we bought some £14 million of stock. By the end of the week, yields had risen to about 7¾%.

The upward pressure on interest rates continued during the following week. At this stage, some large holders of gilt-edged had become disturbed at what was going on: and there were signs that large-scale unloading was contemplated. In addition, the appetites of bear speculators had been whetted. A long-term rate of 8% or more being talked. These were signs of incipient disorder; and we had ourselves then to consider with more precision at what level it might be possible to stabilise the market and/or when to step in more actively as a buyer in order to head off a disorderly situation. If we had ourselves not become aware that better news was in the offing, it is probable that we would have felt obliged to take fairly strong supporting action at some rate between 7¾% and 8%. But we began to become aware that we could well be dealt two aces: namely, a favourable announcement from Basle during the weekend of 6th/7th July [a $2 billion credit facility to be used to offset fluctuations in overseas sterling balances], to be followed by more favourable trade figures, to be announced on Thursday, 11th July. In the light of this we felt able to take greater risks with the market; and it was decided to offer little resistance to a further sharp fall in prices in the very short run, because we felt some confidence that an abrupt turn-round was

BOX 11.1 (cont.)

approaching. So we again retreated very readily, though finding we were buying less stock. By Friday, 28th June, yields had reached 8% – with the assistance of fairly large-scale bear operations, of which we were aware.

As the prospects for better news became firmer, we needed to make plans against a substantial turn-round in the market. The question then was how far we should let this go. It was concluded that the subsequent health of the market would be improved if a substantial rebound were permitted, and certain speculators partially discomforted. In addition there were signs that private-sector issues were being cancelled or postponed on a rate basis corresponding to 7¾% on Government stocks. So 7¾% still looked 'about right'. Accordingly the principal jobbers were warned in advance that they should not expect us to be ready sellers of stock at yields much above 7¾%. The object of this was to ensure that jobbers made very wide prices, come the rebound, and did not accept large buying orders at the low prices initially ruling (if they had done so, the bears would have been unduly rewarded and it would have been the jobbers who would have suffered unless they could have got stock from us at the low prices).

The market's response to the announcement from Basle was just as we hoped. There was a scramble for stock and prices rose abruptly. This seemed an ideal moment for <u>heavy</u> stabilising action on our part. It is not possible to do this very easily or quickly by sales of non-tap stocks from the Issue Department, because the market is inclined to run away ahead of us. Heavy stabilising action has therefore to be effected through adjusting the 'official' price of the relevant tap stock. [Footnote in original: The 'official' price of a tap stock is the price at which the Government Broker is known to be a seller. When there is an upward adjustment in yields, the <u>market</u> price of the tap stock falls below the 'official' price, and the tap is said to be 'inoperative'.] At the time, this price was far out of line with the market, it having been last fixed before the upward adjustment of rates had occurred. In accordance with our policy, therefore, the Government Broker declared a new price for the long tap stock (Treasury 6¾% 1995/98) during the morning of Tuesday, 9th July. At this price the stock yielded just under 7¾%. This action effectively halted the upward move in market prices; and was greeted with some dismay. It was, however, followed by the favourable trade figures announced on Thursday, 11th July. The market responded very well and the long tap stock then became operative at its new price and substantial quantities were sold. At that point, this episode may be said to have ended. During the period from 18th June to 5th July we bought £46 million of medium and long-dated stocks. During the next few days, from 8th–12th July, we sold £117 million. Taking the whole period of upward adjustment from 24th May to 5th July, we bought £63 million. Between then and 12th August we sold £185 million. One should conclude by repeating the warning given at the outset. This whole episode was one of rare clarity and precision. Everything worked in favour firstly of an abrupt upward adjustment and secondly of a quick consolidation. In addition, our own objectives were unusually clear throughout. This should be

> **BOX 11.1 (cont.)**
>
> contrasted with situations in which uncertainty and obscurity are prolonged and
> in which it is also much more difficult, at the outset and subsequently, to define
> our own objectives with any precision.[36]

like short-term interest rate policy during the same period, were *prima
facie* in conflict with the main objective of monetary policy. They super-
sterilised official sales of foreign exchange and gold. Likewise, the post-
devaluation support operations of 1968 were undertaken at a time when
the exchange rate was weak.

After the pound was devalued on 18 November 1967, the government
asked the International Monetary Fund for a standby credit of $1.4 billion,
partly to finance the current account deficit until the expected benefits of
devaluation manifested themselves, and partly to refinance some of the debts
that had been accumulated in the defence of sterling's old parity.[37] The IMF
wished to impose an upper limit on Domestic Credit Expansion (DCE) – that
is, lending by banks to the public and domestic non-bank private sectors – as a
condition of the loan, but encountered fierce objections from the United
Kingdom. The objection as regards bank credit to the private sector was
that an upper limit would be incompatible with the .long-established practice
of banks providing flexible overdraft facilities to their customers. As regards
bank credit to the public sector, the objection was that it was impossible for
the authorities to determine how much government debt was sold to the
banks; moreover, the practice of official intervention in the gilt-edged market,
which sometimes caused bank credit to the public sector to fluctuate unpre-
dictably, was essential in order to preserve the structure of the market.[38]

The 1967 discussion ended without a meeting of minds, but the IMF
nevertheless provided the standby with the agreed vague statement that the
'expectation at present that bank credit expansion will be sufficiently limited to
ensure that the growth of the money supply will be less in 1968 than the present
estimate for 1967'.[39] This vagueness provoked criticism from other members of
the IMF, who doubted that they would have been allowed similar latitude.[40]

---

[36] Fforde, 'Some observations on official operations in the gilt-edged market', 15 October
1968, BOE 3A92/16.

[37] Schenk (2010, ch. 5) gives a detailed and interesting account of the UK's relations with the
IMF and the United States in 1964–69.

[38] Goodhart and Needham (2017).

[39] Extract from Letter of Intent to IMF, 23 November 1967, quoted by Needham (2014, p. 37).

[40] Needham (2014, p. 38).

The Bank of England stuck to its guns and Fforde defended the current policy succinctly in July 1968 as follows:

Rightly or wrongly, this willingness to intervene, which has developed into the accepted convention that we will always be prepared to deal at a price if the market so requests the Government Broker, has rendered gilt-edged securities much more 'marketable' than any other securities in the U.K. This marketability is due entirely to the fact that we are prepared to deal in very large sums; such that any large holder of gilt-edged knows that he can buy or sell very large quantities in one day without disrupting the market or driving prices very far against himself. All this renders gilt-edged more liquid to the holder; and also gives the opportunities for profitable switching operations. Almost certainly the result is that on average more gilt-edged are held outside official hands than would otherwise be the case and are held at a lower yield (relative to the stocks of other public authorities and the private sector) than would otherwise be the case.[41]

The debate was resumed in October 1968, when Jacques Polak of the IMF conducted a seminar in London with representatives of the Treasury and the Bank of England.[42] The Bank of England had submitted a paper before the seminar, making the case for continuous market intervention in order to preserve the marketability of gilts. It acknowledged that 'we have to be careful not to be oversolicitous. Intervention to preserve marketability can easily turn into, first, a refusal to allow anything but small price movements over a day, and second into generalised official support for the market in conflict with other objectives of policy.'[43] At the seminar itself, Fforde, the main representative of the Bank of England, was vigorously supported by Nicholas Kaldor of the Treasury.

According to the minutes of the meeting, produced by the Treasury, the IMF did not address the Bank's argument in detail. They were

inclined to question whether the factors mentioned by the U.K. participants need necessarily inhibit the strategy of the authorities as much as had been implied. Rises in interest rates, with consequential capital losses, had been experienced universally in the post-War world. Moreover, the violent fluctuations to which the equity market was liable did not deter investors in that market. There was no evidence that the appetite of either persons or institutions for equities had been spoiled. Was the case for continuous intervention in the gilt-edged market really made out?[44]

---

[41] Fforde, 'The Bank of England and the gilt-edged market', 26 July 1968, BOE 3A92/16.

[42] See Tew (1974, p. 247), James (1996, pp. 190–1), Needham (2014, pp. 38–9).

[43] 'Some observations on official operations in the gilt-edged market', 15 October 1968, BOE 7A353/1, reproduced in part in Box 11.1.

[44] A.J.C. Edwards, 'Monetary seminar (International Monetary Fund), minutes of proceedings', third day, 2 January 1969, BOE 7A353/1.

The IMF had not convinced the Governor of the Bank of England. In November Sir Leslie O'Brien wrote a ferocious letter to Sir Douglas Allen, responding to suggestions from some Treasury officials that the Bank should withdraw from the secondary market in gilts and let the market find its own level. O'Brien thought that would be 'a catastrophic error of policy':

I must warn you that I regard this wishful thinking as dangerous in the highest degree. In saying this, I would not want you to think that my views were in any way influenced by the concern of a market manager for the market for which he is responsible. Rather they are determined by a sense of the responsibility which devolves on the Bank of England for advising H.M. Government on how best its financing and refinancing needs can be met; and by the duty of the Bank to warn H.M. Government of the consequences which so radical a change in the marketability and status of gilt-edged would have on financial institutions which have acquired stocks on the presumption that H.M. Government's concern for their marketability would be maintained.

O'Brien foresaw four likely results of such a withdrawal: first, a long period of readjustment, during which it would be impossible for the government to refinance maturing gilts or budget deficits, and the floating debt would expand greatly; second, gilt prices would fall very sharply, endangering the solvency of some of the holders, with 'simply incalculable' consequences, there would be no long-term government or industrial borrowing for an extended period, and the government debt would be steadily monetised; third, the government would be accused of bad faith; and fourth, sterling would become less attractive as an investment currency and London's position as a financial centre would be damaged.

Finally, O'Brien ruled out any compromise:

Here, I must advise that the half-way house is a mirage. The withdrawal of the Government Broker, even if supposed to be temporary and intermittent, would in practice prove to have effected an irreversible change in the status of gilt-edged. Once the first step had been taken, investors would be bound to presume that they could no longer rely on the maintenance of the present arrangements. All the consequences that I have outlined would then follow, except that the re-appearance of the Government Broker on some subsequent occasion would merely give investors a heaven-sent opportunity to sell their stock to him while the going was good.[45]

As already noted (section 11.1.3), the Bank adjusted its dealing tactics very shortly after O'Brien wrote his letter; and within two-and-a-half years,

---

[45] O'Brien–Allen, 'Gilt-edged market', 28 November 1968, BOE G41/2.

O'Brien would be initiating a major change in the Bank's operating procedure which was exactly the kind of half-way house that his letter had denounced as a mirage.

11.3 The Pattern of Support Operations

When the demand for gilts weakened, the Bank experienced increased offers of gilts from the jobbers and observed that the prices being quoted by the jobbers were falling. As the jobber's jobber, it had to decide how much of the pressure to absorb by purchasing gilts, and how much to deter by allowing prices to fall. From the spring of 1967 until 1970, gilt yields increased by very large amounts (Figure 11.1). For example five-year yields went up from 6.46% at the end of March 1967 to 8.05% at the end of 1970, while 20-year yields went up from 6.50% to 9.79%.[46]

The increase was not continuous: there were periods when yields stabilised and fell, but they were short-lived. The Bank of England's reactions to market movements followed a pattern which, it is plausible to think, destabilised the market. Specifically, the Bank's characteristic initial reaction to an upward movement in yields was to intervene quite heavily to resist it, perhaps in order to test its strength. Typically in 1967–70, the resistance failed to end the upward movement quickly, and the Bank then reduced the scale of its intervention as yields continued to rise. This pattern can be perceived by inspecting Figures 11.2, 11.4 and 11.5. Its existence is corroborated by regression analysis: equation (1) below, estimated by ordinary least squares, shows that the Bank's weekly net gilt purchases (excluding forthcoming maturities) contribute significantly positively to the statistical explanation of the change in the yield of War Loan over the following four weeks (Table 11.2).

$$Y(t) - Y(t-4) = a + b \times NGS(t - 5)$$

where: $Y(t)$ = yield of War Loan at the end of the week;
$NGS(t)$ = net official sales of gilts (+), excluding forthcoming maturities, during the week, in both primary and secondary markets.

Net gilt sales by the Bank of England explain only a small part of the variation in the four-week changes in War Loan yields (very low R^2); nevertheless their contribution to the explanation is statistically significant at the 5% confidence level (two-tailed test). If the Bank's support operations had been effective, the coefficient would have had a positive sign; if

---

[46] Bank of England Statistical Abstract, 1970, table 30.

Table 11.2 *Estimate of Equation Relating Yield Changes to Official Operations, 1967–70*

	Estimated coefficient	Standard error	t statistic
Constant	0.0685	0.0157	4.36
NGS(t-5)	− 0.00038	0.00017	2.27
R^2	0.023		

Note: Estimated by OLS on weekly data from the week beginning Friday 10/02/1967 to the week beginning 25/12/1970. Data sources: BOE C11/33–47, FTHA, author's calculations.

they had had no effect, the coefficient would have been about zero; the fact that it is negative suggests that the support operations were counter-productive.

Because yields were rising, it was attractive for dealers to be short of gilts for nearly all of 1967–70. The existence of this statistical relationship demonstrates that it was more attractive than usual to be short at times when the Bank was bidding strongly for gilts, and the Bank's willingness to buy meant that selling orders could be executed easily. The Bank's habit of resisting an upward move in yields strongly in its early stages, but then retreating, meant that once a rise in yields had begun, it was likely to continue for a period. Thus, perhaps, were created the extrapolative expectations that the Bank identified as a feature of the market in 1969, and which it cited as a reason for intervening in the market.

The Government Broker was concerned that the Bank's dealing tactics had been destabilising. He noted in September 1970 that:

Before December 1968/January 1969 we were normally willing to deal at once at a figure very close to the middle market price. Since that date, however, in accordance with Government policy of restricting the money supply, we have sometimes tended to bid a price well below the middle market price which has probably fallen already since the offer was made. This encourages sales by institutional investors who expect to repurchase at a considerably lower level and thus results in violent price fluctuations in response to comparatively minor occurrences. These wide swings have introduced an undesirable speculative element to the Gilt Edged market and it might be helpful to revert to the former practice under which we were always ready to buy stock (and sell if available) at near the market price. This should smooth out violent fluctuations and increase confidence in the market. It might well result in less support being required than under the current policy.[47]

[47] Government Broker (Gore-Browne), 'Memorandum – market management', 9 September 1970, BOE C132/12.

The Government Broker recognised that the gilt market was malfunctioning: he had, a little earlier, noted that 'I have become increasingly worried about the fact that the Gilt Edged Market is now not only a gambler's paradise but is so volatile that it is getting a terrible name everywhere.'[48] His proposed solution, however, was simply to reverse the operational changes that had been made in the interests of monetary policy.

11.4 Addressing the Conflict with Monetary Policy

As already noted (section 11.1.3), the first move in the direction of moderating gilt market operations came in December 1968, less than a month after O'Brien's ferocious letter. The *Bank of England Quarterly Bulletin* reported in its gilt market commentary that

When the foreign exchange markets had calmed down after the meeting [of the Group of Ten Finance Ministers in Bonn, on 20–22 November], a rise in U.K. interest rates other than the very shortest was seen as an appropriate accompaniment to the measures which had been taken to restrain domestic demand; and the authorities reverted to a policy of allowing any weakness to be fully reflected in prices.[49]

Thus yields rose during the first ten days of December. However, this change was only temporary:

Though the market then strengthened for a time in the expectation, soon confirmed, of improved trade figures for November, the rising trend in dollar interest rates – acknowledged by the increase of Federal Reserve discount rates – soon brought further selling and the market became very unsettled. It seemed that against this background a further very sharp fall in prices could well cause an increase in selling pressure. In their response to offers of stock the authorities therefore sought to exert a steadying influence, by lowering relatively slowly the prices at which they were prepared to deal; and in the event their purchases of medium and longer-dated stocks were minimal.[50]

A little later, in February–April 1969, amid 'tighter monetary conditions, renewed misgivings about the economy, continuing uncertainties about the international monetary system, and the rise in key international interest rates', 'the authorities generally allowed yields to rise.'[51] The Bank thus explained to the public that it was adjusting its tactics flexibly to market conditions, but the note by the Government Broker

---

[48] Government Broker (Gore-Browne), 'Our role in the market' 18 August 1970, BOE C132/12.
[49] BEQB (1969Q1, pp. 15–16).   [50] BEQB (1969Q1, p. 16).   [51] BEQB (1969Q2, p. 138).

quoted in section 11.3 implies that there was a permanent change, made for monetary policy reasons.[52] Moreover, the decrease between 1968 and 1969 in the estimated sensitivity of the Bank's net secondary market operations to yield changes, as reported in Table 13.1, corroborates the view that the change was permanent.

The paucity of archival material on the policy change of late 1968/early 1969 suggests that the Bank did not discuss the change with the Treasury, as does the understatement of its significance in the published account in the *Quarterly Bulletin*. Perhaps the change represented such a rapid retreat from the extreme position that O'Brien had taken in his letter of 28 November that it would have been intolerably embarrassing to acknowledge it.

At a meeting with the Chancellor on 22 April 1969, the Bank reported that there had been net gilt purchases of £10 million since the Budget a week earlier. O'Brien outlined three options:

   i. For the Bank to stay out of the market entirely. 'This would be a very radical move by the Bank and entirely alter the rules of the game. The Governor would be extremely reluctant to adopt such a course.'
  ii. To 'establish a firm floor to the gilt-edged market. But it would be very rash to attempt this in present circumstances when no-one could be sure that any floor could be maintained.'
 iii. 'The third possibility was to continue edging along with the market as at present, allowing yields to increase but trying to bring about a reversal in market expectations.'

The first two options were pretty obviously straw men, and it is not surprising that there 'was general agreement that the Governor's third possible course of "edging along" was the only feasible policy in the immediate future.' However, 'If the Bank were to acquire large sums of gilts the Government would be placed in a very difficult position in negotiation with the I.M.F. It was very important at this stage to avoid large purchases even at the expense of big increases in interest rates.' Therefore, shamelessly mixing metaphors, 'edging along' was to be 'pursued with a higher degree of brutality than in the past.'[53]

---

[52] Government Broker (Gore-Browne), 'Memorandum – market management', 9 September 1970, BOE C132/12

[53] Hancock, 'Note of a meeting held in the Chancellor of the Exchequer's room at the Treasury at 3.15 p.m. on Tuesday, 22nd April, 1969', 22 April 1969, BOE 3A92/16.

Some brutality was demonstrated on 13 May, when disappointing trade figures were released at noon. The jobbers marked gilt prices down. By lunchtime the Bank had purchased £5.5 million of gilts, bought at prices below the prevailing market level.

The market was quieter in the afternoon but at about 3 p.m. we were asked to make bids for some £5 million of medium dated stocks, all of which were some ¼ down on their opening price. Yields on medium dated stocks are, for various reasons, lower than on short dated stocks; but Mr. Gore Browne and myself took the view that we need do nothing to prolong this state of affairs if there existed a pressure to sell medium dated stock. We therefore bid $^3/_8$ below the ruling market price (making an implied fall of $^5/_8$ on the day). The Jobbers complained that these bids represented a 'change of policy'. They asserted, when confronted with Mr. Gore Browne's explanation, that we had never previously been interested in relative yields. Mr. Gore Browne replied that the bids were perfectly reasonable in the circumstances and that if the Jobbers did not like them they need not accept them. The result was that we did not get the stock, while the Jobbers 'retaliated' by lowering their prices a little at the medium and long end.[54]

Meanwhile the Chancellor, perhaps prompted by his officials, had asked for a note setting out the guidelines on which official operations in the gilt-edged market should be based.[55] The guidelines seem to have been agreed fairly easily between the Bank and the Treasury. The main features were:

The primary objectives for official operations in gilt-edged securities is [*sic*] over time to maximise net sales or minimise net purchases (as the case may be) of stock
...

Medium and long-dated stock
3. At times of weakness in market conditions, the Bank will not refuse to bid for stock offered to them. It will not, however, be an objective of policy to avoid a rise in rates of interest, and the Bank will be prepared to bid at prices sharply below going market levels if it is judged that the primary objective will be best served by their doing so . . ..

Short-dated stock
7. The primary objective of official policy will be the same at the short end as at the long end: to minimise net purchases or maximise net sales, as the case may be . . . The official attitude to yields at the short end of the market is likely to be taken as an indicator of intentions for Bank Rate, and the implications of allowing or encouraging expectations in this regard will be one of the factors affecting the tactics of debt management at the short end.[56]

---

[54] Fforde, 'The gilt-edged market, Tuesday May 13th', 13 May 1969, BOE 3A92/16.

[55] R.T. Armstrong, 14 May 1969, BOE 3A92/16.

[56] R.T. Armstrong, 'Guidelines for official operations in gilt-edged', 14 May 1969, BOE 3A92/16.

The parts of the document which are not quoted above are mainly acknowledgements that the primary objective might at times not be best served by the Bank bidding very low prices for gilts offered to it.

It does not seem that the guidelines made any perceptible difference to the Bank's reaction to rising market yields. The estimated scale of the Bank's reaction to rising yields was much the same after the guidelines as it had been before (Chapter 13, 13.1; Table 13.1).[57] The big change had come at the end of 1968. The Bank found it easy to comply with the guidelines because it was already doing so. Short gilt yields peaked in the spring and summer of 1969, and fell on balance for the following two years, although long yields did not peak until November 1970 (Figure 11.1). Domestic credit contracted in the financial year 1969/70. Official operations in the gilt market continued to be a source of anxiety, however, as monetary growth accelerated and became a matter of concern to the Conservative government elected in June that year, and as the Bank, seemingly unconsciously, reverted to a policy of supporting the gilt market more generously (section 11.1.5 above).

---

[57] The specification and estimation of the equations is discussed in Chapter 13.

12

Competition and Credit Control, 1970–72

12.1 Introduction

The Bank of England and the Treasury had become increasingly concerned about money supply, partly on account of academic criticism of UK monetary policy, and partly on account of their own research which suggested that they had underestimated its importance.[1] Concern about money supply implied concern about how to control it.

The problem fell into two parts, as seen from the perspective of the credit counterparts to money supply, which was the prevailing method of analysing the money supply process in the United Kingdom.[2] One was bank credit to the private sector, which had been subject to quantitative controls from 1955 to 1958 and since 1965. The control technique was tested to destruction when the clearing banks exceeded their lending ceilings in 1968–69. The other was bank credit to the public sector, the control of which required the government to borrow sufficient amounts from outside the banking system to finance maturing debt and its continuing deficit, if any. The Bank of England could not impose a specific upper limit on bank credit to the public sector while acting as jobber of last resort in the gilt market.

The solution to both parts of the problem was seen as greater reliance on the price mechanism, in keeping with the philosophy of the new Conservative government, and rationing credit by price was the theme of the Competition and Credit Control programme which the Bank of England introduced in 1971. It was followed by an unexpected explosion of bank credit to the private sector, which naturally attracted widespread

[1] Goodhart and Crockett (1970).   [2] Goodhart and Needham (2017).

attention, but the problem of bank credit to the public sector was largely solved.[3]

12.2 Negotiations

Jenkins and O'Brien agreed in October 1969 to the formation of a Bank-Treasury Working Group on Control of Bank Credit, which re-formed in 1970 as the Monetary Policy Group.[4] A paper written for the group by Charles Goodhart summarised the liquidity problem in the gilt market succinctly:

If the authorities should abdicate the role of stabilising the gilt market in the short run, would professional speculators emerge from the private sector to take over this role? Would private sector institutions find the necessary capital resources to enable them to play this role?[5]

The Bank considered how it might limit its liability to buy gilts in the event of market weakness and the Government Broker, alarmed by the possible implications for the gilt market, submitted a memorandum on possible alterations in technique. It noted that:

1. From our records it would appear:

    a). In the period 1952/58 we virtually only bought short-dated stocks and occasionally when necessary made a bid if one of the big Banks was a seller.
    b). In the period 1959/62 we still concentrated on the above policy but were prepared to make bad bids for stock when the market was overloaded.
    c). From 1962 onward the policy of always being prepared to buy any stock offered gradually developed.

2. It would appear reasonable to revert, at any rate in some degree, to the policies prevailing before 1962 so as to avert 'orders from on high' to abandon the Gilt-Edged Market in toto. This would inevitably mean some contraction of the scope of the market as it is now but in many ways this would not be a bad thing as so much of the present turnover is purely speculative.

---

[3] For more on Competition and Credit Control, see Gowland (1984, chs. 5–8), Moran (1984), Capie (2010) and Goodhart (2015).

[4] This draws heavily on Needham (2014, p. 52).

[5] Goodhart, 'The relationship between the techniques of monetary operations and the level and stability of interest rates', 23 July 1970, BOE 6A74/4.

The memorandum went on to set out three possible alternative plans:

a). Never buy anything outright with a maturity of over one year; switch freely but only to a shorter maturity [i.e. when switching, always lengthen the maturity of the debt outstanding in the market]; and be prepared to sell when prices are suitable and the stock was wanted.

b). The same, except with a maturity limit for outright purchases of five years.

c). Maintain a maturity limit for outright purchases except when it is known that the seller is a clearing bank; switch freely in either direction within specified maturity bands; sell as in the other plans.[6]

The Bank's behaviour as regards market support changed radically in 1971. Demand for gilts remained strong in January, but O'Brien was worried about a possible reversal of demand, and wrote in a manuscript note to his colleagues that he wanted 'to reach early agreement with you as to the precise nature of our response to any short-term turn-round in the gilt-edged mkt. I am certainly not prepared just to stand there and take what is thrown at us even at declining prices.'[7] He was perhaps concerned to prevent a repetition of the backsliding that had taken place after the 1970 Budget (see Chapter 11, 11.1.5).

The Bank was still uneasy about the state of the jobbing system. Even John Page, who opposed any major changes in operational techniques, commented in replying to O'Brien that:

Indeed, that part of our present technique which involves a willingness to deal in almost any gilt-edged stock at a price is of comparatively recent origin; and we have changed other elements of our technique in the last two years. Up to 1962 our operations were confined to selling tap stocks, both short and long, and buying only short-dated stocks, especially near-maturing stocks. Your [O'Brien's] knowledge of how we moved from there to our present position will be much better than mine. But my understanding is that two considerations governed the change: first, the increasing incapacity of the jobbing system to cope with the volume of transactions in gilt-edged and a desire to prevent that increasing incapacity from damaging the marketability of gilt-edged which has been regarded as one of its principal attractions in comparison with other assets. The second consideration, as I understand it, was that a willingness to deal in a wider range of stocks increased the efficiency with which we could carry out refinancing. Typically, or at any rate frequently, holders or [sic] near-maturing gilt-edged will not wish to reinvest

---

[6] Government Broker, 'Notes for possible alterations in our role in managing the gilt-edged market', 6 November 1970, BOE 3A/9. As earlier chapters have shown, there are reasons to doubt the completeness of this summary of operations in 1952–58 and 1959–62.

[7] O'Brien, ms. note to Hollom, Fforde and Page, 22 January 1971, BOE C40/1481.

directly in the two (occasionally three) maturities which we have available on tap. They will wish rather to go into other maturities, the holders of which may be prepared to sell in exchange for our tap stocks . . .

The disadvantage of our willingness to deal at a price in almost any gilt-edged stocks are, first, the possibilities of short run changes in the money supply which it opens up . . . The second disadvantage is that it provides a greater scope than would otherwise be available to the short-term operator, especially in periods when we wish to allow a significant change in the level of yields in either direction . . . Personally I do not find this situation intolerable but others may. If they do find it intolerable and if it is judged that short period fluctuations in the money supply are also highly undesirable it does not necessarily follow that the remedy is the complete abandonment of present techniques. We need rather to examine the possibility of reverting to our pre-1962 mode of operation or something close thereto . . .

One final point: I think it would be much less difficult to curtail sharply the range of our intervention in the gilt-edged market if somehow or other the capacity of the jobbing system could be substantially enlarged. There is no doubt that having two large jobbers only with resources which are exiguous in relation to the volume of transactions nowadays conducted, is highly unsatisfactory. I believe that we should explore by consultation with the Government Broker in the first instance what are the possibilities of improving this situation. For example, it might be possible to interest one of the larger industrial jobbers in taking over a small gilt-edged jobber and developing a large scale business if we could also interest a few large insurance companies in providing capital.[8]

The Government Broker articulated a variant of his earlier possible plans for new dealing arrangements: no outright purchases of maturities longer than a year, except at discretion; always be prepared to sell if the price is suitable; as to switching, always be prepared to buy shorter to sell longer stocks, but buy longer to sell shorter only within defined maturity bands. He noted that 'it would obviously be preferable to have three large jobbing firms rather than two but I feel that if there is a real need this might well evolve and should certainly not be imposed, even if this were possible.'[9]

After further discussion Page sent to the Treasury a letter describing the Bank's proposed change in technique:

The essence of our suggestions is that the Bank would declare that they no longer regarded themselves as obliged to buy outright stocks other than those with a year or less to run to maturity but that they would continue to undertake switches within certain limits . . . As to the limits on exchanges, we would clearly be

---

[8] Page, 'The gilt-edged market', 26 January 1971, BOE C40/1481. As already noted, the pre-1962 mode of operation was not quite as the Government Broker had described it in his note of 6 November 1970, and was therefore not perhaps quite what Page had in mind.

[9] Daniell, 'Memorandum', 8 February 1971, BOE C40/1481.

prepared to engage in any which tended to lengthen the average life of the debt or left the average life more or less unchanged.[10]

At a meeting in the Treasury, Alan Neale (Second Permanent Secretary) was concerned about the effects of the proposed changes on the marketability of gilt-edged. The Bank of England representatives conceded that the changes might 'lead to some shortening in the average life of the debt', and possibly to higher interest rates.[11]

The Deputy Government Broker, Thomas Gore-Browne, was not persuaded:

This morning I was shown a draft of what I gather is to be a public document referring to the 'new plans'. I naturally was only shown that part pertaining to the Gilt Edged Market.

I am afraid I had to say, and I hope as tactfully as I could, that it was about as muddled a paragraph as I had ever seen and that it really should be re-written. The Chief Cashier took this very well and I then spent the rest of my time trying to persuade everybody that the less that was put on paper about this matter, in my opinion, the better.[12]

The Bank consulted market participants about the proposed changes. All expected seriously adverse consequences. The consultees included the two leading jobbers:

Their initial reaction was that they could not begin to operate, even on the basis of a very much smaller turnover in the market than at present, without some recourse to a facility to take them out of excessive bull positions.[13]

The representative of the discount market (Harry Goodson of Union) thought that the proposed changes would reduce the houses' willingness to hold gilts; he also inquired about the possibility that they might deal directly with the Bank of England in under-one-year maturities. The latter provoked an adverse reaction from the Government Broker and was not pursued, even after a further approach from the discount market in July.[14]

Fforde concluded from the consultations that:

a. We have not been encouraged to change our view that the current degree of marketability of short-dated stocks is of great importance to institutional

[10] Page–Painter, 18 March 1971, BOE 3A8/12.
[11] 'Minutes of a meeting held on Friday, 26 March 1971', BOE 3A8/12.
[12] Gore-Browne, 24 March 1971, BOE 3A8/12.
[13] 'Official management of the gilt-edged market', 5 April 1971, BOE C40/1482.
[14] Daniell, 'The Gilt Edged Market', 14 April 1971, BOE C40/1482; Page, 'Direct dealing in gilt-edged with the discount market', 15 July 1971, BOE 3A8/17.

holders of them, though there is some suggestion ... that it is not quite as important as we may have thought.

b. ... we would have to be prepared to see some shortening-down of the average life of the existing short-term debt.

c. ... some members of the Discount Market and some of the merchant banks would be prepared to continue moderately-invested in short-dated stocks and to develop as dealers rather than speculators once our main proposals were put into effect.

d. Our proposals have brought very much into the open the question of our continuing to conduct our gilt-edged operations exclusively through jobbers in the Stock Exchange ... But whatever the ultimate answer, we cannot go from Stock Exchange to Over-the-Counter in a week ... Maybe we should make a move here [in the under 12-month area] ab initio, and be prepared to deal in under-12-month stocks through the money market as well as the Stock Exchange.

e. As regards the <u>long</u> end of the market, we have <u>not</u> been encouraged in our belief that the current degree of marketability is of prime importance to most institutional investors and that it significantly reduces the cost of Government long-term borrowing.

f. Mr. Ginsburg [of Legal and General Assurance Society Ltd], whose views may admittedly be somewhat unrepresentative, supports those of us who consider that our present technique ... has called forth a volume and type of speculation which has made the market <u>disorderly</u> and <u>less attractive</u> to long-term investors.

g. The likelihood of investors in long-dated stocks wishing to switch into short-dated stocks on a large scale, as a consequence of the proposed change, does not seem very great.

h. The jobbers are as anxious as anyone else to shake off the type of speculation that causes us trouble .... It cannot be achieved unless we change our own technique. The jobbers are prepared, not unnaturally with great reluctance, to go along with this, <u>provided we do not totally abandon all our last-resort help</u>. This does not seem unreasonable.

i. The jobbers had put forward a proposal for last-resort arrangements with the Bank, which needed to be examined.

j. All agreed that it would be better if bull positions were liquidated before introduction of the new arrangements.[15]

The jobbers' proposal was set out in a two-page letter from Hugh Merriman, the senior partner of Akroyd and Smithers, to the Deputy Government Broker. The main feature was that 'our two firms [Akroyd and Smithers, and Wedd, Durlacher, the two large gilt jobbers] would

---

[15] Quotations from Fforde–O'Brien, 'Gilt-edged market', 8 April 1971, BOE C40/1482.

have a right each day to sell to you a specified quantity of stock at a level of the market to be laid down by you the previous day.' Merriman also asked for a form of repurchase agreement for tap stocks to be considered.[16]

In commenting on the results of the Bank's consultations, the Government Broker suggested that:

Finally, I would think a reversion to our old method of Tap selling would be of great assistance to the Jobbers, particularly in a rising market. This would mean that they knew the price at which we were prepared to sell and that we would always 'let them out' before putting the price up. The result of this might well be that they could run a considerable bear in these stocks which would give them considerable room for manoeuvre, e.g. switching into other stocks they might wish to sell.[17]

In other words, the jobbers would have a free option to buy tap stocks at a known price.

At a meeting in the Bank on 14 April, the jobbers' proposals were largely rejected, to their dismay. Hollom 'was rather keen on the idea of [the Bank of England] taking some Equity stake in each of the two big Jobbing firms', but was 'shot down'.[18]

Page then produced proposals of his own. He said that the jobbers' proposals 'for an undertaking on the part of the Bank to buy each day a stated amount of stock at prices specified at the close of business on the previous day are not acceptable, principally because they undesirably limit our room for manoeuvre in the light of developments in the market each day.' However, he was in favour of something very similar, namely:

A stop-large-loss arrangement which would take the form of our being prepared at their [the jobbers'] request each morning to indicate the volume of stock we would be prepared to take off them outright at the close of business if necessary and an indication of the price at which we would be prepared to do so.

In addition, Page proposed a financial facility, which could be either an advance facility or a sale and repurchase facility, 'on terms to be agreed, but

---

[16] Merriman–Gore-Browne, 8 April 1971, BOE C40/1482.
[17] Daniell, 'The Gilt Edged Market', 14 April 1971 BOE C40/1482. The proposed change is described as a reversion to an earlier technique, but I have been unable to discover when the earlier technique was changed.
[18] Daniell, 'The Gilt Edged Market', 15 April 1971, BOE C40/1482.

fairly favourable'; 'a willingness on our part to contemplate ... any switches where both stocks had over five years to run'; 'possibly, a reversion to the system of announced tap prices'; 'agreement by the jobbers to disclose to us, daily if we require it, the state of their books'; and the 'whole understanding to be subject to review after three months and to be extensible to another large gilt-edged jobber if one were to be created.'[19] The financial facility and the requirement for the jobbers to disclose the state of their books were presumably linked: the Bank wanted to know about the financial condition of its debtors.

It was agreed that Page's proposals could be tried out as an experiment for three months. It was thought 'that there would be some pressure for direct dealing outside the stock exchange in up to 12 months paper; and [we] would leave the door open for this, but refuse to examine the idea till after the experimental 3 months.'[20] Page wrote to the Treasury about it, describing the stop-large-loss facility as a 'safety net', and not setting a time limit but saying that 'In due course and gradually we would hope to be able to withdraw the safety net as the breadth of the market made by others than ourselves grows.'[21] The Treasury agreed to the proposals.[22]

The details of the safety net, as set out by Page, were that the Bank would be prepared to buy up to £20 million money value of stocks from each of the two main jobbers 'at prices quoted by us before the opening of business on the same day.' The arrangement was to be subject to review at any time and in any case at the end of three months.[23] In fact, the safety net, and the other main features of the arrangements, remained until 1986. It was a well-kept secret.

The new arrangements were announced on Friday 14 May and became effective the following Monday. The text of the Government Broker's announcement to the jobbers is reproduced in Box 12.1.

Finally, and probably prompted by Page, the Government Broker suggested in June to the equity jobbers Pinchin Denny that they might enter the gilt-edged market, but they declined.[24]

---

[19] Page, 'Gilt-edged market', 19 April 1971, BOE C40/1482. In 1944, the jobbers had refused the Bank's request for disclosure of their books, because they had reason to suspect that the Bank would not buy gilts from them until they were already full up (Chapter 6, 6.3).

[20] Hollom m/s note, 19 April 1971, C40/1482.

[21] Page–Painter, 20 April 1971, BOE C40/1482.

[22] 'Minutes of a meeting held on Friday, 23rd April 1971', BOE C40/1481.

[23] Page, 'The new approach: the gilt-edged market', 5 May 1971, BOE 3A/13.

[24] Gore-Browne, 8 June 1971, BOE C132/13.

12.3 After the Change

The scale of the Bank's operations in the gilt market did fall after 17 May: its turnover fell from a weekly average of £205 million in the period from the beginning of 1971 up to 13 May, to £130 million in the period from 21 May to the end of the year. Moreover, to everyone's surprise, market turnover did not shrink, as Figures 12.1 and 12.2 make clear. Peter Cooke considered the figures for the first five weeks reassuring, but added that 'since 17th May the market has been generally steady to firm; the test of the authorities' new stance when there is a general expectation that rates are on a downward [*sic*] path has yet to come.'[25]

The change in gilt dealing arrangements was only part of Competition and Credit Control; the other part was the removal of the credit ceilings applied to banks and the replacement of the 28% minimum liquidity ratio with a reserve asset ratio, of 12.5% of defined eligible liabilities, which took effect in September 1971. At the outset, the clearing banks' liquid asset ratios were well above 12.5%, to which was to be added £382 million of Special Deposits which were to be released. In order to get their reserve asset ratios down, there was a special issue of £1,300 million of gilts

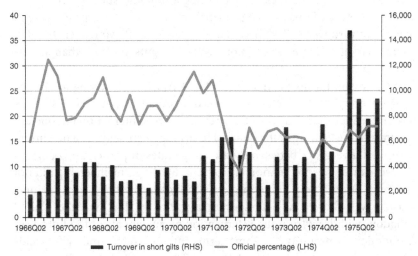

Figure 12.1 Turnover in Short Gilts (£m, Quarterly) and Percentage Accounted for by Official Holders

[25] Cooke, 'Gilt-edged market turnover', 1 July 1971, BOE 3A8/17.

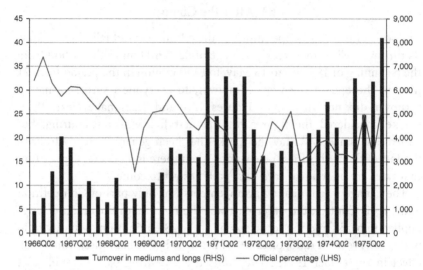

Figure 12.2 Turnover in Medium and Long Gilts (£m, Quarterly) and Percentage
Accounted for by Official Holders

maturing in 1973, 1974 and 1977 to absorb the excess. One consequence of
this was that the London clearing banks' gilt holdings suddenly increased
by nearly 70%, and this in turn probably accounts for the large increase in
banks' gilt turnover (+74% between 1970 and 1972). Moreover, the discount market became much more active in gilts in 1971 than in the
preceding years.

It was by no means plain sailing. On 24 April 1972 sterling joined the
'snake' arrangement, which was intended to provide exchange rate stability
in Europe after the collapse of the Bretton Woods international monetary
system and the floating of the dollar. The arrangement allowed a maximum
permitted divergence between the exchange rates of participating currencies, supported by intervention obligations. Sterling's membership did not
last long. 'After a very heavy outflow of funds in the third week of June,
sterling was allowed as a temporary measure to float and the United
Kingdom withdrew from the intervention arrangements of the European
Economic Community.'[26] Short-term interest rates and gilt yields
increased sharply during June. Between 27 April, just after sterling joined
the snake, and 22 June, the day before sterling floated, five-year yields
increased from 6.0% to 8.2%. In the week beginning 16 June, the Bank

[26] BEQB (1972, p. 303).

made 'special purchases' – i.e. purchases greater than required by the safety net provision – and total purchases that week, excluding forthcoming maturities, amounted to £151.5 million, nearly all of them shorts.

In its summer *Quarterly Bulletin*, the Bank of England compared the experience of 1972 thus far with that of 1969, before Competition and Credit Control, when the market had also been weak:

After January 1972 yields moved up slowly until mid-May, and then rose very sharply indeed. As already explained, the weakness of the market in this period reflected growing anxieties about inflation, depressing industrial news, and the outlook for the balance of payments; and the steepness of the rise in yields cannot be ascribed solely to the change in the authorities' policy towards the market. Nevertheless the new official tactics were no doubt among the influences behind an increase which occurred at this time in the size of fluctuations in the Financial Times [Government Securities] index. The index moved by more than 0.20 on 61 days (on 13 of which the movement exceeded 0.60) out of 127 working days of February to July 1972, compared with 46 days (and 2 days) out of the 124 working days in the first six months of 1969, the last period in which there had been a substantial and sustained rise in the yield on gilt-edged stocks. Wider swings in interest rates were always expected to be a consequence of the new system.[27]

The Government Broker became uneasy:

The recent very sharp falls which took place at unprecedented speed have made jobbing in the market a precarious business. As a result two firms, Smith Brothers and Pyke and Bryant, have felt obliged to stop trading and Francis and Praed are known to be contemplating going in the near future.[28]

He added that

the market ... rests entirely with two firms, Akroyd and Smithers and Wedd Durlacher. Both are very competent and deal in very large amounts, but both have lost big money recently and without our "safety net" things would be far worse. I can visualise them giving up if we altered this materially and would strongly recommend that this is not done.[29]

He later suggested that the safety net be enlarged to a possible maximum of £30 million per jobber, and that the Bank should conduct switches freely in either direction, i.e. longer or shorter, but only within defined maturity bands.[30] I can find no record of whether his proposals were adopted.

[27] BEQB (1972, p. 319).
[28] Daniell, 24 July 1972, BOE 3A92/1. Smith Brothers had been active in gilts for only three months, and Francis and Praed had been in decline for many years.
[29] Daniell, 24 July 1972, BOE 3A92/1.
[30] Daniell, 'The Gilt Edged Market', 7 September 1972, BOE 3A92/2.

12.4 Postscript: After 1972

The main narrative ends in 1972, but it should be noted that the arrangements set up in 1971 in the gilt market survived largely unchanged for the next 15 years, until Big Bang, which was motivated by competition considerations, and not by concern about government debt management.[31]

The Bank of England raised short-term interest rates at times to historically high levels, at least in nominal terms, partly in order to get gilt yields up enough to stimulate sales. The strategy became known as 'The Grand Old Duke of York' after the nursery rhyme of the same name. It had something in common with the strategy recommended by the Radcliffe Report, set out in Chapter 8, 8.5 above.[32]

The market continued to be dominated by the two big jobbers, Akroyd and Smithers and Wedd Durlacher Mordaunt and Co, reinforced from 1978 by Pinchin Denny, who regretted their earlier decision not to join the gilt market, and by a group of jobbing firms specialising in smaller transactions.[33] In a period of high and unstable inflation, market conditions were at times extremely difficult, notably in the two years after August 1972, when long gilt prices fell by about 40% without the Bank providing significant support to the market, other than through the 'safety net'. I recall from my own experience in 1982–86 that the standard size of the safety net at that time was £20 million per jobber per day, but that occasionally, on days when prices had fallen very heavily, a 'double net' was provided at the Bank's discretion – i.e. £40 million per jobber.[34]

Competition and Credit Control did not make debt management easy, but it achieved a better balance between the competing objectives of maintaining the structure of the market intact and managing monetary policy.

---

[31] Dutta (2018) claims that the regulatory actions which led to Big Bang were motivated by the desire to facilitate government debt management, but provides no convincing supporting evidence.

[32] Radcliffe Committee (1959, para. 562).   [33] Interview with V.A.L. Powell, CMH.

[34] Tony Coleby, who had been responsible for Bank of England gilt operations in the mid-1970s, described the post-1971 safety net. See Coleby (2006).

BOX 12.1 The Government Broker's Announcement to the Jobbers on Competition and Credit Control

Announcement to Jobbers of Proposed New Gilt-Edged Methods

Gentlemen,

An important announcement on changes in credit control is being made tonight and among the changes to be announced will be some relating to the Bank of England's dealing in the Gilt Edged Market. I have therefore asked you all to come here so that I can explain them to you personally.

1. The first, and the most important, one from your point of view is that from today the Bank will no longer feel obliged to bid outright for any stock with a maturity over one year. The Bank will, however, reserve the right to buy any stock outright at its sole discretion.
2. The Bank of England will be prepared to switch freely in certain areas of the market provided they have the stock available and, although they will in the main try to aim at lengthening the debt in public hands, reverse switching within certain limits will be possible although, of course, at prices of the Bank's own choosing.
3. The Bank will be prepared to sell stock as hitherto but will revert to the old method of Tap selling, i.e. announcing the price and allowing you, the Jobbers, to close your bears before a change takes place.

If you will all now refer to paragraph 13 on page 5 of the document that I have given you you will see from the final paragraph that this alteration in the Bank's method of operation in the Gilt Edged Market is all part of the general subject of credit control.

This is being put forward now so that further discussion on the changes in credit control can be made with the knowledge of our new position in the Gilt Edged Market and will prevent the Banks from adjusting their ratios by being able to sell unlimited stock to the Bank of England when it suits them.

I think I should point out that the new system is only returning to the methods employed by the Bank of England prior to 1962 and although the amount of stock in issue has, of course, increased, the change is not as revolutionary as it might at first appear. Of course it will have an effect on the market as a whole and will, among other things, prevent the vast

BOX 12.1 (cont.)

speculative operations that have been enabled to take place by the Bank's willingness to deal. Having been intimately connected with these proposed changes for many months I still cannot assess what the effect will be. I am, however, sure that in the long run we will have a healthier and more genuine market although albeit not quite such a large one.

In view of this the Bank of England feel it is essential to give some assistance to the market if this is needed during the 'teething period' so they are prepared:

a). To clear all Jobbers' books if this is desired at tonight's middle market price;

b). To offer a money facility to all Gilt-Edged Jobbers at a special rate subject, of course, to certain conditions;

c). To provide for a limited period some facility to prevent a breakdown in the market.

As this last point must be a very delicate matter it is felt right to grant this facility only to the two largest Firms, i.e. Wedd and Akroyd, on the understanding that they will guarantee to provide facilities to all the other Jobbers should these be desired. I have spoken to Wedd and Akroyd earlier this afternoon and they will explain this to you after I have finished. This facility will inevitably be extremely nebulous, therefore it would be quite wrong of me to give any details at all but I felt it right that you should be aware that it will exist, if only temporarily.

I can, however, assure you that apart from T.A.G.B., K.G.H. and myself, my own Firm will be completely ignorant of this and therefore I would humbly suggest that it is not broadcast to other Brokers. At the same time it would be helpful if you did not tell the outside world that your books had been cleared. Last time we did this for the market at the time of devaluation we got into such trouble with the Discount Market and other organisations for treating the Jobbers in a special way that there was serious consideration given to never doing such a thing again and I feel that if this should happen again the Bank may well say "a plague on all your houses".

I am sure you all realize that if we cannot make the Gilt Edged Market continue to work following the Bank's modifications another market, quite possibly outside the Stock Exchange, will inevitably arise, perhaps somewhat on the American pattern. This cannot be a good thing for us in

BOX 12.1 (cont.)

this room, therefore let us please all try and co-operate to make this new system work well.

NOTE: T.A.G.B. and K.G.H. were Thomas Gore-Browne, the Deputy Government Broker and Kenneth Hill, the dealing partner of Mullens responsible for government operations, respectively.

Source: *BOE 3A/13*

13

The Bank of England's Contribution to Market Liquidity

In a hypothetical perfectly liquid bond market, the government could sell any amount of debt that it wanted to, at any time, at a price very close to the previously ruling price. This is subject to the proviso that the announcement of the new borrowing did not change the market's view of the public finances or the sustainability of the government's debt. In such a hypothetical market, there would be no correlation between gilt sales and gilt yields, or changes in gilt yields over the period, whether a day, a week, a month, or a year, in which the sales took place (unless, implausibly, the government was systematically better than the market at forecasting future bond yields). In such a market, the government would be using the liquidity provided by the market to sell bonds at times of its choosing.

13.1 Routine Operations

The gilt market in the years after Big Bang came closer to that ideal than it had done previously. Before then, as already noted, liquidity was often deemed inadequate and the Bank of England supplemented it through its own operations. Supplementing market liquidity meant concentrating its offers of gilts at times when bidders predominated, and prices were rising, and abstaining from offering, and sometimes bidding, at times when offerors predominated, and prices were falling. It took various specific forms, for example:

a. Until March 1940, and again from the late 1940s, new issues were normally sold at fixed-price tenders, which were underwritten by the Issue Department of the Bank of England. The portion acquired in underwriting was sold later, gradually, in the secondary market. Thus new issues put less strain on market liquidity than they would have done if, for example, they had been offered for sale at auctions in which all the bonds had been sold at whatever price cleared the market.

b. At times, the Bank bought gilts when prices were falling, thereby supplementing the liquidity of the gilt market.

c. The Bank undertook switches in the market from the 1950s onwards, presumably in response to investor demand and supplementing market liquidity.

It is open to question whether these liquidity-supplementing operations damaged market liquidity in the longer term by reducing the incentives for commercial market-making. That question is discussed in Chapter 15. This section aims merely to describe and where possible quantify the Bank of England's contribution to liquidity in the gilt market during various periods between 1928 and 1972. The quantification is both incomplete and rough.

It is incomplete because I have not attempted to quantify the liquidity contribution of the switches that the Bank undertook between different gilt-edged stocks, though the volume of switches increased greatly in the 1950s and 1960s. To do so, one might estimate the coefficients of a set of equations, one for official transactions in each gilt-edged stock, in each of which the independent variables included the yields of all other gilt-edged stocks, and one or more variables representing the liquidity of the market in each stock. Although it might be possible to find acceptable simplifications, such an enterprise is beyond the scope of this book.

Instead, I have concentrated on net official sales of gilts, excluding transactions in forthcoming maturities, defined as stocks maturing in the next nine months, this being a single, simple aggregate relevant to monetary policy. Transactions in under-nine-month gilts, though executed on the Stock Exchange, were akin to money market transactions, owing to the short maturities of the gilts concerned, and their size depended more on the incidence of maturities and the precise price that the Bank was willing to pay, relative to other money-market yields and the price it was willing to bid for other short-term money-market assets such as Treasury bills in its open-market operations. There is a question as to whether net official sales in the secondary market alone should be included, or whether the measurement should also include primary market sales, i.e. amounts of new issues sold at tenders. In the estimated equations reported below, the dependent variable is secondary market net sales, because secondary market sales are less difficult to explain (in a statistical sense) with the chosen independent variables than are total net sales.

The amount of liquidity that the Bank provided to the market is measured by the estimated reaction of net official sales in the secondary market to a given change in yields: the larger the reaction, the more liquidity the Bank was providing. The regression equations are estimated over selected time periods from 1928 to 1972.

It is necessary to decide which yield or yields to use for estimation purposes. Essentially the issue is whether the chosen yield should be short or long. I have addressed the question empirically by trying both; long yields performed generally better, which is surprising, bearing in mind that the Bank's transactions were disproportionately concentrated in short gilts (less than five years to maturity). The reported results therefore use changes in long yields as a dependent variable.

It is also interesting to investigate whether the Bank's reaction to rises and falls in gilt yields was symmetrical; I have addressed that question empirically, too, by reporting two sets of estimated equations: in one, changes in yields, regardless of sign, are a single variable; in the other, rises and falls in yields are separate independent variables. I test whether the latter fit the data significantly better than the former.

In order to assess the Bank's responsiveness to yield changes, it is not sufficient to estimate the coefficients of changes in yields in equations whose dependent variable is net official sales. The reason is that on occasions, for example in 1951–52, 1957, 1961, 1964, 1966, 1967 and 1969, the Bank increased its discount rate (Bank rate) as a signal that it was tightening monetary policy, and simultaneously reduced the prices at which it was willing to sell gilts. On some such occasions, an increase in gilt yields was followed very quickly by net sales of gilts, often in large amounts. For this reason, changes in Bank rate need to be included as additional independent variables.

Of course, the government's need to borrow to finance its deficit, to refinance maturing gilts and perhaps to absorb surplus liquidity, also affected the rate of gilt sales. However, most of the equations whose estimation is reported in this chapter have estimation periods of a year or so, over which those factors do not vary much and can be regarded as being captured adequately by the constant term. The equations estimated on pre-war data are an exception, because the estimation periods are longer, but budget balances varied little in that period until the late 1930s, by which time the Bank of England's secondary market turnover had become very small (see Chapter 5).

The estimation is done using ordinary least squares. The technique is not ideal, because gilt yields were endogenous when the Bank was performing a significant market-making role, as it was in much of the 1950s and all of the 1960s. Instrumental variables would be a better technique, but no obviously suitable instrument is available. That is one reason why the quantification is rough; another reason is that I have articulated no structural model of official gilt sales.

The results are summarised In Table 13.1.

Table 13.1 *Estimated Relationships between Net Official Secondary Market Gilt Sales and Yield and Rate Changes, 1928–72*

A. **Dependent variable:** net official sales in the secondary market, excluding forthcoming maturities; **independent variables**: constant, changes in long gilt yield (1928–54, 2½% Consols; thereafter 3½% War Loan), changes in Bank rate.[1]

Standard errors in brackets.

Units £ million

Period	Constant	Coefficient of change in yields	Coefficient of change in Bank rate	R^2
Equations estimated on monthly data				
Dec 1928–Dec 1936	10.3^a	-33.3^c	-4.6	0.13
	(1.4)	(13.2)	(3.9)	
Jan 1937–May 1940	4.3^a	$+1.3$	-0.1	0.00
	(1.3)	(10.6)	(3.4)	
Jul 1945–Oct 1949	11.2^b	-58.0^d		0.04
	(3.5)	(40.3)		
Nov 1949–Oct 1951	26.5^a	$+100.1$		0.13
	(5.8)	(55.2)		
Nov 1951–Jul 1954	49.6^a	-183.8^c	-42.9^d	0.28
	(7.6)	(70.1)	(25.8)	
Equations estimated on weekly data				
1950	7.8^a	-73.3		0.16
	(1.2)	(24.0)		
1951	2.5^c	-28.2	-2.0	0.03
	(1.2)	(22.0)	(16.7)	
1952	4.1^a	-70.6^b	-6.3	0.21
	(1.2)	(20.5)	(5.6)	

(continued)

---

[1] 3½% War Loan was a much bigger and more liquid issue than 2½% Consols. Both allowed the government a call option, but the call option was more valuable to the government in the case of War Loan, on account of its higher coupon, and more likely to affect the market price of the stock. However, by 1955, there was no prospect of War Loan being called in the foreseeable future, and I judge that the existence of the option did not materially affect the market price.

Table 13.1 (*continued*)

Period	Constant	Coefficient of change in yields	Coefficient of change in Bank rate	R^2
1953	14.2[a]	−110.9	−31.5	0.08
	(2.2)	(70.7)	(30.7)	
1954	18.9[a]	+3.4	+2.8	0.01
	(6.8)	(5.3)	(39.6)	
1955	8.4[a]	−58.0[c]	−4.5	0.12
	(1.6)	(24.9)	(10.8)	
1956	15.3[a]	−88.9[c]	−3.4	0.10
	(2.0)	(41.0)	(15.3)	
1957	17.6[a]	−155.7[a]	+16.2	0.25
	(2.9)	(40.1)	(12.4)	
1958	15.1[a]	−118.3[b]	−5.0	0.17
	(2.3)	(38.2)	(11.9)	
1959	5.9[a]	−140.0[a]		0.24
	(1.9)	(35.9)		
1960	12.2[b]	−267.8[b]	+5.5	0.20
	(3.7)	(80.9)	(17.3)	
1961	12.9[b]	−168.4[b]	−7.4	0.16
	(4.0)	(57.9)	(13.5)	
1962	14.1[a]	−154.3[b]	−9.8	0.16
	(3.8)	(50.1)	(30.6)	
1963	7.1[b]	−181.6[a]		0.32
	(2.3)	(37.3)		
1964	10.4[b]	−417.3[a]	+72.9[a]	0.46
	(3.8)	(80.5)	(13.2)	
1965	23.1[a]	−275.3[a]	−0.2	0.24
	(4.6)	(68.6)	(33.4)	
1966	15.2[a]	−293.2[b]	−3.2	0.21
	(4.3)	(85.6)	(32.3)	
1967	22.8[d]	−741.8[a]	+193.4[a]	0.36
	(11.4)	(200.6)	(44.3)	
1968	13.6	−716.0[a]	−138.1	0.46
	(8.7)	(130.4)	(88.9)	
1969	29.5[a]	−309.3[a]	−74.1[d]	0.54
	(6.1)	(41.7)	(43.1)	
3 Jan–9 May 1969	5.9	−247.5[b]	−49.0	0.38
	(10.3)	(81.4)	(40.3)	
16 May–26 Dec 1969	40.8[a]	−296.3[a]		0.57
	(7.4)	(47.8)		
1970	25.6[b]	−439.6[a]	−39.0	0.58
	(7.8)	(54.5)	(78.5)	

(*continued*)

Table 13.1 (*continued*)

Period	Constant	Coefficient of change in yields	Coefficient of change in Bank rate	R^2
1971 pre-CCC	90.9[a] (19.6)	−337.3[c] (130.8)	−40.2 (75.9)	0.35
1971 post-CCC	55.1[a] (11.8)	−180.3[c] (102.1)	−26.1 (68.9)	0.10
1972	29.3[a] (6.3)	−90.1[c] (42.9)	−221.4[b] (72.9)	0.41

B. **Dependent variable**: net official sales in the secondary market, excluding forthcoming maturities; **independent variables**: constant, rises in long gilt yield (1928–54, 2½% Consols; thereafter 3½% War Loan), falls in long gilt yield, changes in Bank rate.
Standard errors in brackets.
Units £ mn

Period	Constant	Coefficient of rise in yields	Coefficient of fall in yields	Coefficient of change in Bank rate	R^2
Equations estimated on monthly data					
Dec 1928–Dec 1936	9.6[a] (1.9)	−23.0 (23.9)	−40.2[c] (18.8)	−5.0 (4.0)	0.13
Jan 1937–May 1940	5.4[b] (1.9)	−12.9 (21.7)	+11.5 (17.4)	−0.7 (3.5)	0.02
Jul 1945–Oct 1949	14.8[b] (4.7)	−106.3[c] (59.1)	+23.7 (83.7)		0.06
Nov 1949–Oct 1951	23.9[c] (9.8)	+131.6 (110.3)	+69.8 (107.5)		0.13
Nov 1951–Jul 1954	72.6 (11.6)	−441.6[a] (121.9)	+80.1 (124.0)	−44.9 (23.8)	0.41[g]
Equations estimated on weekly data					
1950	7.7[a] (1.5)	−70.8[d] (41.7)	−75.3[c] (36.0)		0.16
1951	3.3[c] (1.6)	−45.2 (31.2)	+69.6 (50.8)	−1.3 (16.8)	0.05
1952	4.2[b] (1.6)	−72.9[c] (31.7)	−67.5[d] (38.4)	−6.4 (5.6)	0.21
1953	16.1[a] (2.8)	−333.2[d] (220.2)	−59.3 (85.6)	−31.3 (30.7)	0.10
1954	24.1[a] (3.0)	−462.5[b] (144.3)	+5.6 (4.9)	−40.0 (38.7)	0.18[f]

(*continued*)

Table 13.1 (*continued*)

Period	Constant	Coefficient of rise in yields	Coefficient of fall in yields	Coefficient of change in Bank rate	R^2
1955	7.3^b	-35.3	-80.4^c	-6.1	0.13
	(2.3)	(43.3)	(42.8)	(11.1)	
1956	18.5^a	-158.5^c	$+8.9$	$+2.6$	0.13
	(3.2)	(68.7)	(87.8)	(15.9)	
1957	16.0^b	-126.5^d	-183.5^b	$+11.5$	0.25
	(4.6)	(76.9)	(74.2)	(16.4)	
1958	13.8^a	-90.0^d	-146.2^c	-5.7	0.18
	(3.4)	(68.7)	(67.9)	(12.1)	
1959	2.1	-22.7	-215.1^a		0.28^h
	(3.0)	(77.6)	(56.6)		
1960	16.1^b	-377.2^c	-162.6	$+8.9$	0.20
	(5.7)	(147.1)	(143.2)	(17.8)	
1961	11.6^c	-141.7^d	-193.9^c	-8.1	0.17
	(5.9)	(103.9)	(100.7)	(13.8)	
1962	20.3^a	-306.9^b	-71.3	-4.3	0.20
	(5.8)	(119.0)	(77.0)	(30.5)	
1963	7.4^c	-188.7^b	-173.0^b		0.32
	(3.3)	(62.2)	(71.0)		
1964	-3.8	-114.7	-931.5^a	$+60.7^a$	0.56^f
	(5.6)	(118.4)	(173.9)	(12.6)	
1965	26.2^a	-344.4^b	-221.5^c	-0.0	0.25
	(7.2)	(139.8)	(117.4)	(33.6)	
1966	28.2^a	-647.5^a	-8.0	$+19.2$	0.29^g
	(7.0)	(174.7)	(148.8)	(32.4)	
1967	49.7^b	$-1,363.2^a$	-140.6	$+205.8^a$	0.42^g
	(17.2)	(361.2)	(352.9)	(43.3)	
1968	3.8	-527.2^b	-992.0^a	-109.4	0.48
	(11.3)	(192.2)	(244.7)	(90.8)	
1969	16.9^c	-219.2^a	-458.4^a	-65.3^d	0.57^h
	(9.1)	(64.1)	(91.5)	(42.3)	
3 Jan–9 May 1969	7.6	-260.2^c	-208.0	-49.7	0.38
	(14.5)	(112.8)	(249.5)	(41.7)	
16 May–26 Dec 1969	28.1^c	-211.1^b	-426.5^a		0.60
	(11.3)	(74.6)	(100.5)		
1970	30.6^b	-475.2^a	-377.0^b	-34.7	0.58
	(12.3)	(86.1)	(128.6)	(79.5)	
1971 pre-CCC	88.7^c	-316.7	-352.8	-42.1	0.35
	(36.9)	(321.5)	(256.7)	(83.5)	
1971 post-CCC	80.1^a	-440.3^c	$+84.2$	-21.4	0.16
	(20.4)	(201.6)	(204.3)	(67.7)	
1972	2.2	-64.1	-684.5^a	-38.9^c	0.58^e
	(9.3)	(82.0)	(106.1)	(21.0)	

C. **Dependent variable**: net official sales in the secondary market, excluding forth-coming maturities; **independent variables**: constant, rises in long gilt yield (2½% Consols up to 1954, 3½% War Loan from 1955), falls in long gilt yield, changes in Bank rate, compensation issues of known timing. Equations are estimated by OLS.

Standard errors in brackets.

Units £ mn

Equations estimated on weekly data.

		Coefficient of				
Period	Constant	Rise in long yields	Fall in long yields	Change in Bank rate	Compensation issues	R^2
1950	7.4^a	−70.2	$−76.7^c$		+0.31	0.18
	(1.6)	(42.0)	(36.2)	(0.28)		
1951	3.7^c	−47.2	+12.8	−1.8	−0.04	0.07
	(1.7)	(31.1)	(50.9)	(16.8)	(0.04)	
1952	4.7^b	$−54.5^d$	$−61.0^d$	−6.6	$−0.62^b$	0.35
	(1.5)	(29.9)	(35.7)	(5.2)	(0.20)	
1953	17.1^a	−21.1	−46.0	−30.2	$−1.32^a$	0.30
	(2.5)	(20.2)	(76.6)	(27.4)	(0.37)	
1954	24.3^a	$−444.9^b$	+5.6	−37.6	−0.57	0.19
	(3.0)	(146.6)	(4.9)	(39.0)	(0.73)	
1955	7.8^b	−37.6	$−76.0^d$	−6.3	−0.86	0.14
	(2.3)	(43.3)	(43.0)	(11.2)	(0.89)	
1956	18.1^a	$−166.4^c$	+3.4	+4.0	+9.4	0.17
	(3.2)	(68.1)	(86.8)	(15.8)	(6.4)	

Notes: in the weekly regressions, the first week of the 'year' for present purposes begins on the first Friday of the calendar year, and the last week begins on the last Friday of the calendar year.

[a] = significantly different from zero at 99.9% confidence level (one-tailed test).

[b] = significantly different from zero at 99% confidence level (one-tailed test).

[c] = significantly different from zero at 95% confidence level (one-tailed test).

[d] = significantly different from zero at 90% confidence level (one-tailed test).

[e] = fit of estimated equation is significantly closer than that of corresponding equation in panel A at 99.9% confidence level.

[f] = fit of estimated equation is significantly closer than that of corresponding equation in panel A at 99% confidence level.

[g] = fit of estimated equation is significantly closer than that of corresponding equation in panel A at 95% confidence level.

[h] = fit of estimated equation is significantly closer than that of corresponding equation in panel A at 90% confidence level.

The main features of the results are as follows:

i. The fit of the equations for the earlier years is generally poor. Changes in yields and Bank rate explained only a small part of the variation in net official sales of gilts in the secondary market. From the mid-1960s onwards, however, the fit improves, which suggests that intervention policy was more consciously directed at smoothing price movements.

ii. From 1928–36, and from 1952 onwards, the Bank's secondary market operations were in some degree sensitive to changes in market yields. In other words, the Bank added liquidity to the market.

iii. From January 1937 to May 1940, the Bank does not appear to have added liquidity to the market.

iv. The amount of liquidity that the Bank added to the market appears to have increased rapidly from the mid-1950s to its peak in 1968. The increase was far greater than the increase of 38% in the outstanding total of gilts between 1955 and 1968.

v. There is evidence that the Bank's responsiveness to rises and falls in yields was asymmetrical in only a few periods. In 1954, 1966 and 1967, it was much more responsive to rises in yields than to falls; in 1959, 1964, 1969 and 1972, it was more responsive to falls than to rises. The 1972 result is not surprising bearing in mind the implementation of Competition and Credit Control the previous year.

vi. Increases in Bank rate appear to have stimulated gilt sales independently of yield changes in 1964, 1967 (when the increase was accompanied by devaluation), 1969 and 1972 (when the biggest increase was again accompanied by devaluation).

vii. The Bank reduced the scale of its liquidity provision after 1968 and after CCC (the post-CCC reduction is evident in the results for 1972, but not in those for the post-CCC part of 1971).[2]

viii. The dealing guidelines agreed between the Bank of England and the Treasury in May 1969 (Chapter 11, 11.4) had little effect: the estimated coefficients of yield changes before and after the guidelines were agreed are not very different.

ix. The Bank absorbed substantial parts of quite small coal nationalisation compensation issues in 1952 and 1953 (see Chapter 8, 8.4). In 1952 roughly 60% of compensation issues were offset by the Bank's secondary market operations in the week of issue, and in 1953 more than 100% of them were thus offset.

---

[2] The fall in the Bank's share of market turnover, which occurred immediately after CCC (see Chapter 12), suggests that the scale of the Bank's provision of liquidity through undertaking switches diminished sharply. Switches of course do not affect net sales.

13.2 Rescuing the Jobbers

In September 1931, when gilt prices fell heavily as the United Kingdom left the gold standard and Bank rate was increased, the Bank provided liquidity support to the jobbers by lending money to them, contrary to its normal practice.[3] I have found no records explaining its actions, but surmise that the jobbers had bought large amounts of gilts on the Saturday of the fateful weekend, and that their normal sources of financing were insufficient, or had dried up. It also provided emergency liquidity assistance to the discount house Smith St Aubyn at the end of the month (Chapter 5, 5.4; Appendix A).

On five later occasions, the Bank provided capital support, free of charge, as well as liquidity support, to the market-makers by buying gilts from them at above-market prices. This happened in March 1952, September 1957, February 1960, November 1964 and November 1967. All but one of them followed a rise in Bank rate. The total amount of capital provided, taking all the operations together, was about £650,000 (Appendix A). Very little was committed to paper about these operations, but an internal note by Maurice Allen described the 1960 operation, Mullens' files refer to the 1964 and 1967 operations, and the Government Broker referred to the latter in his remarks to the gilt-edged jobbers on the eve of CCC.[4] I have collected information about them by inspecting the Issue Department daily ledgers for the dates of possible rescue operations, and compared the prices at which the Bank bought gilts with the close of business prices recorded in the *Financial Times*.

In 1952, 1957 and 1960, the Bank alleviated the losses on the market-makers' bull (i.e. positive) positions, but did not cover them completely: the prices it paid were below the levels prevailing before the rise in Bank rate (in the 1960 case, gilt yields).[5] In 1964 and 1967 they covered the jobbers' losses in full by buying whatever gilts the jobbers had on their books at prices close to the levels prevailing just before the rise in Bank rate. It is not clear what account was taken of the jobbers' bear (i.e. negative) positions, the size of which would normally have been unknown to the

---

[3] Details of all the operations described in this section are provided in Appendix A.

[4] Allen, 'Committee on internal statistics. Gilt-edged market: 19th February 1960 onwards', 3 March 1960, BOE C42/13; untitled note, 23 November 1964, BOE C132/6; 'Devaluation – 1967', 21 November 1967, BOE C132/9. The Government Broker's remarks to the jobbers are reproduced in Box 12.1.

[5] The jobbers Francis and Praed were said to have been particularly badly hurt by the rate rise in 1957, despite the Bank's assistance. Interviews with Angus Ashton and Sir Nigel Althaus, CMH.

Bank. If the Bank simply ignored bear positions, then the jobbers would have been compensated for their bull position losses but allowed to enjoy their bear position profits.

Were the rescue operations confined to the Stock Exchange jobbers, or were the discount houses allowed to take part as well? It is impossible to tell from the Issue Department ledgers, because they do not identify counterparties. In logic, the discount houses should have been allowed to take part, at least in the 1950s, because they were recognised market-makers in short gilts. In September 1957, just before the rise in Bank rate, Union Discount Company alone had £80 to £85 million of gilts, presumably all or nearly all shorts.[6] Yet the Bank of England bought only £5.2 million of shorts from the entire gilt market in the rescue operation, so any help provided to the discount market can have relieved only a small proportion of their losses. There is clear evidence that the discount market was not included in the 1967 rescue operation.[7]

I did not discover evidence of any rescue operations in September 1949 (devaluation), January or February 1955, June 1960, July 1961, July 1966 or February 1969 (Bank rate rises).

I did not consider days when gilt prices rose sharply, thereby exposing any jobbers who were short, because the Bank was normally ready to sell gilts at prices close to the current market. That this was the case was affirmed by the Government Broker in a discussion with the stockbrokers Greenwells in 1971. Asked 'when we had had to buy a lot of stock why did we let it go at ¼ profit instead of allowing the price to go up much higher? I told them the usual story about how the Jobbers would go broke if we did not look after them in this way.'[8] It should be remembered, though, that in November 1949, the Bank did not resist the price rise that it had provoked until the rise had extended to about 4% for some long maturities (Chapter 7, 7.7), and that in July 1968 the Bank allowed prices to rise in order to 'discomfort certain speculators' (Box 11.1).

The objective of the rescue operations was not written down, but it seems clear that it was to ensure the continued presence of a group of committed market-makers, even if their effectiveness depended heavily on the Bank of England's willingness to act as the ultimate market-maker. If either of the two big gilt jobbing firms (there were only two by the mid-

[6] Evidence to Parker Tribunal (1958, Q8959).
[7] See the Government Broker's announcement to the gilt-edged jobbers at the time of Competition and Credit Control, reproduced in Box 12.1.
[8] 'Notes on a meeting between certain members of Messrs Greenwell and Co. and P.A.D. in the Stock Exchange on 28th January 1971', 29 January 1971, BOE 3A8/10.

1960s) had failed or withdrawn from the market, then the market structure would have been compromised and the government's ability to borrow would have been seriously impaired for however long it took for an alternative market structure to emerge; and these were, in any case, difficult times for government financing. It is therefore understandable that the Bank encouraged the Stock Exchange in its attempts to secure additional capital from private sources for the jobbers (see Chapter 9, 9.5).

But until the jobbers' capital had been reinforced, there was no obvious option but to bail out the jobbers at times of dire stress. All bailouts create moral hazard, and there is no way of knowing how the jobbers' behaviour was affected. It can be argued that the Bank behaved in a way which minimised moral hazard. The risk-taking capacity of the jobbers was limited by the quantity of their own resources, and by the margins of surplus collateral which were required by those who lent money and gilts to them. Had those lenders been assured that the Bank would bail the jobbers out *in extremis*, they might have relaxed their surplus collateral requirements and enabled the jobbers to take more risk.

The Bank of England tried to keep the bailouts a very close secret; the lenders would have been aware of no reason to relax. Even so, a belief became widespread in the City that the Bank would not let a big gilt jobber fail, and that the big jobbers would not let a small jobber fail.[9] The belief was well-founded, but a commercial bank considering a credit limit could not be certain of it. The Bank of England seems to have been quite discriminating in deciding when to mount rescue operations: as far as I can tell, every rescue followed an action by the Bank which depressed gilt prices, and the Bank did not, for example, try to resist the long decline of Francis and Praed, which ended in 1972 when the firm was wound up because of the retirement of partners, and big losses.[10]

I have found no evidence that the Bank demanded any *quid pro quo* for the capital which it, in effect, provided to the jobbers. Could it or should it have done so? Under the pre-1966 Stock Exchange rules, a non-member could not take an interest in a member firm (see Chapter 9, 9.5). After 1966, it would have been possible, but the interest would have had to be notified to the Stock Exchange and made public, thus violating the secrecy of the operation and aggravating moral hazard. It might have been possible for the Bank to support the jobbers by means of unsecured loans. However, the need to service the loans would have increased the financial risks being run

---

[9] I am grateful to Graeme Gilchrist for this information.
[10] Interview with Angus Ashton, CMH.

by the partners, who might have preferred to go out of business rather than accept them: they had shown no interest in Norman's offer in 1944 (Chapter 6, 6.3). If they had accepted unsecured loans, the existence of the debt might have caused the jobbers either to behave more cautiously, and thus fail even more egregiously to make liquid markets in gilts, or to take extravagant risks. For the sake of the relatively small amounts involved, it cannot have seemed worth the trouble to the Bank.

Were the bailouts a proper use of public money? They certainly were not transparent. Yet allowing the jobbers to fail would certainly have added to the government's financing costs, at least temporarily, and the bailouts were quite likely the least-cost and least-risk policy. There is no record of any analysis or debate on the subject. The bailouts solved the immediate problem of keeping the market going, but not the longer-term problem of achieving a sustainably liquid gilt market.

14

Governance in Practice

The governance of the Issue Department was recast in 1928, when the Treasury note issue was incorporated into the Bank of England issue and the Issue Department's balance sheet accordingly enlarged (Chapter 4). The principles were set down in the Currency and Bank Notes Act 1928, supplemented by a letter from the Bank of England to the Treasury. Relevant clauses of the former, and the latter, are reproduced in the box at the end of this chapter.

The main features of the new arrangements were that the Treasury would receive all of the profits of the note issue, net of expenses; that the Treasury should be fully informed about the assets of the Issue Department and about transactions in them; and that in managing the assets, the Bank would act in 'personal consultation' with the Treasury. The meaning of 'personal consultation' is unclear, neither the Bank nor the Treasury being natural persons, but the Bank used the phrase to describe its relationship with the Treasury over the Issue Department for many years (e.g. O'Brien quoted it in 1971, when he was Governor).[1] In practice, it seems to have meant that the consultation was to a great extent oral, and there were plenty of opportunities for Treasury and Bank of England officials to meet: for example, it was customary for a Treasury official (not a minister) to attend the Treasury bill tender at the Bank at 1 p.m. every Friday, followed by lunch.

The Bank's letter also enjoined strict secrecy regarding the assets and transactions of the Issue Department.[2] Thus secrecy was hard-wired into the management of the Issue Department. It led to a practice of making decisions informally and largely orally, and to the exclusion from the

[1] O'Brien–Allen, 3 August 1971, BOE G41/2.   [2] See documents reproduced in Box 14.1.

discussion of people whom those involved did not believe had a 'need to know'. This was unfortunate not only for historians, but also for the quality of the decisions. Certainly there were policy actions which seem doubtfully wise in retrospect and were questioned at the time, but only, as far as one can tell from the archives, by people who were not members of the small inner circle. The support operations of 1961 are a case in point.

Secrecy was part of the Bank's culture. The then Deputy Governor, Sir Ernest Harvey, told the Macmillan Committee in 1929 that 'It is a dangerous thing to start to give reasons.'[3] Was all the secrecy really necessary? It certainly was in wartime, and I have argued elsewhere that in the 1950s the United Kingdom's financial situation was so precarious, on account of the massive overhang of debts incurred in time of war, and the available remedies, such as explicit default, so few and unattractive, that secrecy was justifiable.[4] By the 1960s, that justification no longer applied in general: the government debt/GDP ratio had fallen below 100% by the early 1960s, for example. And the introduction of the *Bank of England Quarterly Bulletin* in 1960, and the collection and publication of a greatly expanded range of financial statistics, both following recommendations of the Radcliffe Committee, created a new degree of openness. Nevertheless, as already noted, the strict secrecy surrounding the bailouts of the jobbers must have limited moral hazard usefully. In any event, the post-Radcliffe openness did not survive the long, vain struggle to maintain sterling's exchange rate parity at $2.80. In that struggle, it was understandably deemed essential not to disclose to the market how much of the reserves, and how much external borrowing, had been used to support the exchange rate.[5] And maintaining secrecy about foreign exchange and gold operations necessitated maintaining secrecy also about domestic market operations, since the details of the latter, if carefully examined, would have revealed a great deal about the former.

By and large, the Treasury took an interest in the gilt market when its ministers were concerned about it, or when there were problems in selling gilts. It was compelled to pay attention when the Issue Department began

---

[3] Macmillan Committee (1931b, Q435), reproduced in Sayers (1976, Appendix 21, p. 156).

[4] Allen (2014, p. 211).

[5] After the pound had been devalued, some people in the Bank wanted to publish an article in the *Quarterly Bulletin* giving a full account. The article was drafted but never published, on the grounds that full disclosure of the support given to sterling before devaluation would have embarrassed some of the lenders. Sangster, 'Bulletin article "Special assistance for the reserves 1964–1970"', 29 April 1971, and comments thereon, BOE 6A179/1. Naef (2017, figure 5) provides estimates of the amount of support.

to lose money in the second half of the 1930s as bond prices fell (Chapter 5, 5.8). The Treasury largely took over debt management policy from 1945, when the Bank was not invited to participate in the National Debt Enquiry, but its interest was less for most of the 1950s.[6] It was interested in the attempt to manage long-term interest rates in 1962–64, and it became very interested in 1968 when the IMF drew attention to the conflict between the Bank's role as the 'jobber of last resort' and the objectives of monetary policy. However, it does not seem to have paid much attention to the growing inadequacy of the market-making structure in the 1950s and 1960s, and the increasing role of the Issue Department in compensating for it, though it was aware of what was going on (Chapter 9, 9.4). These matters were largely left to the Bank, where debt management was conducted in great secrecy by about half a dozen people, assisted by the Government Broker, his deputy, and his dealing partner. Much of the discussion was conducted only orally. The leaving of few written records was, at times at least, deliberate. For example, in November 1949, after the Bank had supported gilt prices (Chapter 7, 7.7), the Chief Cashier of the Bank, Percival Beale, sent to his deputy a draft letter to the Treasury, which he said had been seen by Sir Kenneth Peppiatt, at that time an executive director of the Bank:

Sir Kenneth thinks it unwise to have on the records at the Treasury a letter from the Bank dealing with

a) borrowing of stock, and
b) the nature of our intervention operations over recent weeks/months.[7]

In the United Kingdom, the managers of the central bank had very considerable discretion in debt management – far more, for example than in the United States. There, the Federal Reserve has been periodically forbidden by law to buy US Treasury securities directly on issue; moreover, operations in the secondary market were, and are, subject to authorisation by the Federal Open Market Committee, whose decisions have been minuted since it was created in 1936.[8] The Committee gives fairly precise directions to the Federal Reserve Bank of New York, which conducts operations on its behalf, and does not always accept the New York Fed's advice, as in the case of bills-only (Chapter 8).

---

[6] On the National Debt Enquiry, see Fforde (1992, pp. 326, 335), Howson (1993, pp. 45–54).
[7] Beale–Excell, 29 November 1949, BOE C40/422.
[8] Garbade (2014). The minutes of the FOMC, and its executive committee, from its establishment, are available on the FRASER website of the Federal Reserve Bank of St Louis.

In the United Kingdom, no attempt was made, e.g. by the Treasury, to evaluate the effectiveness of debt management by calculating the cost of funding to the government – though it was, of course, recognised that the financing of the First World War had been very costly. But even if the calculations had been made, interpreting the results would have been problematic, because it would not have been clear with what benchmark the actual costs were to be compared. Some kind of average of secondary market yields over the period? It would not have been possible for the government to sell debt in such a way that the cost was equal to the average gilt yield over any period: that would have presupposed the ability to sell a roughly equal amount of gilts each day, which was precluded by the limited capacity of the market-makers. Precise performance evaluation was logically impossible, and was rightly not attempted.

The bailouts of the jobbers in 1952, 1957, 1960, 1964 and 1967 raised serious questions about the use of Issue Department funds, even though, as I have suggested, respectable answers could have been given (Chapter 13, 13.2). Were the operations reported to the Treasury? I have found no written evidence of it either in the Bank of England archives or the National Archives, where the Treasury's files are to be found. Yet I cannot conceive that the Bank would have omitted to mention an operation of this kind, especially in view of the undertakings on information that it had given in 1928. I think it most likely that the operations were disclosed to the Treasury orally, but not in writing, that only one or two Treasury officials were told about them, and that they were asked to keep it to themselves.[9] Treasury officials would have been more frightened by the probable serious disruption of the gilt-edged market than they were dismayed by the loss of Issue Department profits.

The Bank's accounts were audited, although until 1971 no auditor's statement or certificate was published. It is possible that the auditors were told in confidence of the bailouts, but in any case it would be unrealistic to think that an auditor would have checked the price of every purchase against market prices at the time of purchase.

---

[9] My view is informed by advice from Lord Armstrong of Ilminster, for which I am very grateful. He doubts whether any Treasury officials were told.

BOX 14.1 Amalgamation of the Note Issues, 1928: Documents.

i. Currency and Bank Notes Act, 1928: selected clauses

3. Securities for note issue to be held in issue department

   (1) In addition to the gold coin and bullion for the time being in the issue department, the Bank shall from time to time appropriate to and hold in the issue department securities of an amount in value sufficient to cover the fiduciary note issue for the time being.

   . . .

   (3) The Bank shall from time to time give to the Treasury such information as the Treasury may require with respect to the securities held in the issue department . . .

   . . .

5. Transfer to Bank of certain part of assets of Currency Note Redemption Account

   (1) On the appointed day, in consideration of the Bank undertaking liability in respect of the transferred currency notes, all the assets of the Currency Note Redemption Account other than Government securities shall be transferred to the issue department, and there shall also be transferred to the issue department out of the said assets Government securities of such an amount in value as will together with the other assets to be transferred as aforesaid represent in the aggregate the amount of the transferred currency notes. For the purpose of this subsection the value of any marketable Government securities shall be taken to be their market price as on the appointed day less the accrued interest, if any, included in that price.

   (2) Any bank notes transferred to the Bank under this section shall be cancelled.

   . . .

BOX 14.1 (cont.)

6. Profits of note issue to be paid to Treasury

   (1) The Bank shall, at such times and in such manner as may be agreed between the Treasury and the Bank, pay to the Treasury an amount equal to the profits arising in respect of each year in the issue department ...

   (2) For the purposes of this section the amount of the profits arising in any year in the issue department shall, subject as aforesaid, be ascertained in such, manner as may be agreed between the Bank and Treasury.

...

ii. Letter from C.P. Mahon to the Secretary of the Treasury

Confidential

Bank of England
27th July 1928

The Secretary
      Treasury
            Whitehall, S.W.1.

   Sir,

I am directed to refer to the Currency and Bank Notes Act 1928 and to say that, in view of the fact that the Bank have surrendered to His Majesty's Government the entire future net profits of the Issue Department including the whole of that portion which is derived from the issue of Bank Notes of denominations above £1, and further that such profits will be liable to increase or decrease according to any fluctuations which may take place in the value of the Securities held from time to time as cover for the fiduciary issue, the Bank recognise that the Government are entitled to ask that the Treasury shall be kept fully and constantly informed regarding all operations affecting the Securities held from time to time in the Issue Department.

   I am accordingly instructed by the Governors to give their Lordships this undertaking, that in their future management of the Securities in the Issue Department, the Bank will act in personal consultation with

BOX 14.1 (cont.)

the Treasury on lines similar to those hitherto followed in connection with operations affecting the Securities of the Currency Note Account.

The Governors are confident that Their Lordships will be in agreement with them as to the need for the observance of strict secrecy at all times regarding the nature of the Securities held in the Issue Department and of the operations which may take place from time to time in connection therewith.

I am, Sir,

Your obedient Servant,

(Sd.) C.P. MAHON

Chief Cashier

Source: *BOE G14/25.*

15

Conclusions

15.1 Gilt-Market Liquidity and Monetary Policy

John Fforde was the Chief Cashier of the Bank of England from 1966 to 1970, and in that capacity was responsible for managing the heavy gilt-market support operations that were undertaken during that period. He was also largely responsible for enabling the Bank to reduce the extent of its obligation to support the gilt market, which had become unsustainable. Later in his life, when he came to write the official history of the Bank of England from 1941 to 1958, he was evidently troubled by the Bank's management of the gilt market. He quoted Peppiatt's memorandum of 1 January 1952 about the inadvisability of the Bank's becoming a jobber (also quoted in Chapter 8), which he described as a *locus classicus*, and added that 'The opinion of this author, who had to operate the technique of systematic intervention in its later flowering, is that it would have been better if the Bank had stuck to Peppiatt's precepts through thick and thin.'[1]

The Bank of England's attitude to gilt-market liquidity was reactive for most of the time until the late 1960s. In 1939, when it had become concerned about the losses that the Issue Department's gilt portfolio had sustained as yields had risen after 1935, it expressed its uncompromising opposition to providing support to the market, though it was willing to underwrite new gilt issues and to buy gilts that would reach maturity, or be the subject of a conversion offer, in the near future. And in the 1930s, the Bank was very disciplined in selling off the portions of new issues that it had acquired through underwriting (Chapter 5). This hands-off attitude to market support survived until well after the war.

---

[1] Fforde (1992, p. 649).

During the war the Bank, concerned that liquidity in the Stock Exchange was inadequate, had set about establishing a parallel dual-capacity market in short gilts in which the discount houses were the market-makers (Chapter 6, 6.3); in 1945, it reacted very quickly to the threat to the cheap money policy that was posed by the sharp falls in short gilt prices – not by supporting the market itself, but by arranging for the discount houses to raise more capital, so that they would be able to absorb sales without allowing prices to fall by as much (Chapter 7, 7.2).

For several years after the 1945 episode, market liquidity appears not to have concerned the Bank much. It supported the gilt market during the convertibility crisis for reasons that are not clear (Chapter 7, 7.4), but until 1950 did nothing to soften the impact of nationalisation issues on the long market (Chapter 7, 7.5). The concerns which Peppiatt expressed in 1952 about the jobbers (Chapter 8) were conveyed to the Chairman of the Stock Exchange. When no action ensued, the Bank did nothing initially, but later in the 1950s began to fill the market-making gap itself. Likewise in the early 1960s, when the Bank appeared to see even greater inadequacies in the commercial market-making structure, it again found no solution except to expand its own activities. It was probably reassured by the Radcliffe Committee's recommendation that it should have an objective for interest rates at all maturities, which was in a way an echo of the National Debt Enquiry's recommendation of 1945; its adoption of an objective for long-term interest rates in 1962–63 incidentally led it even further into market-making on its own account.

The Bank had good reasons to be concerned about market liquidity. The government debt/GDP ratio, which had been 259% in 1946, was 151% in 1954 and 101% in 1962. Most of the reduction could be attributed to inflation. The budget surpluses of the late 1940s were not sustained, primarily because the democratic process did not assign a high priority to debt repayment. There were heavy gilt maturities each year to be refinanced, and the Bank of England, anxious to avoid the risk that the debt would be monetised, was concerned that the bonds it had to offer should be as attractive as possible. One of the main attractions was a liquid market. The United Kingdom could not risk the apparent insouciance about market liquidity that was implicit in the bills-only policy adopted in 1953–61 in the United States, where the government debt/GDP ratio was less than half as large (Box 8.1).

Academics did not offer very helpful advice. The Keynesian world-view, which had dominated British macroeconomics since the 1940s, was challenged in the 1960s both by long-time dissenters, who drew attention to

evident policy failures, and by monetarists inspired by Milton Friedman of
the University of Chicago. The challengers were critical of both the
Radcliffe Report and the monetary policy of the 1960s, asserting that the
money supply, which was the key to inflation, was being dangerously
neglected. 'Inflation is always and everywhere a monetary phenomenon,
in the sense that it is and can be produced only by a more rapid increase in
the quantity of money than in output.'[2] Academic economists generally
failed to understand the Bank of England's concerns about the microstructure of the gilt market, though these had been set out clearly in an article
published in 1966 (Chapter 10, 10.6).

A group of academics from the London School of Economics
organised a conference in 1969 to mark the tenth anniversary of the
Radcliffe Report.[3] The organisers did not, however, devote much time
to debt management, despite a protest to the Bank of England from
Professor Brian Tew of the University of Nottingham, who quite
reasonably pointed out that the Radcliffe Report had devoted much
attention to the subject, and that its recommendations had not been
implemented.[4] Moreover, there was some academic work in progress
on debt management at the time, including the doctoral thesis of
William White.[5] This was a missed opportunity.

A paper written jointly by the Treasury and the Bank of England for the
conference did, however, restate official concerns about the structure and
liquidity of the gilt market, though much less clearly than in the Bank's
article of 1966:

With gilt-edged maturities currently at a rate of around £1,500 million a year,
a primary official objective must continue to be that described in the Bank of
England *Bulletin* of June 1966, that is to maintain market conditions that will
maximise, both now and in the future, the desire of investors to hold British
government debt. This long-term objective obviously affects the authorities' choice
of tactics in a particular short-run situation. Because the market response to
a moderate price change for gilt-edged has been found to be unstable and often
perverse in the short term, the movement of interest rates required to achieve
adequate liquidity absorption through debt operations may be so large that a rapid
or seemingly arbitrary adjustment could permanently damage the willingness of

---

[2] Friedman (1970). For a perceptive assessment of revolutions in macroeconomics, see
Johnson (1971).
[3] The proceedings were published in Croome and Johnson (1970).
[4] Tew–Thornton, 3 March 1969, BOE 6A72/1.
[5] 'The authorities and the U.K. gilt-edged market 1952–66', PhD thesis, University of
Manchester.

investors to hold gilt-edged, compounding the difficulties of monetary management in the future.[6]

The emphasis on the market's 'unstable and often perverse' response to moderate price changes was unfortunate. The fact that the authorities did not disclose much relevant information made for market instability (Chapter 8, 8.5), and the Bank's dealing tactics had made it rational for the market to sell when the Bank began buying (Chapter 11, 11.3).[7] Equally unfortunate was the absence of any discussion of the market microstructure. The real problem, which the paper did not make explicit, was the extreme difficulty inherent in the Bank combining market-making with monetary policy management. Academic critics (like the IMF mission of 1968, see Chapter 11, 11.2), did not recognise this problem, let alone discuss it. For example William Norton, discussing the alleged instability of the gilt market, concluded, rightly, that 'it is essentially a short-run phenomenon and may well be due to the way the authorities operate in the market.'[8] However, Norton did not explore the reasons why the authorities operated as they did, and his conclusions cannot have made them feel any more confident about changing their technique. In general, and not only in the United Kingdom:

Postwar monetary debate was conducted in a language that may be called 'monetary Walrasianism' – Walrasian in the sense that the economy was conceived as a set of simultaneous equations in which prices move to equate supply and demand for each good, and monetary in the sense that one set of equations was conceived as equating money demand and money supply.[9]

The limitations of 'monetary Walrasianism' were recognised by some economists in the 1960s, but they were not taken seriously by monetarist commentators on monetary policy, or by other mainstream macroeconomists.[10]

---

[6] BEQB (1969Q4, pp. 455–6). For more information about the conference and the Bank of England's paper, see Capie (2010, pp. 459–63).
[7] Gowland (1984, pp. 91–2) says that extrapolative expectations were a central feature of what he calls the 'cashiers' theory' of the gilt market, which he says guided the Bank of England's operations.
[8] Norton (1969, p. 493). Goodhart's studiously neutral account of the Bank's gilt-market operations (published in 1973 but mainly written in 1967) does not discuss market microstructure. Bain (1970, p. 49) did however acknowledge the Bank's function as 'jobber of last resort'.
[9] Mehrling (1998, p. 294).
[10] See, for example Clower (1967), and Johnson's survey of monetary theory for the tenth anniversary of Radcliffe conference (Johnson 1970, pp. 99–100), and the references therein.

Recent research on the United Kingdom's public debt management in the period 1694–2017 by Ellison and Scott (2017) has noted that the average maturity of UK government debt has been, and is, unusually long by international standards, and concluded that, in the twentieth century, 'the UK government would have been better off issuing just three year bonds.' The present study questions the implicit assumption that the market is so reliably liquid that the government can always choose how much to borrow at any particular maturity. There have been times when it would have been impossible to sell gilts without causing a large fall in prices and endangering both the sustainability of the public finances and the market structure. Governments were sometimes forced to borrow on Treasury bills, and accordingly saw great merit in locking in longer-term funding when they could.

Moreover it is far from clear that, even if the market had, somehow, remained liquid throughout, shorter debt really would have been better in the twentieth century. Shorter debt would have meant very heavy maturities immediately after the two world wars, which would have made macroeconomic policy even more difficult than it actually was. Against the pressure of pent-up consumer demand, interest rates would have had to rise to very high levels – even higher than in 1920 – to refinance the maturing debt, and the effect of higher borrowing costs on the government budget would have destabilised the public finances very quickly.[11] The post-1945 dominance of fiscal policy over monetary policy would have become apparent much more quickly than it actually did, and inflation would surely been much higher.[12]

Debt managers need to know how large a yield premium it is worth paying to borrow long when they can. The history related in this book shows that the risk of markets becoming illiquid is a real one. Macroeconomists have not yet made a convincing estimate of the costs of illiquidity in government securities markets, and the debt managers' question about the yield premium remains unanswered.

What could the Bank of England have done differently? Its concerns about the lack of market liquidity were understandable, given the supreme importance of being able to sell bonds and avoid the progressive monetisation of the government debt as outstanding gilts matured. It tried, without success until the 1960s, to interest the Stock Exchange in the question of whether the gilt jobbers had enough capital.

---

[11] On 1920, see Howson (1975, ch. 2).
[12] On fiscal dominance in the 1950s, see Allen (2014, pp. 224–8).

Could, and should, the Bank have helped to establish a gilt market outside the Stock Exchange? In 1942, it empowered the discount houses to act as market-makers in short maturities, and for a long time they seem to have been the main market-makers in short gilts. However, they gradually faded after the reactivation of monetary policy in 1951 and the Bank rate rise of 1957, probably because they lacked distribution capacity. The clearing banks might have been alternative candidates as market-makers, but they gave no reason to think they would be interested.[13] And the failure of the Bolton plan in 1964 to engender a new market-making structure suggests that there were no available options at that time. It is therefore easy to understand how the Bank of England allowed itself to become the jobber of last resort. It is also easy to understand why it felt obliged to bail out the commercial jobbers when its actions threatened their solvency. Of course this involved a subsidy and moral hazard, but, as Benos and Wetherilt say, 'some kind of policy intervention to ensure that markets remain liquid and efficient at a socially optimal level' is justified.[14]

There is, however, some evidence that the Bank was in practice more than a jobber of last resort. The fact cited above, that it was quoting a tight dealing spread for War Loan in July 1960, is one piece of evidence: a genuinely last resort jobber would quote a wide spread, so as to leave room for the commercial market to operate profitably. And the fact that the Bank's share of market turnover became as large as it did is another piece of evidence.

Moreover, the Bank seems not to have recognised that the Stock Exchange jobbers were becoming more profitable in the mid-to-late 1960s, as they relied more on positioning and less on turnover for their income. As the jobbers became more profitable, they became better able to raise capital through mergers and, post-1969, from external sources.

The fact that market liquidity did not suffer after the Bank withdrew in 1971 came as a surprise to all concerned. The main reason must have been the improved capacity of the jobbers; the exemption of gilts from long-term CGT in 1969 might also have been important. It seems likely that hyperactivity on the Bank's part had been stifling the commercial market-

---

[13] The clearing banks proved to be very effective market-makers in foreign exchange after the market was reopened in 1951, but foreign exchange was perhaps more closely integrated with their normal customer business than gilts. Moreover, market-making in gilts would have caused accounting problems for the clearing banks, since they did not use mark-to-market accounting. Atkin (2005) recounts the twentieth-century history of the London foreign exchange market.

[14] Benos and Wetherilt (2012, p. 344).

makers: as Page expressed it in a lecture in November 1971, 'So long as the Bank were prepared in effect to put substantial resources into ensuring the marketability of gilt-edged, there was no particular reason why others should do so.'[15] If the Bank had been a less active market-maker in the early to mid-1960s, and if it had retreated more promptly than it did as the jobbers advanced, the conflicts between its objectives for market liquidity and monetary policy might have been less painful.

15.2 The Age of Intervention

Before 1914, the gold standard seemed to be part of the natural order of things. It was widely thought to be self-adjusting after the Bank Charter Act 1844, but a series of crises led to the Bank of England taking on the functions of a modern central bank. Its main objective was to try to prevent financial crises, or, failing that, to contain their consequences by acting as lender of last resort. Bank of England intervention in financial markets had become well-established by the late nineteenth century.[16]

The gold standard had been inoperative during the First World War, because the cost of transporting gold was prohibitive, and it was suspended immediately afterwards; it must have seemed natural to try to restore it as part of 'the world of yesterday', to use Stefan Zweig's evocative phrase. 'On all sides, the 1925 discussions [on the return to gold] never really got much beyond general theoretical arguments, overlaid with emotion and supported by a few well-chosen statistics.'[17]

After sterling left the new gold standard in 1931, the scale and ambition of market intervention increased radically. Initially, intervention in the gold and foreign exchange markets, conducted by the Bank of England but on behalf of the Treasury, was aimed at accumulating sufficient gold and foreign exchange to repay the short-term borrowings of 1931. However, the statutory function of the Exchange Equalisation Account, set up in 1932, was 'checking undue fluctuations in the exchange value of sterling'.[18] In practice, the objectives of intervention also included maintaining the exchange rate at levels deemed by the

---

[15] BEQB (1971 Q4, p. 478).

[16] See, for example, Sayers (1936 and 1976). Even after the First World War, the gold standard was so much a part of the natural order of things that in the 1931–2 issue of the League of Nations Statistical Yearbook, 'conversion coefficients for currencies' – i.e. exchange rates – were included in the same section as weights and measures.

[17] Moggridge (1972, p. 97).   [18] Quotation from section 24 (3) of the Finance Act 1932.

Treasury to be acceptable, and rebuilding the reserves after the 1931 debacle.[19]

It was implicit that the authorities believed that a purely market-determined rate would exhibit 'undue fluctuations'. The Bank's purchases of foreign exchange and gold in late 1931 and early 1932 for debt repayment must have put additional stress on already-strained market liquidity. Sayers talks of a 'thin market' immediately post-gold standard, and says that the Bank was 'conscious that efforts to maintain an orderly market were going to be necessary for a long while.'[20] The daily range of fluctuation of sterling against the dollar increased radically after the departure from gold, suggesting that the market had become much less liquid.[21] And the market was in 'a state of semi-paralysis' after restrictions on dealing were imposed in January 1939, in anticipation of war.[22]

Exchange market intervention was a vehicle for the extension of state power. The Exchange Equalisation Account was set up partly so that intervention could be carried out beyond the limits imposed by the size of the Bank of England Issue Department, and it was designed so as to insulate the Bank of England's balance sheet from the effects of intervention.[23] The foreign exchange market was closed at the beginning of the war and not reopened until 1951; during that period, foreign exchange was provided by the authorities for approved purposes at a fixed rate, which was devalued from £1 = $4.03 to £1 = $2.80 in September 1949.

The conversion of War Loan in 1932 into a new stock with a yield below pre-conversion market levels was a further demonstration of the state's power, this time as a monopolist in the bond market. It needs to be stressed that the War Loan conversion involved no element of default: the government acted entirely within the prospectus terms of the old War Loan. Conversion apart, debt management policy was aimed at keeping the Treasury bill circulation down; accordingly it super-sterilised the effect of official gold and foreign exchange purchases, not only on the commercial banks' reserves but also on the supply of Treasury bills. There are grounds

[19] See Howson (1980, ch. 5). Montagu Norman denied that keeping sterling cheap was a policy objective, but he was concerned to rebuild the reserves (Clay, 1957, pp. 418, 460). In effect, therefore, he favoured the same policy as those who wanted to keep the exchange rate down.
[20] Sayers (1976, p. 419).
[21] The average range of daily fluctuation was 0.36% in February 1932, compared with 0.08% in August 1931. Source: TDA, author's calculations.
[22] Osborne and Allport (1950, p. 308).
[23] Howson (1980). Similar institutions were established in other countries, notably the United States.

for doubting the wisdom of this policy, but it cannot be denied that intervention in the gilt market was well co-ordinated with intervention in the gold and foreign exchange markets.[24] Operations in the secondary market were mainly confined to market smoothing by purchasing forth-coming maturities, underwriting new issues and a certain amount of jobbing; however, by acting as lender of last resort to the jobbers in September 1931, the Bank prevented the market-makers from collap-sing. The scale of gilt-market intervention decreased after the authorities chose to reduce the fiduciary note issue in 1933 and 1936, thus lowering the upper limit of the Issue Department's gilt holdings, and even more after 1937, following the losses that the Issue Department's gilt portfolio had sustained as bond yields rose.

As from 1940, it became the objective of debt management to achieve a particular structure of yields, within which the quantity of gilt sales was to be maximised (Chapter 6). The objective of achieving a predetermined yield structure was endorsed in 1945 by the National Debt Enquiry. However, the desired structure was lowered by 0.5% at all maturities in late 1945, and it became clear in 1947 that the new structure was unsus-tainable without a shortening in the average maturity of the debt that would have been regarded as dangerous (Chapter 7). Both during and after the war, yield objectives were pursued with only modest help from intervention in the secondary market, but controls over private issues and external flows were crucial. Gilt-market intervention was deployed as a weapon of monetary policy in 1948 in an attempt to contain the growth of bank deposits, even though it entailed putting upward pressure on long-term yields, and supporting successive attempts to restrain bank deposits or bank credit was to remain an objective of debt management thereafter.

The market environment changed in two important ways in 1951: the foreign exchange market reopened, and monetary policy was 'reactivated', in the sense that the Bank of England ceased to be willing to buy Treasury bills in unlimited amounts at a fixed discount rate. Foreign exchange intervention was directed at maintaining the sterling exchange rate close to the Bretton Woods parity. In the gilt market, by contrast, one principal concern was to limit the commercial banks' ability to create credit by selling gilts to absorb the Treasury bills which they could count as liquid assets; another concern, sometimes in conflict, was to contain the severity of falls in market prices and, occasionally, to protect the solvency of the

---

[24] On the doubtful wisdom of the policy see Balogh (1947, p. 67 fn. 2), Nevin (1955, pp. 142–54), Howson (1975, pp. 143–4), Sayers (1976, pp. 493–5).

Stock Exchange jobbers. There was no target for the level of yields, the attempt to manage long-term interest rates in 1962–4 being a temporary exception, though new issues were confined to short maturities at times when yields were thought, usually mistakenly, to be temporarily high. But in addition, gilt-market intervention became a means of maintaining liquidity in the secondary market for gilts. As far as I am aware, liquidity in the foreign exchange market was not a major preoccupation for the Bank of England after the war, possibly because the Bretton Woods commitment to maintain the exchange rate within the fluctuation band was a commitment to provide unlimited liquidity to the market at the limits of the band.[25]

In the 1930s, the objectives of intervention in the gold and foreign exchange markets were clear, and intervention in the gilt market was co-ordinated with that intervention. After the war, there was no conscious co-ordination. The Bank of England in effect continued to super-sterilise external flows, but now buying gilts which incidentally sterilised sales of foreign exchange. Its activities in the gilt market aggravated the convertibility crisis of 1947; and they destabilised monetary policy in 1961 and in 1967–8 when the Bank bought gilts at times when the exchange rate was under pressure. And the attempt to maintain the exchange rate parity of $2.80 from 1964 to 1967, which required massive intervention in foreign exchange, forced the government to pursue monetary policies which were clearly not to its liking and which, in the spring of 1967, it relaxed prematurely.

The Bank and the Treasury were far too ready to believe that domestic and foreign exchange markets could be kept separate by the extensive and complicated array of controls that were in operation. Furthermore the microstructures of the markets for gilts, short-term money and foreign exchange were very different; that of the gilt market, in particular, increasingly being thought incapable of providing adequate liquidity unaided. Intervention was most of the time conducted in related markets, by separate groups of people, with separate and sometimes incompatible objectives.

The age of intervention ended gradually in the foreign exchange and gold markets from the late 1960s onwards as official operations became

---

[25] In a debate with Milton Friedman in 1967, when exchange rates were pegged under the Bretton Woods system, Robert Roosa predicted that foreign exchange markets would not be liquid enough to support international trade and investment if exchange rates were allowed to float. Events proved him wrong. Roosa (1967).

decreasingly effective against the growing power of private market participants, and abruptly in the gilt market in 1986, when Big Bang in the Stock
Exchange created a much more liquid market. The authorities lost whatever power they still had to influence exchange rates and bond yields. In the
bond market, the authorities got in exchange the ability to sell gilts as and
when they needed, and were to a large extent able to stop worrying about
whether debt management would interfere with monetary policy. The need
for official intervention in the secondary market was eliminated. And in
foreign exchange, large exchange rate adjustments could take place with
very little of the political humiliation that accompanied a formal
devaluation.

16

Epilogue: Bearing the Cost of Providing Liquidity

The Stock Exchange did not adapt to the rapidly changing needs of the gilt-edged market during or after the war. Its governance was idiosyncratic, and the obstacles to change were formidable: 'each member, whatever volume of business he undertook or capital he commanded, had equal power.'[1] However, it would be facile to dismiss the liquidity problems of the gilt-edged market in that period as a historical accident. During the Second World War, the Bank of England set up an alternative market for short gilts, centred on the discount houses. It seems to have worked well for several years, but then faded away. Official attempts to find new market-makers for gilts outside the Stock Exchange in the 1960s came to nothing. And in the United States, the market for medium and long-dated government securities was not very liquid after the Accord between the US Treasury and the Federal Reserve. It would be a serious mistake to assume that there will always be a liquid market for government securities.

Immediately after Big Bang in 1986, there were 27 committed gilt-edged market-makers; they were required to be separately capitalised companies and they had, between them, capital resources of £595 million, vastly more than had previously been available to the jobbers. An industry that found it very hard to get capital before Big Bang attracted a glut of it afterwards. The market proved to be overcrowded and over-capitalised, so that by the end of 1989 the market-makers were down to 19 in number and £395 million in capital, the reduction in capital being entirely accounted for by trading losses.[2] The market-makers were mostly subsidiaries of large banks. They had easy access to credit collateralised against gilts, and their separate capitalisation and regulatory oversight by the Bank of England provided their creditors and counterparties with some assurance about

---

[1] Michie (1999, p. 200).　[2] BEQB (1990Q1, p. 68).

their financial strength. Moreover the arrangements for settling gilt transactions had been made much safer by the introduction of 'assured payments', greatly reducing settlement risk. With this better-capitalised
market infrastructure, it was possible to sell new gilt issues through auctions with no formal underwriting, and to reduce radically the scale of
official operations in the secondary market.

The requirement for separate capitalisation was removed in 1997, but
most of the market-makers were subsidiaries of large banks and broker-
dealers, and before the financial crisis, they were widely thought either to
have plenty of capital, or at least to be 'too big to fail'.[3] A gilt repo market
was introduced in 1996, and delivery-versus-payment for gilt settlements
was introduced in 2001, making settlements safer still. In these circumstances, market liquidity was ample and the task of debt management
much simpler than before 1986.

Since the financial crisis, things have changed again. The main gilt-
edged market-makers, being mostly banks, are subject to the large amount
of new regulation that has followed the financial crisis, and no doubt also to
closer scrutiny by share- and bond-holders. These developments have
reduced the market-makers' ability to carry inventories of bonds in the
periods between the regular auctions and the emergence of demand from
final investors, and there is evidence that market-makers' balance sheet
constraints impaired gilt market liquidity during and after the financial
crisis of 2008–09.[4]

The UK Debt Management Office, which succeeded the Bank of England
in 1998 as the agency responsible for public debt management, has
responded to this change in various ways, including by syndicating the
distribution of some issues, and paying syndication fees, and by making gilt
auctions smaller and more frequent, so as to ease the burden of the market-
makers. It has also introduced a post-auction option facility, which offers
market-makers the option of buying additional gilts at each auction. These
changes have made the pace of official sales responsive in some degree to
market conditions, so that the DMO is using less market liquidity, in the
sense of Benos and Wetherilt, than previously.[5]

---

[3] BEQB (1997Q1, p. 74).
[4] The International Monetary Fund devoted a chapter of its *Global Financial Stability Report*
of October 2015 to the subject. See also Duffie (2012), Committee on the Global Financial
System (2014), Fender and Lewrick (2015), Goldman Sachs (2015), Powell (2015), Benos
and Zikes (2016), Fischer (2016), Anderson and Stulz (2017).
[5] See Debt Management Office (2017, pp. 23–6). Benos and Wetherilt (2012, p. 344) provide
justification for the according of privileges to committed market-makers.

Market liquidity has a cost. In the 1950s and 1960s, the commercial market could not bear the cost of providing adequate liquidity. The Bank of England increasingly filled the gap, and went too far in doing so, creating a conflict with monetary policy. The conflict was largely resolved in 1971, but the Bank continued to provide liquidity, on a less extravagant scale, until 1986. For the 20 years or so after 1986, commercial banks provided ample liquidity, but it is possible that that period will come to be regarded as a historical anomaly, inseparable from the long boom in financial market activity that ended abruptly in 2007.[6] Governments and central banks will need to make heavy use of bond markets, particularly if they want to unwind quantitative easing, and some contingency planning for a permanently less liquid gilt market would be no more than prudent.

[6] Shin (2016).

Cast of Characters

Allen, Sir Douglas (1917–2011)	Permanent Secretary, HM Treasury, 1968–74.
Allen, Maurice (1908–88)	Adviser to the Governors, Bank of England, 1954–64; Executive Director 1964–70.
Althaus, F.R. (1895–1975)	Senior Partner, Pember and Boyle, and witness to the Radcliffe committee.
Amory, Derick Heathcoat (1899–1981)	Chancellor of the Exchequer, 1958–1960.
Anderson, Sir John (1882–1958)	Chancellor of the Exchequer, 1943–45.
Armstrong of Ilminster, Lord, formerly R.T. Armstrong (1927–)	Secretary of the Radcliffe Committee, 1957–59; Under Secretary (Home Finance), HM Treasury, 1968–70.
Armstrong, Sir William (1915–80)	Joint Permanent Secretary, HM Treasury, 1962–68.
Barber, Anthony (1920–2005)	Chancellor of the Exchequer, 1970–74.
Beale, Percival (1906–81)	Chief Cashier, Bank of England, 1949–55.
Bolton, Sir George (1900–82)	Director, Bank of England, 1948–68.
Butler, R.A. (1902–82)	Chancellor of the Exchequer, 1951–55.
Callaghan, James (1912–2005)	Chancellor of the Exchequer, 1964–67.
Chamberlain, Neville (1869–1940)	Chancellor of the Exchequer, 1923–24, 1931–37, Prime Minister, 1937–40.
Clay, Henry (1883–1954)	Adviser, Bank of England, 1930–41.
Cobbold, Cameron (1904–87)	Deputy Governor, Bank of England, 1945–49; Governor, 1949–61.
Cooke, Peter (1932–)	First Deputy Chief Cashier, Bank of England, 1970–73.
Cripps, Sir Edward (1885–1955)	Government Broker, 1937–48.

(continued)

(*continued*)

Cromer, Lord (1918–91)	Governor of the Bank of England, 1961–66.
Dalton, Hugh (1887–1962)	Chancellor of the Exchequer, 1945–47.
Daniell, Sir Peter (1909–2002)	Deputy Government Broker, 1950–63; Government Broker, 1963–73.
Dobby, Ambrose	Dealing partner, Mullens and Co., 1964–71.
Ellen, Eric C. (d 1955)	Manager, Union Discount Company of London, 1940–46; Chairman, London Discount Market Association, 1941–46.
Fforde, John (1921–2000)	Chief Cashier, Bank of England, 1966–70; Executive Director, 1970–82; later wrote the official history of the Bank from 1941 to 1958.
Francis, Herbert (1880–1968)	Secretary and Comptroller-General of the National Debt Office, 1938–46.
Glendyne, Lord (1878–1967)	Partner, Nivison & Co.
Goldman, Sir Samuel (1912–2007)	Third Secretary, HM Treasury, 1962–68; Second Permanent Secretary, 1968–72.
Goodhart, Charles (b 1936)	Adviser, Bank of England, 1968–85.
Goodson, Harry (b 1909)	Manager, Union Discount Company of London Ltd, 1963–72.
Gore-Browne, Sir Thomas (1918–88)	Deputy Government Broker, 1963–73; Government Broker, 1973–81.
Harrod, Sir Roy (1900–78)	Economist, influential private adviser to Harold Macmillan.
Harvey, Sir Ernest (1867–1955)	Deputy Governor, Bank of England, 1929–36.
Hawker, Sir Cyril (1900–91)	Executive Director, Bank of England, 1954–62.
Holland-Martin, Edward (1900–81)	Executive Director, Bank of England, 1933–48.
Hollom, Jasper (1917–2014)	Chief Cashier, Bank of England, 1962–66; Executive Director 1966–71; Deputy Governor 1971–81.
Hopkins, Sir Richard (1880–1955)	Second Secretary, HM Treasury 1932–42; Permanent Secretary 1942–45.
Jarrett, Jack	Senior Partner, Francis and Praed, in 1960.
Jay, Douglas (1907–96)	Parliamentary Private Secretary to the Chancellor of the Exchequer, 1947; Economic Secretary to the Treasury, 1947–50; Financial Secretary, 1950–51.
Jenkins, Roy (1920–2003)	Chancellor of the Exchequer, 1967–70.

(*continued*)

(continued)

Kaldor, Nicholas (1908–86)	Adviser to HM Treasury, 1964–70.
Keynes, John Maynard (1883–1946)	Economist; adviser to HM Treasury 1940–41; Director, Bank of England, 1941–46.
King, Wilfred (d 1965)	Historian of the London discount market; editor of *The Banker*, 1946–65.
Lloyd, Selwyn (1904–78)	Chancellor of the Exchequer, 1960–62.
Macmillan, Harold (1894–1896)	Prime Minister, 1957–63.
Martin, William McChesney (1906–98)	Chairman, Federal Reserve Board, 1951–70.
Maudling, Reginald (1917–79)	Chancellor of the Exchequer, 1962–64.
Merriman, Hugh (1910–83)	Second senior partner, Akroyd and Smithers, at the time of the Parker tribunal; later senior partner.
Mullens, Sir Derrick (1909–75)	Government Broker, 1950–63.
Mynors, Sir Humphrey (1903–89)	Deputy Governor, Bank of England, 1954–64.
Neale, Sir Alan (1918–95)	Second Permanent Secretary, HM Treasury, 1971–72.
Niemeyer, Sir Otto (1883–1971)	Director, Bank of England, 1938–52.
Norman, Montagu (1871–1950)	Governor of the Bank of England, 1922–44.
O'Brien, Leslie (1908–95)	Chief Cashier, Bank of England, 1955–62; Executive Director, 1962–64, Deputy Governor, 1964–66; Governor, 1966–73.
Page, John (1923–2005)	Chief Cashier, Bank of England, 1970–81.
Parsons, Sir Maurice (1910–78)	Deputy Governor, Bank of England, 1966–70.
Peppiatt, Sir Kenneth (1893–1983)	Chief Cashier, Bank of England, 1934–49; Executive Director, 1949–57.
Phillips, Sir Frederick (1884–1943)	Third Secretary (Finance), HM Treasury 1939–42, Second Secretary 1942–43.
Polak, Jacques (1914–2010)	Economic Counsellor and Director of Research, International Monetary Fund, 1966–79.
Priestley, Jimmy (1915–2008)	Partner, Wedd Jefferson.
Radcliffe, Viscount Cyril (1899–1977)	Chairman, Committee on the Working of the Monetary System (1957–59).
Radice, Italo de Lisle (1911–2000)	Under secretary, H.M Treasury, 1961–68.
Simon, Sir John (1873–1954)	Chancellor of the Exchequer, 1937–40; (as Viscount Simon) Lord Chancellor, 1940–45.

(continued)

(continued)

Stevens, John (1913–73)	Director, Bank of England, 1957–65, 1968–73.
Thompson-McCausland, Lucius (1904–84)	Adviser to the Governor of the Bank of England, 1949–65.
Trinder, Arthur (1901–59)	Manager, Union Discount Company of London Ltd, 1947–58.
Wilkins, Dick (d 1989)	Partner, Wedd Jefferson, Wedd Durlacher Mordaunt and Co.
Wincott, Harold (1906–69)	Journalist, *Financial Times*.

Appendix A

Bailing Out the Jobbers

This appendix sets out the evidence from the Bank of England's daily ledgers pertaining to the bailing-out of jobbers and discount houses after sharp falls in gilt prices caused by increases in Bank rate or other Bank of England actions.

A.1 September 1931

The United Kingdom suspended the gold standard on Sunday 20 September, and Bank rate was increased from 4.5% to 6% on Monday 21st.

The Issue Department records show that in the whole of September 1931, net purchases of gilts from the market were £9,320,000, of which £3,745,000 were of 4½% Treasury 1930/32, due to mature in April 1932.[1] This was an unusually large monthly amount. The Bank settled gilt purchases from the market of £1,105,000 on Monday 21 September and £500,000 on Friday 25th. No sales were settled on those days. The deals settled on Monday would have been contracted on Friday or Saturday, before the Gold Standard was suspended. Gilt prices fell very heavily on the Saturday, and some of the purchases were at above that day's middle closing prices quoted in the press. Of the four deals settled on Friday 25th, two were at prices a little below Thursday's middle closing market price quoted in the press, and two above. It is possible that some of the transactions were intended as a rescue operation, but the evidence is not conclusive, bearing in mind the likely range of price fluctuations. As Table A.1 shows, the difference between the cost to the Bank of these purchases and the value of the stocks bought at the closing middle price on the date of purchase was a bit less than £3,400,

[1] BOE C40/579.

Table A.1 *Issue Department Gilt Purchases Settled on Monday 21 and Friday 25 September 1931*

Stock	Amount purchased (nominal, £)	Purchase price	Closing price on Thursday 17 September	Closing price on assumed dealing date	Difference between purchase cost and value at closing mid price (£)
Settled on Monday 21 September					
4½% Treasury 1930/32	180,000	99 7/8		99¾–100 (Friday and Saturday)	0
4% Treasury 1931/33	250,000	98	98–98¼	97½–¾ (Saturday)	937
4½% Treasury 1932/34	325,000 200,000 150,000	97 5/8 98 97 7/8	98 1/16–98 5/16	97 3/8–5/8 (Saturday)	1,969
Settled on Friday 25 September					
4½% Treasury 1930/32	200,000 100,000	£99:6s:7d £99:6s:3d		£99¼–¾	−529
4% Treasury 1931/33	100,000	£96 3/4		£96 1/8–3/8	500
4½% Treasury 1932/34	100,000	£96 1/2		£95 7/8–96 1/8	500

Sources: BOE C40/579, FTHA, TDA, author's calculations.

which suggests that if the purchases did represent a rescue operation, it was only modest in scale.

In addition to the Issue Department's gilt purchases, the Banking Department of the Bank of England made secured loans to Stock Exchange member firms as shown in Table A.2.

I have found no other written material relating to these loans. My interpretation is that the usual sources of credit to the jobbers were insufficient to finance gilt purchases due for settlement on Monday 21 September, or had dried up, and that:

Table A.2 *Selected Banking Department Advances, September 1931*

Date of advance	Date of repayment	Borrower	Amount
Monday 21/09/1931	Tuesday 22/09/1931	Mullens, Marshall, Steer, Lawford & Co.	£2,200,000
Tuesday 22/09/1931	Tuesday 29/09/1931	Francis and Praed	£750,000
Tuesday 29/09/1931	Tuesday 06/10/1931	Francis and Praed	£250,000

Source: BOE ADM9/223.

a. the initial loan to Mullens, Marshall, Steer, Lawford & Co., the Government Brokers, on Monday 21 September, was for passing on to the gilt jobbers;
b. all of the jobbers except Francis and Praed were able to repay the next day;
c. Francis and Praed needed, and got, £750,000 for the following week, and £250,000 for the week after that.

This operation represented last-resort liquidity support rather than capital support.

In addition, on 30 September, the Bank of England provided the discount house Smith St Aubyn with a facility to borrow against the security of £1,000,000 of 4% Treasury 1934/36 and, if necessary, £1,250,000 of 4½% Treasury 1932/34, at the penal rate of 2% above Bank rate, subject to a minimum of 6%. The first £100,000 of the loan could be left unsecured for one night 'to meet their immediate needs'.[2] In fact, Smiths borrowed £50,000 on 30 September, £450,000 on 1 October and £100,000 on 5 October. They repaid the entire £600,000 on 31 October.[3]

A.2 March 1952

The Budget speech, which included the news of the increase in Bank rate from 2.5% to 4%, was delivered after trading hours on Tuesday 11th. The Issue Department's transactions settled on 13 March, which would have been contracted on the 12th, the first trading opportunity after the Budget, were as follows. They were all purchases; there were no sales.

[2] Committee of Treasury minutes, 30 September 1931, BOE G8/60.
[3] Source: BOE ADM9/223.

Table A.3 *Issue Department Gilt Purchases Settled on 13 March 1952*

Stock	Nominal amount (£)	Purchase price	Closing middle prices		Difference between purchase cost and value at closing mid price (£)
			11 March	12 March	
2½% Savings 1964/67	500,000	82½	84 1/8	82¼	1,250
2½% Funding 1956/61	550,000	90 xd	92 1/8 xd	89½ xd	2,750
2½% National	1,000,000	99½	100 9/32	99 3/8	1,250
War	7,500,000	99 23/32			25,781
Bonds 1951/53	850,000	100			5,313
1¾% Serial Funding 1952	1,000,000	99 5/32	100	99¼	−938
Total	11,400,000				
Loss to Issue Dept					35,406

Sources: BOE ADM18/55, FTHA, author's calculations.
Note (**to this and the following tables in this Appendix**): after 1944, the prices for under-five-year stocks were conventionally quoted ex-accrued or rebate interest ('clean'), while those of over-five-year stocks were quoted including accrued or rebate interest ('dirty'). The cost and valuations are on the same basis as the prices are quoted 'xd' means ex-dividend.

The prices which the Bank paid to purchase gilts were below the previous day's closing prices, but above the closing prices on the day of the Bank rate increase. Thus the Bank ameliorated the market-makers' losses, but did not cover them entirely.

I discovered no evidence of unusual loans to the gilt market in March 1952.

A.3 September 1957

Bank rate was increased from 5% to 7% on 19 September. The Issue Department's transactions settled on 20 September, which would have been contracted on the 19th, were as follows. They were all purchases; there were no sales.

Table A.4 *Issue Department Gilt Purchases Settled on 20 September 1957*

Stock	Amount purchased (nominal, £)	Purchase price	Closing middle prices		Difference between purchase cost and value at closing mid price (£)
			18 September	19 September	
3½% Conversion 1961 or after	300,000	61	63 5/8	59	6,000
3% Transport 1968/73	250,000	71	73 1/8	70	2,500
4% Gas 1969/72	400,000	82	83 7/8	81	4,000
3% Savings 1960/70	750,000	75	77¼	74	7,500
4½% Electricity 1967/69	500,000	90	91 15/16	89	5,000
3½% Conversion 1969	900,000	81½	83 5/8	81	4,500
3% Funding 1966/68	400,000	79¾	81½	78½	5,000
4½% Conversion 1962	500,000 2,500,000	95 96	98 1/8	94	5,000 50,000
2½% Funding 1956/61	950,000	90¼	92 23/32	89	11,875
2% Exchequer 1960	300,000	92	94 7/16	91	3,000
3% War 1955/59	300,000	95	97 7/32	94	3,000
2¼% Serial Funding 1957	694,000	99:7s:11d	99 11/16	£99 13/32	−72
Total	8,744,000				
Loss to Issue Dept					107,303

Source: BOE ADM18/61, FTHA, author's calculations.

It might be thought that the gilt purchases of 19 September were made before the Bank rate announcement at the prices then ruling in the market. However, Angus Ashton, formerly of the gilt jobbers Francis and Praed, made it clear in his interview with Bernard Attard in 1990 that the deals were done after the Bank rate announcement.[4]

---

[4] Interview with Angus Ashton (CMH).

As in 1952, the Bank ameliorated the market-makers' losses, but did not cover them entirely.

I discovered no evidence of unusual loans to the gilt market in September 1957.

A.4 February 1960

On 24 February 1960, the Bank responded to an offer of £29¾ million of gilts by Midland Bank by bidding 1% below the prevailing market price. This amounted to a discretionary increase in gilt yields, and the Bank bought gilts from the jobbers 'at broadly opening prices' to 'enable jobbers to square their books before price [*sic*] to be established for the Midland sale was allowed to have its full impact on the market'.[5] The transactions thus spared the jobbers a loss that they would otherwise have incurred. The Issue Department's gilt purchases settled on 25 February were as shown in Table A.5; there were no sales.

The Bank's purchases limited the losses that the jobbers sustained on their long positions on 24 February 1960, but it did not eliminate them.

Table A.5 *Issue Department Gilt Purchases Settled on 25 February 1960*

Stock	Nominal amount (£)	Purchase price	Closing middle prices		Difference between purchase cost and value at closing mid price (£)
			23 February	24 February	
2 ½% Funding 1956/61	1,000,000	98 33/64	98½	98 7/16	781
3% Exchequer 1962/63	750,000	95½	95 9/16	95 5/16	1,406
2½% Exchequer 1963/64	500,000	92 15/32	92½	92 3/8	469
4½% Conversion 1964 A	1,000,000	99 33/64	99 3/16	98 31/32	5,469
3% Savings 1955/65	700,000	92 3/8	92 9/16	91¾	4,375
5½% Exchequer 1966	500,000	102 3/8	102½	102 7/8	2,500

(continued)

[5] Allen, 'Committee on internal statistics. Gilt-edged market: 19 February 1960 onwards', 3 March 1960, BOE C42/13.

Table A.5 (*continued*)

| Stock | Nominal amount (£) | Purchase price | Closing middle prices | | Difference between purchase cost and value at closing mid price (£) |
			23 February	24 February	
2½% Savings 1964/67	250,000	85 3/8	85½	84½	2,188
	15,000,000	84 13/32			
	5,500,000	84 3/8			
3% Funding 1966/68	500,000	85 1/16	85 3/16	84 1/8	4,688
4½% Electricity 1967/69	1,000,000	95 1/8	95¼	94½	6,250
3½% Conversion 1969	500,000	87 7/16	87 11/16	86¾	3,438
	9,250,000	86½			
4% Victory Bonds	615,850	95 5/8	95¾	95¼	2,309
3% Electricity 1968/73	250,000	77¾	79 1/8	77 1/8	1,563
5% Treasury 1986/89	1,000,000	95 15/16	96	95¼	6,875
3½% Funding 1999/2004	250,000	70½	70 11/32	69 7/8	1,563
Total	38,565,850				
Loss to Issue Dept					43,872

Sources: BOE ADM 18/64, TDA, author's calculations.

A.5 November 1964

Bank rate was increased from 5% to 7% on 23 November, and gilt prices fell sharply. The Bank sold £20.25 million of gilts at close to the new, lower, level of prices, and it bought £19.61 million, nearly all at prices above the new market levels. The purchases settled on 24 November were:

Three of the recorded purchases, for a total of £300,000 nominal, were at prices in line with closing levels on 23 November and therefore not part of the rescue operation, but the other purchases were made at prices very close to closing levels on 20 November, before the Bank rate rise.

The Government Broker commented that after the Bank rate rise had been announced:

Table A.6 *Issue Department Gilt Purchases Settled on 24 November 1964*

Stock	Amount purchased (nominal, £)	Purchase price	Closing middle prices		Difference between purchase cost and value at closing mid price (£)
			20 November	23 November	
2½% Treasury 1975 or after	650,000	40¼	40 7/8	39¾	6,500
3½% Conversion 1961 or after	75,000	56 13/16	56¾	55½	984
3½% War Loan 1952 or after	350,000	56¼	56¼	55	4,375
5½% Treasury 2008/12	350,000	90¾	90¾	89¼	5,250
3½% Funding 1999/2004	750,000	64¼	64 3/8	63	9,375
3% Redemption 1986/96	68,200	60 3/8	60½	59¼	767
3% Gas 1990/95	650,000	60 3/8	60 3/8	59	8,937
5¾% Funding 1987/91	1,800,000	95 5/8	95 3/8	94	29,250
4% Funding 1960/90	50,000	92¼	92 1/8	91	625
5% Treasury 1986/89	100,000	85	86 3/8	85	0
	200,000	86 3/8			2,750
3% Transport 1978/88	1,050,000	64¼	64¼	63	13,125
3½% Treasury 1979/81	100,000	73¾	75 1/8	73¾	0
	33,600	75 1/8			462
3½% Treasury 1977/80	100,000	73¾	75	73¾	0
	80,000	75			1,000
3½% Electricity 1976/69	395,000	75 7/8	75 7/8	74½	5,431
4¼% Electricity 1974/79	60,000	83½	83½	82¼	750
4% Transport 1972/77	82,000	81 7/8	81 7/8	80 ¾	922
3% Savings 1965/75	55,000	77 7/16	77 7/16	76¼	653
5¼% Conversion 1974	50,000	95¼	95 5/16	93¾	750
3% Electricity 1968/73	650,000	81 1/8	81 3/16	79 7/8	8,125
3% Transport 1968/73	50,000	81 1/8	81 3/16	79 7/8	625

(*continued*)

Table A.6 (*continued*)

Stock	Amount purchased (nominal, £)	Purchase price	Closing middle prices 20 November	Closing middle prices 23 November	Difference between purchase cost and value at closing mid price (£)
4% Gas 1969/72	1,010,000	89¾	89 7/8	88¾	10,100
5% Conversion 1971	1,500,000	97 5/8	97 11/16	96¼	20,625
3% Savings 1960/70	50,000	86 13/16	86 7/8	85 3/8	719
4½% Electricity 1967/69	72,000	95¼	95 5/16	94	900
3% Funding 1959/69	105,000	90 5/16	90 5/16	89	1,378
3½% Conversion 1969	653,000	91¼	91 5/16	90	8,162
2½% Savings 1964/67	415,000	92 5/8	92 9/16	91 3/8	5,187
5½% Exchequer 1966	3,776,000	100	100	99 1/8	33,040
4% Treasury 1965	26,000	99:16s:10d	99:16s:10d	99½	89
3% Savings 1955/65	366,000	98 13/32	98 11/32	97 5/8	2,859
5% Exchequer 1976/78	1,500,000	91 5/16	91¼	90¼	15,937
5% Exchequer 1967	1,060,000	98 19/32	98 9/16	97¼	15,237
3% Funding 1966/68	186,000	90 5/8	90 9/16	89¼	2,441
4% Exchequer 1968	543,000	94 5/16	94 5/16	93	7,127
5¼% Funding 1978/80	600,000	91 9/16	91½	90½	6,000
Total	19,610,800				
Loss to Issue Dept					232,852

Source: BOE ADM18/72, FTHA, author's calculations.

We then sent the Dealers round the Market to clear all the Jobbers' books, dealing at our middle closing price for Friday. The total cost of this was somewhere about £17 million.[6]

This makes it clear that the Issue Department bought all the gilts that the jobbers held at the time of the rate rise, and thus covered all their gilt losses.

I discovered no evidence of unusual loans to the gilt market in November 1964.

A.6 November 1967

The pound was devalued over the weekend 18–19 November, and Bank rate was increased from 6.5% to 8%. The Stock Exchange was closed on Monday 20 November. The Government Broker recorded on Tuesday that 'We also got the agreement of the Bank to take out the Jobbers from their position of Friday at Friday night's prices, although I pointed out that out attitude in the market had been such last week that I did not think this was really a necessity. However, the Bank were anxious to be as helpful as possible.'[7] The Issue Department bought £64.8 million of gilts on Tuesday, for settlement the next day, as shown in Table A.7.

Table A.7 *Issue Department Gilt Purchases Settled on 22 November 1967*

Stock	Amount purchased (nominal, £)	Purchase price	Closing price		Difference between purchase cost and value at closing mid price (£)
			17 November	21 November	
3½% Conversion 1961 or after	50,000	50 5/16	50 3/8	49¾	281
4% Consols 1957 or after	500,000	57 3/8	57 5/8	57	1,875
3½% War Loan	10,000,000	48¾	49½	48¾	0
	3,575,000	49 7/16			24,578
5½% Treasury 2008/12	1,300,000	80	80	78½	19,500

(continued)

[6] Daniell, 23 November 1964, BOE C132/6.
[7] Government Broker, 'Devaluation – 1967', 21 November 1967, BOE C132/9.

Table A.7 (*continued*)

Stock	Amount purchased (nominal, £)	Purchase price	Closing price 17 November	Closing price 21 November	Difference between purchase cost and value at closing mid price (£)
3½% Funding 1999/2004	900,000	56 3/8	56 3/8	55¾	5,625
6¾% Treasury 1995/98	10,500,000	94¼	96	94¼	0
5¾% Funding 1987/91	250,000	85¾	85 3/8	83¾	5,000
4% Funding 1960/90	150,000	95 5/8	95 5/8	94¾	1,312
5% Treasury 1986/89	1,900,000	77 5/8	77¾	76¼	26,125
6½% Funding 1985/87	750,000	92 7/8	93	91½	10,312
5½% Funding 1982/84	4,000,000	86	86 7/8	85¾	10,000
	100,000	86¾			1,000
3½% Treasury 1979/81	1,000,000	70½	71 3/8	70½	0
5½% Funding 1978/80	3,000,000	82¾	84 1/8	82¾	0
	400,000	84			5,000
3½% Treasury 1977/80	500,000	73½	73 5/8	73	2,500
3½% Electricity 1976/79	200,000	71 3/8	71 3/8	70¼	2,250
4¼% Electricity 1974/79	250,000	77 5/8	77 5/8	76¼	3,437
4% Transport 1972/77	200,000	77½	77 5/8	76¾	1,500
3% Electricity 1974/77	550,000	72 5/8	72 5/8	71½	6,188
6½% Treasury 1976	2,500,000	97½	98 5/8	97¾	−6,250
	250,000	98½			1,875
3% Savings 1965/75	1,000,000	74¾	76	74¾	0
	425,000	76			5,312
5¼% Conversion 1974	250,000	90 1/8	90¼	89	2,813
3% Electricity 1968/73	500,000	80¾	82	80¾	0
	250,000	82			3,125
4% Gas 1969/72	70,000	87 5/8	87 5/8	86¼	962
6¼% Exchequer 1972	150,000	96 1/16	96 1/8	94 5/8	2,156

(*continued*)

Table A.7 *(continued)*

| Stock | Amount purchased (nominal, £) | Purchase price | Closing price | | Difference between purchase cost and value at closing mid price (£) |
			17 November	21 November	
6% Conversion 1972	700,000	96 1/16	96 1/16	94½	10,938
6¾% Exchequer 1971	4,200,000	98½	98 9/16	97 9/16	39,375
5% Conversion 1971	50,000	93¼	46,625	92 5/8	312
6½% Treasury 1971	1,300,000	97 27/32	93¼	96 13/16	13,406
3% Savings 1960/70	215,000	89 5/16	89 9/16	88 7/16	1,881
6% Exchequer 1970	1,500,000	96 3/8	97 5/16	96 3/8	0
	2,820,000	97¼			24,675
4½% Electricity 1967/69	500,000	96¾	96 3/16	95 3/8	6,875
6½% Exchequer 1969	1,000,000	98 1/8	99 1/16	98 1/8	0
3% Funding 1966/68	7,000,000	97	97 7/32	97	0
Totals	64,755,000				
Loss to Issue Dept					233,941

Source: BOE ADM18/76, FTHA, author's calculations.

More than half of the Bank's purchases – £35.5 million nominal – were made at the closing price on Tuesday 21 November, and therefore involved no subsidy to the jobber. As to the remaining £22.3 million, they were made at prices close to the closing levels of Friday 17 November, and, again assuming that it bought all the gilts the jobbers wanted to sell, the Bank thus covered virtually all of their losses.

Appendix B

Sources of Data

B.1 Issue Department Transactions

Pember and Boyle (1950 and 1976) provide compendious information about gilts, including detailed histories of individual issues. All of it comes from the public domain, so it includes no information about the activities of the Bank of England in the secondary market.

The Bank of England archives provide information as follows.

B.1.1 1928–54: Monthly Returns to the Treasury (C40/579–86)

The returns are of two kinds. From December 1928 to March 1943 the Bank sent to the Treasury, after the end of each month, a statement of 'alterations effected in the securities held in the Issue Department' during the month. Until February 1932, it gave a detailed list of individual transactions, including in gilts, identifying the nominal amounts bought or sold, stock by stock, the price and the counterparty. Market counterparties were described simply as 'market', the CRND was separately identified, as were colonial accounts – e.g. 'Sec. of State in Council of India' – and other public bodies – e.g. 'Clearing office for enemy debts'.

From March 1932, the statements identify neither individual transactions, nor the nature of the counterparty, nor the prices at which deals were done. They provide total purchases and sales over the month, stock by stock, together with nominal amounts transacted and cash proceeds or costs. One can of course calculate an average price for the month by dividing the proceeds or cost of the transaction by the nominal amount transacted. The March statement, which was not sent to the Treasury until 16 July, was accompanied by a letter explaining that it had 'been held up pending a decision as to the new form that it should take . . . '[1] The change of format was presumably precipitated by the establishment of the Exchange Equalisation Account, into which the gold and foreign exchange reserves were transferred from the Issue Department. These returns continued in their 1932 format until March 1943, when they were dropped.[2]

The other kind of return is the Note Issue Income account (NII), which the Bank sent each month to the Treasury, accompanied by a Note Issue Expenses account, which is of no interest for present purposes. Note Issue Income, for the purposes of the return, included accrued and rebate interest paid and received on gilts that the Issue Department bought or sold, and expenses incurred in the purchase or sale (presumably brokers' fees). The NII statements listed total transactions during the month, stock by stock, specifying in each case the nominal amount, as well as the amount of accrued or rebate interest plus expenses.

Some transactions did not incur any expenses. It is tempting to suppose that those included transactions with the CRND, but separate evidence on the Issue Department's transactions with the CRND shows that they did incur expenses in the 1930s. However, there is a fairly close correspondence between data from other sources on transactions with the CRND in 1943–45 and transactions incurring no expenses identified from the NII statements.[3] Evidently brokerage charges on transactions between the Issue Department and the CRND were dropped at some point. It also seems likely that transactions between the Issue Department and the Bank of England's customers were free of brokerage charges. Those might have included certain public bodies, and some Empire central banks and currency boards.

It is not certain that the NII returns capture all of the Issue Department's transactions. An expense-free transaction settled on a dividend date would involve neither accrued nor rebate interest; and it is possible that in the case of some other transactions, expenses cancelled out accrued or rebate interest. Nevertheless the NII returns provide useful information up to July 1954; from August 1954 onwards, they cease to provide any information about the particular gilts that were bought and sold.

---

[1] Redfern–Secretary of the Treasury, 16 July 1932, BOE C40/580.
[2] Wynn-Williams–Chadwick, 20 April 1943, BOE C40/583.
[3] Note by Francis, 8 August 1945, BOE C40/438.

B.1.2 Weekly Internal Bank of England Reports (C11/1–55)

Cobbold instituted in 1949 a weekly report of gilt transactions which was provided to him for discussion each Friday (the 'Friday story'). The reports include information about the Issue Department's purchases and sales, stock by stock, from Friday a week earlier to Thursday. They identify separately transactions with the CRND, and in some cases overseas central banks, but do not identify other counterparties, nor give the prices at which deals were done.

B.1.3 Daily Account Books (C1/76–98, available on Bank of England Internet Site)

The daily account books provided a handwritten summary of the Bank's accounts for the deputy governor. Until 1950, there were one or two volumes for each year; afterwards, one volume covered two years. They show, for example, the amount of banknotes in issue each day, and the amount held in the Banking Department. They also show bankers' balances at the Bank of England each day. Each volume, up to 1950 at least, has a page listing the assets in the Issue Department, including holdings of individual gilt-edged stocks. The entries are hard to read, and it appears that they have been made in pencil and repeatedly altered during the year; I infer that the figures that now appear are as at the end of the year.

B.1.4 Daily Ledgers

The daily ledgers (ADM9 series for the Banking Department, ADM18 for the Issue Department) record in manuscript each transaction done by the Bank. Borrowers from the Bank are identified, but not the interest rates which they paid, or details of any collateral. The prices at which securities were bought and sold are specified, but the counterparties are not identified.

B.2 Discount Houses' Holdings of Gilts

Just after the end of each year from 1939–68, the Principal of the Bank of England Discount Office wrote a review of the year just ended for internal circulation, including tables showing each discount house's holdings of each gilt-edged stock with one to five years to run to maturity. The tables also showed each house's capital and reserves, and details of its other assets and contingent liabilities (BOE C47/39 and 40).

B.3 Yields

Each day's closing gilt prices were reported in the *Financial Times* and *The Times* (except during the newspaper strike of April 1955), and are available in the digital archives of those newspapers (FTHA, TDA). Yields can be calculated from the prices using readily available software.

Appendix C

New Gilt Issues for Cash or Conversion

Table C.1 *Tender Issues, 1928–40*

Date of prospectus	Stock	Amount (£ m)	Terms	Amount (£m) subscribed by Bank of England Issue Department	Amount (£m) subscribed by National Debt Commissioners
28/11/1928	4½% Treasury 1932/34	46	Cash (£99)	25	
		54	Conversion of 5% National War Bonds 1929 (£106.25 for £100 NWB),	3	
		2	Conversion of 4½% NWB 1929 (£101.25 for £100)	0	
		47	Conversion of 4½% Treasury bonds due 1929 (£101.25 for £100)	17	
02/11/1929	5% Conversion 1944/64	155	Cash (£100; special placing of £30mn at £99.5)	41	
		88	Conversion of 5% War Loan 1929/47 (£100)	0	
		79	Conversion of 5½% Treasury 1930 (£100, plus £0.75 cash bonus)	12	
22/02/1930	4½% Conversion 1940/44	61	Cash (£95)	30	
		32	Conversion of 5½% Treasury 1930 (£105.5 Conversion for £100 Treasuries)	19	
02/10/1930	4% Treasury 1934/36	105	Cash (average price £100:11s:6.89d)	70	
16/03/1932	4½% Conversion 1940/44	42	Conversion of 4½% Treasury bonds due 1932 (£97.625 Conversion for £100 Treasuries)	36	
16/03/1932	4% Consols 1957 or after	73	Conversion of 4½% Treasuries due 1932 (£107 Consols for £100 Treasuries)	55	
29/04/1932	3% Treasury 1933/42	110	Cash (average tender price £97:16s:1.97d)	66	
10/10/1932	2% Treasury 1935/38	77	Cash (£100)	62	
		73	Conversion of 4½% Treasury 1932/34	20	
03/11/1932	3% Conversion 1948/53	302	Cash (£97.5)	74	

(continued)

Table C.1 (*continued*)

Date of prospectus	Stock	Amount (£ m)	Terms	Amount (£m) subscribed by	
				Bank of England Issue Department	National Debt Commissioners
30/06/1932, offer open until 30/09/1932	3½% War Loan 1952 or after	1,921	Exchange for 5% War Loan 1929/47 (£100)	32	
17/03/1933; sale by weekly tenders from 24/03/1933 to 26/05/1933, and tender on 26/09/1933.[a]	2½% Conversion 1944/49	164 43	Cash Conversion of 4% Treasury 1934 (£106.375 of new issue for £100 of old)	120 20	
August 1933	2½% Treasury 1937	30	Conversion of 5½% US$ bonds due 01/02/1937		
03/04/1934	3% Funding 1959/69	150	Cash (£98)	97	
02/12/1935	1% Treasury 1939/41	100	Cash (£98)	12	
02/12/1935	2½% Funding 1956/61	200	Cash (£96.5)	160	
17/11/1936	2¾% Funding 1952/57	101	Cash (£98.5)	60	
27/04/1937	2½% National Defence 1944/48	100	Cash (£99.5)	85	
13/06/1938	3% National Defence 1954/58	321	Cash (£98)	26	
17/01/1940; 08/02/1940[b]	2% Conversion 1943/45	245	Conversion of 4½% Conversion 1940/44	65	28
05/03/1940	3% War Loan 1955/59	303	Cash (£100)	116	30

Sources: Bank of England C40/580, 581, 582, Pember and Boyle (1950), Osborne and Allport (1950, p.97), 'The wartime administration of the National Debt Commissioners 1939–45', February 1946, BOE C40/438.
Notes: [a] See Box 5.1 for further details. [b] Closing date of offer to pay cash on redemption.

Table C.2 *Tap Issues, 1940–45*

Dates on tap	Stock	Amount (£m)	Amount subscribed by	
			Bank of England Issue Department (£m)	National Debt Commissioners (£m)
25/06/1940–31/12/1940	2½% National War Bonds 1945–47	444	0	19
02/01/1941–14/08/1941	2½% National War Bonds 1946–48	493	20	49
09/10/1941–30/11/1942	2½% National War Bonds 1949–51	714	10	106
01/12/1942–31/08/1943	2½% National War Bonds 1951–53	522	35	54
01/09/1943–06/11/1944	2½% National War Bonds 1952–54	810	20	119
13/06/1945–15/12/1945	2½% National War Bonds 1954–56	426	0	29
02/01/1941–30/04/1942	3% Savings 1955–65	713	0	22
01/05/1942–05/08/1944	3% Savings 1960–70	1,009	32	17
08/08/1944–15/12/1945	3% Savings 1965–75	1,057	0	83
07/11/1944–12/06/1945	1¾% Exchequer 1950	327	225	11

Sources: Osborne and Allport (1950, pt I ch. 5).
Note: Osborne and Allport (1950, p. 1411) provide a list of gilts issued directly to the National Debt Commissioners between 1941 and 1945.

Table C.3 *Tap Issues, 1945–46*

Dates on tap	Stock	Amount (£mn)	Amount subscribed by:		
			Bank of England Issue Department (£m)	National Debt Commissioners (£m)	
08/12/1945 (date of conversion offer)	1¾% Exchequer 1950	176 (conversion of 2½% Conversion 1944/49) + 284 (conversion of 2½% National War Bonds 1945/47).	100	74 (out of 1944/49s) + 180 (out of 1945/47s)	
16/05/1946–16/07/1946	2½% Savings 1964/67	418 (cash) + 334 (conversion of 2½% National War Bonds 1946/48	40 (converted; author's estimate)	154 (converted) +75 (bought from Issue Department and converted)	
25/10/1946–11/01/1947	2½% Treasury 1975 or after	482 (reinvestment of proceeds of 3% Local Loans and cash offer)	96 (out of Local Loans) 0 (cash)	96 (out of Local Loans) + 68 (cash)	

Sources: Osborne and Allport (1950, p. 190); Howson (1993, p. 137); note issue income account statement, April 1946, BOE C40/584; correspondence between Francis and Holland-Martin, 21–23/02/1946, BOE C40/438; Peppiatt-Bamford, 'Local Loans', 9 December 1946, BOE C0/473; Compton, 'Stock market transactions by government departments', 25 November 1947, NA T233/143, author's calculations.

Table C.4 *Tender Issues, 1946–October 1951*

Date of prospectus	Stock issued	Amount (£m)	Terms	Amount subscribed by Bank of England Issue Department (£m)
19/10/1948	3% British Electricity 1974/77	100	Cash (£99½)	0
03/12/1949	2¼% Exchequer 1955	735	Conversion of 1¾% Exchequer 1950	398
02/05/1950	3½% British Electricity 1976/79	150	Cash (£99)	59
06/06/1950	2½% Funding 1956/61	100	Cash (£99½)	77
		506	Conversion of 2½% National War Bonds 1949/51	218
31/10/1950	3% Funding 1966/68	250	Cash (£100)	106
		88	Conversion of 2½% National War Bonds 1949/51	81
09/07/1951	3½% British Gas 1969/71	75	Cash (£98)	51

New Gilt Issues for Cash or Conversion

Table C.5 *Tender Issues, November 1951–59*

Date of prospectus	Stock issued	Amount (£m)	Terms	Bank of England Issue Department	National Debt Commissioners
			Amount (£m) subscribed by		
08/11/1951	1¾% Serial Funding 1952	450	Conversion of £1 billion	26	
	1¾% Serial Funding 1953	200	Treasury bills	27	
	1¾% Serial Funding 1954	350		7 4	
23/04/1952	4¼% British Electricity 1974/79	150	Cash (£99)	92	
01/10/1952	1¾% Serial Funding 1953	242	Conversion of 1¾% Serial	28	
	1¾% Serial Funding 1954	68	Funding 1952 (£345 million)	0	
	3% Serial Funding 1955	35		0	
	3% Serial Funding 1955	374	Conversion of 2½% National War Bonds 1951/53 (£374 million)	233	
	1¾% Serial Funding 1953	135	Cash (£98 7/8)	0	
	1¾% Serial Funding 1954	67	Cash (£97 7/8)	20	
	3% Serial Funding 1955	115	Cash (£100)	0	
03/11/1952	4% British Transport 1972/77	60	Conversion of 1¾% British Transport 1952		
	4% British Transport 1972/77	60	Cash (£95½)	37	
26/02/1953	3% Exchequer 1960	100	Cash (£99½)	70	
20/04/1953	4¼% British Electricity 1974/79	125	Cash (£100)	84	

(continued)

Table C.5 *(continued)*

Date of prospectus	Stock issued	Amount (£m)	Terms	Amount (£m) subscribed by	
				Bank of England Issue Department	National Debt Commissioners
15/06/1953	3% Exchequer 1960	100	Cash (£100)	52	
07/07/1953	2½% National War Bonds 1954/56	398	Conversion of 2½% National War Bonds 1952/54	153	
04/08/1953	4% British Gas 1969/72	80	Cash (£99)	66	
30/09/1953	1¾% Serial Funding 1954	49	Conversion of 1¾% Serial Funding 1953	0	
	2½% Serial Funding 1957	503		259	
	3% Exchequer 1962/63	341	Cash (£99½)	190	
25/01/1954	3½% Conversion 1969	341	Conversion of 2½% National War Bonds 1952/54	311	
15/02/1954	4% British Transport 1972/77	80	Cash (£101)	77	
31/05/1954	2% Conversion 1958/59	292	Conversion of 3% National Defence Loan 1954/58	39	
	2% Conversion 1958/59	300	Cash (£99½)	157	
05/07/1954	2½% Exchequer 1963/64	274	Conversion of 1¾% Serial Funding 1954	214	
	3½% Funding 1999/2004	143		90	
13/08/1954	3½% British Electricity 1976/79	100	Cash (£100½)	97	
26/11/1954	2% Exchequer 1960	448	Conversion of 2¼% Exchequer 1955	181	
	3% Funding 1966/68	202		160	

(continued)

Table C.5 (*continued*)

				Amount (£m) subscribed by	
Date of prospectus	Stock issued	Amount (£m)	Terms	Bank of England Issue Department	National Debt Commissioners
20/06/1955	4% British Transport 1972/77	42	Cash (£96½)	16	
11/07/1955	4% British Gas 1969/72	100	Cash (£98)	90	
08/08/1955	4½% British Electricity 1967/69	200	Cash (£98½)	178	
10/10/1955	4% Conversion 1957/58	250	Cash (£99½)	185	
	4% Conversion 1957/58	426	Conversion of 3% Serial Funding 1955	278	
02/03/1956	5% Exchequer 1957	300	Cash (£100)	196	
20/04/1956	3½% Treasury 1979/81	250	Cash (£81)	244	
06/07/1956	4½% Conversion 1962	657	Conversion of 2½% National War Bonds 1954/56	581	33
11/02/1957	3½% Funding 1999/2004	300	Cash (£80)	269	30
03/05/1957	4½% Conversion 1962	100	Cash (£99)	38	
09/01/1958	5½% Exchequer 1966	500	Cash (£99½)	342	
11/02/1958	5½% Funding 1982/84	300	Cash (£98½)	274	
25/04/1958	4¾% Conversion 1963	353	Conversion of 4% Conversion 1957/58	270	
	5¼% Conversion 1974	299		269	

(*continued*)

Table C.5 (*continued*)

Date of prospectus	Stock issued	Amount (£m)	Terms	Amount (£m) subscribed by	
				Bank of England Issue Department	National Debt Commissioners
28/11/1958	4½% Conversion 1964	250	Conversion of 2% Conversion 1958/59	217	
07/08/1959	4½% Conversion 1964	54	Conversion of 3% War Loan 1955/59	45	
	5% Conversion 1986/89	144		120	18
	5% Conversion 1986/89	157	Cash (£98)	150	5
30/12/1959	5% Conversion 1971	412	Conversion of 2% Exchequer 1960 (309)	292	3
			Conversion of 3% Exchequer 1960 (105)	90	9

Table C.6 *Tender Issues, 1960–72*

Date	Stock issued	Amount (£m)	Terms	Bank of England Issue Department	National Debt Commissioners
				Amount (£m) subscribed by	
26/01/1960	4½% Conversion 1964	200	Cash (£99.25)	185	
12/07/1960	5½% Treasury 1962	300	Cash (£99)	76	
30/09/1960	5½% Treasury 2008/12	500	Cash (£95)	491	7
31/01/1961	4¾% Conversion 1963	300	Cash (£99.375)	285	
	5½% Exchequer 1966	483	Conversion of 2½% Funding 1956/61	400	
08/12/1961	6% Conversion 1972	301	Conversion of 4½% Conversion 1962	268	
	5½% Funding 1982/84	200	Conversion of 4½% Conversion 1962 (£110 for £100)	199	
04/05/1962	5% Treasury 1986/89	300	Cash (£84.5)	299	
15/06/1962	5% Exchequer 1967	400	Cash (£98)	249	
30/08/1962	5½% Treasury 2008/12	500	Cash (£95)	500	
28/09/1962	4% Treasury 1965	100	Cash (£99.5)	3	
		291	Conversion of 5½% Treasury 1962	271	
18/04/1963	5% Exchequer 1976/78	400	Cash (£96)	348	
20/09/1963	4% Exchequer 1968	500	Cash (£98)	433	
14/02/1964	5¼% Funding 1978/80	400	Cash (£96.5)	399	
20/04/1964	5¾% Funding 1987/91	400	Cash (£97)	398	

(*continued*)

Table C.6 *(continued)*

Date	Stock issued	Amount (£m)	Terms	Amount (£m) subscribed by	
				Bank of England Issue Department	National Debt Commissioners
03/02/1965	5%Exchequer 1967	450	Cash (£96.5)	431	
15/06/1965	6½% Exchequer 1969	100	Cash (£100)	28	
		312	Conversion of 3% Savings 1955/65	223	33
	6½% Treasury 1976	100	Cash (£100)	97	
		200	Conversion of 3% Savings 1955/65	145	16
22/09/1965	6% Funding 1993	600	Cash (£96)	600	
26/10/1965	6% Exchequer 1970	500	Cash (£99)	437	
07/10/1966	6¾% Exchequer 1971	700	Cash (£99.25)	495	
24/10/1966	6¾% Treasury 1995/98	400	Cash (£97.5)	394	
31/01/1967	6¼% Exchequer 1972	400	Cash (£98.5)	319	
		515	Conversion of 2½% Savings 1964/67	432	
	6½% Funding 1985/87	500	Cash (£98.75)	493	
		59	Conversion of 2½% Savings 1964/67	25	
21/11/1967	6¾% Treasury 1995/98	600	Cash (£94.5)	599	
13/02/1968	6¾% Exchequer 1973	700	Cash (£97.25)	605	
17/07/1969	9% Treasury 1994	400	Cash (£96.5)	325	
03/10/1969	8¾% Treasury 1997	400	Cash (£95)	392	
30/12/1969	6¾% Exchequer 1971	200	Cash (£96.3125)	116	

(continued)

Table C.6   (*continued*)

Date	Stock issued	Amount (£m)	Terms	Bank of England Issue Department	National Debt Commissione-rs
				Amount (£m) subscribed by	
23/01/1970	8½% Treasury 1980/82	600 261	Cash (£96.25) Conversion of 3% Savings 1960/70	548 104	
06/08/1970	6¾% Treasury 1974	300	Cash (£98.25)	293	
	8½% Treasury 1984/86	600	Cash (£95)	524	12
07/01/1971	6½% Treasury 1976	600	Cash (£94.25)	563	32
14/01/1971	9% Treasury 1994	500	Cash (£94.5)	489	
17/02/1971	6½% Exchequer 1976	600	Cash (£95.5)	569	13
05/03/1971	9% Treasury 1992/96	600	Cash (£95.5)	589	7
07/07/1971	8¾% Treasury 1997	400	Cash (£95)	376	
09/07/1971	6% Treasury 1975	500	Cash (£98.5)	411	42
03/09/1971	8¼% Treasury 1987/90	600	Cash (£96)	553	
10/09/1971	5¼% Treasury 1973	550	Cash (£99.25)	199	70
	5½% Treasury 1974	400	Cash (£98.69)	131	10
	6¼% Treasury 1977	350	Cash (£97.94)	73	15
15/10/1971	8% Treasury 2002/06	600	Cash (£95)	596	
21/01/1972	7¾% Treasury 2012/15	600	Cash (£96)	560	
28/04/1972	6¼% Treasury 1977	500	Cash (£101.25)	472	7
	7¾% Treasury 1985/88	500	Cash (£97.5)	428	

Note C.4, C.5 and C.6: the tables do not include issues of stock as compensation for nationalised assets.

Sources (C.4, C.5 and C.6): Pember and Boyle (1976), Bank of England and National Archives, author's calculations.

Further details of the sources are available from the spreadsheets which are available on the internet, at Cambridge.org, niesr.ac.uk, eh.net, bankofengland.co.uk and researchgate.net.

Appendix D

Official Turnover, 1951–72

Table D.1 *Issue Department Turnover by Maturity Bands, 1951–72*
(A) in £ million (nominal)

Year	Purchases				Sales			
	Forthcoming maturities (<9m)	Other shorts (<5y)	Mediums (5–15y)	Longs (>15y)	Forthcoming maturities (<9m)	Other shorts (<5y)	Mediums (5–15y)	Longs (>15y)
1951	23.3	190.6	18.2	129.1	0.0	101.3	165.2	175.2
1952	110.2	134.2	20.4	126.5	3.5	154.0	32.1	289.5
1953	510.5	184.6	95.7	171.2	5.0	567.4	298.8	406.0
1954	912.7	228.8	237.5	175.1	93.8	589.1	641.7	396.2
1955	229.8	230.7	135.7	96.0	77.5	328.6	315.5	199.3
1956	608.8	238.5	102.3	38.4	20.1	674.0	334.7	137.1
1957	711.6	282.6	163.4	183.7	29.0	676.8	361.8	439.6
1958	750.2	447.5	311.4	186.3	9.0	549.3	514.3	710.8
1959	365.8	514.0	295.6	109.6	29.9	589.9	370.3	236.1
1960	321.7	773.7	501.5	213.0	0.0	952.5	695.8	332.2
1961	524.9	1,089.5	358.0	251.2	18.7	1,317.6	428.5	396.9
1962	395.8	1,166.2	716.1	628.0	2.5	1,038.4	1,094.8	1,282.0
1963	494.6	591.7	419.5	256.9	0.0	634.8	454.2	501.6
1964	484.6	761.8	379.2	322.2	10.2	934.8	319.3	723.8
1965	901.6	681.8	380.1	207.1	0.0	1,435.7	736.1	299.0
1966	364.1	993.5	516.7	318.6	0.0	1,198.3	385.6	960.8

(continued)

Table D.1 (*continued*)

Year	Purchases				Sales			
	Forthcoming maturities (<9m)	Other shorts (<5y)	Mediums (5–15y)	Longs (>15y)	Forthcoming maturities (<9m)	Other shorts (<5y)	Mediums (5–15y)	Longs (>15y)
1967	602.5	1,653.6	560.4	553.9	0.0	1,679.1	1,042.9	1,128.1
1968	505.6	1,592.0	232.3	490.3	0.0	1,486.8	181.0	864.8
1969	589.2	718.2	212.3	393.0	0.0	1,231.9	282.4	999.9
1970	842.9	1,189.2	581.8	908.5	2.4	1,107.5	1,263.7	1,223.9
1971	856.5	963.6	540.7	448.7	0.0	1,878.5	1,153.2	2,782.4
1972	830.7	581.7	316.5	336.4	27.8	649.2	312.9	1,241.4

(B) *as percentage of gilts in the maturity band outstanding.*

Year	Purchases			Sales		
	Shorts (up to 5y)	Mediums (5–15y)	Longs (>15y)	Shorts (up to 5y)	Mediums (5–15y)	Longs (>15y)
1951	10.3	0.6	1.3	4.9	5.7	1.7
1952	7.0	0.8	1.2	4.5	1.3	2.8
1953	19.0	3.0	1.6	15.6	9.2	3.9
1954	32.2	5.9	1.8	19.3	15.9	4.0
1955	13.2	3.2	1.0	11.6	7.4	2.0
1956	21.5	1.9	0.4	17.6	6.1	1.4
1957	21.7	3.4	2.1	15.4	7.6	4.9
1958	31.7	5.7	2.0	14.8	9.5	7.6

1959	27.5	5.1	1.2	19.4	6.4	2.5
1960	36.2	8.4	2.3	31.5	11.7	3.6
1961	33.4	6.2	2.7	27.6	7.4	4.3
1962	41.4	11.6	7.3	27.6	17.7	14.9
1963	21.7	7.4	3.0	12.7	8.0	5.8
1964	23.2	7.4	3.5	17.6	6.2	7.9
1965	31.3	7.2	2.2	28.3	14.0	3.1
1966	25.6	9.1	3.4	22.6	6.8	10.3
1967	35.7	9.9	6.3	26.6	18.4	12.8
1968	29.6	5.1	5.1	21.0	4.0	8.9
1969	19.4	4.6	3.8	18.3	6.2	9.8
1970	35.8	11.3	9.3	19.6	24.6	12.6
1971	28.8	11.6	4.3	29.8	24.7	26.6
1972	19.0	7.4	2.8	9.1	7.3	10.2

Sources: BOE C11/3–55, Pember and Boyle (1976), author's calculations.

References

Archives

BOE	Bank of England
EHA	Economist Historical Archive
FTHA	Financial Times Historical Archive
NA	National Archive
TDA	Times Digital Archive

Oral History

Centre for Metropolitan History (CMH), University of London Institute of Historical Research, 'The jobbing system of the London Stock Exchange: an oral history' available at www.history.ac.uk/projects/research/jobbing. The archive consists of aural and written records of interviews conducted in 1989 and 1990 with former jobbers by Bernard Attard and Olwen Myhill.

Published Works

Alford, R.F.G. (1959), 'London's money brokers', *The Banker*, June, 380–9.

Allen, W.A. (2014), *Monetary policy and financial repression in Britain, 1951–59*, London: Palgrave Macmillan.

Allen, W.A. (2016), 'The British attempt to manage long-term interest rates in 1962–64', *Financial History Review*, **23**(1), 47–70.

Anderson, M. and R. Stulz (2017), 'Is post-crisis bond liquidity lower?', NBER working paper 23317.

Arrow, K.J. (1959), 'Towards a theory of price adjustment', in M. Abramowitz and others, *The allocation of economic resources*, Stanford CT: Stanford University Press.

Atkin, J. (2005), *The foreign exchange market of London: development since 1900*, Abingdon: Routledge.

Attard, B. (2000), 'Making a market. The jobbers of the London Stock Exchange, 1800–1986', *Financial History Review*, 7(1), 5–24.

Bach, G.L. (1949), 'The Federal Reserve and monetary policy formation', *American Economic Review*, 39(6), 1173–91.

Backhouse, R.E. and M. Boianovsky (2013), *Transforming modern macroeconomics: exploring disequilibrium microfoundations, 1956–2003*, Cambridge: Cambridge University Press.

Bain, A.D. (1970), *The control of the money supply*, London: Penguin Modern Economics.

Balogh, T. (1947), *Studies in financial organization*, Cambridge: Cambridge University Press.

Bank for International Settlements (1939), Ninth Annual Report, Basel.

Bank of England (1966), 'Official transactions in the gilt-edged market', BEQB (*Bank of England Quarterly Bulletin*), 141–8.

Bank of England (1967), 'The London discount market: some historical notes', BEQB 144–56.

Bank of England (1969), 'The operation of monetary policy since the Radcliffe report', BEQB 448–60.

Bank of England (1989), 'The gilt-edged market since Big Bang', BEQB 49–58.

Benos, E. and A. Wetherilt (2012), 'The role of designated market-makers in the new trading landscape', BEQB 343–53.

Benos, E. and F. Zikes (2016), 'Liquidity determinants in the UK gilt market', Bank of England staff working paper no. 600.

Bernholz, P. (2015), *Monetary regimes and inflation*, 2nd edn, Cheltenham: Edward Elgar.

Binder, S. and M. Spindel (2017), *The myth of independence: how Congress governs the Federal Reserve*, Princeton NJ: Princeton University Press.

Blaug, M. (1962), *Economic theory in retrospect*, Cambridge: Cambridge University Press.

Board of Governors of the Federal Reserve System (1948), Thirty-fourth annual report covering operations for the year 1947.

Board of Governors of the Federal Reserve System (1954), Fortieth Annual Report covering operations for the year 1953.

Bordo, M. and E.N. White (1993), 'British and French finance during the Napoleonic Wars' in M.D. Bordo and F. Capie (eds.), *Monetary regimes in transition*, Cambridge: Cambridge University Press.

Boyle, A. (1967), *Montagu Norman*, New York: Weybright and Talley.

Bremner, R.P. (2004), *Chairman of the Fed: William McChesney Martin Jr and the creation of the modern American financial system*, Harvard NJ: Yale University Press.

Buiter, W. and A. Sibert (2008), 'The central bank as the market-maker of last resort: from lender of last resort to market-maker of last resort', in *The first global financial crisis of the 21st century*, Centre for Economic Policy Research.

Cairncross, A. (1985), *Years of recovery: British economic policy 1945–51*, London: Methuen.

Cairncross, A. and B. Eichengreen (1983), *Sterling in decline*, Oxford: Blackwell.

Capie, F.H. (2010), *The Bank of England: 1950s to 1979*, Cambridge: Cambridge University Press.

Capie, F.H., T.C. Mills and G.E. Wood (1986), 'Debt management and interest rates: the British stock conversion of 1932', *Applied Economics*, **18**, 1111–26.

Chandler, L.V. (1949), 'Federal Reserve policy and the Federal debt', *American Economic Review*, **39**(2), 405–29.

Clay, Sir H. (1957), *Lord Norman*, London: Macmillan.

Cleaver, G. and A. (1985), 'Union discount: a centenary history', privately published.

Clower, R. W. (1967), 'A reconsideration of the microfoundations of monetary theory', *Western Economic Journal*, **6**, 1–9.

Cohen, C.D. (1971), *British economic policy 1960–1969*, London: Butterworth.

Coleby, A. L. (2006), Statement at witness seminar on 'The old gilt-edged market', 22 March 2006, symposium transcript published by Lombard Street Research.

Committee on the Global Financial System (2014), 'Market-making and proprietary trading: industry trends, drivers and policy implications', Bank for International Settlements, CGFS papers no. 52.

Conti-Brown, P. (2016), *The power and independence of the Federal Reserve*, Princeton NJ: Princeton University Press.

Coombs, C.A. (1976), *The arena of international finance*, Abingdon: John Wiley and Sons.

Cottrell, P.L. (1995), 'The Bank in its international setting', in R. Roberts and D. Kynaston (eds.), *The Bank of England: money, power and influence, 1694–1994*, Oxford: Oxford University Press.

Cristiano, C. and P. Paesani (2017), 'Unconventional monetary policy ante litteram: Richard Kahn and the monetary policy debate during the works of the Radcliffe Committee', *Cambridge Journal of Economics*, https://doi.org/10.1093/cje/bex072.

Croome, D.R. and H.G. Johnson (eds.) (1970), *Money in Britain 1959–1969, the papers of the Radcliffe report – ten years after conference at Hove, Sussex, October 1969*, Oxford: Oxford University Press.

Debt Management Office (2017), Annual Review 2016–17.

Dow, J.C.R. (1964), *The management of the British economy, 1945–1960*, Cambridge: Cambridge University Press.

Drummond, I.M. (1981), *The floating pound and the sterling area, 1931–1939*, Cambridge: Cambridge University Press.

Duffie, D. (2012), 'Market making under the proposed Volcker rule', https://papers.ssrn.com/sol3/papers.cfm?abstract_id=1990472 (last accessed 16 July 2017).

Dutta, S. J. (2018), 'Sovereign debt management and the globalization of finance: recasting the City of London's "Big Bang"', *Competition and Change*, **22**(1), 3–22.

Eichengreen, B. (2008), *Globalizing capital*, 2nd edn, Princeton NJ: Princeton University Press.

Ellison, M. and A. Scott (2017), 'Managing the U.K. national debt 1694–2017', CEPR discussion paper DP 12304.

Fender, I. and U. Lewrick (2015), 'Shifting tides – market liquidity and market-making in fixed income instruments', *BIS Quarterly Review*, March.

Ferguson, N. (2001), *The Cash Nexus*, London: Allen Lane, the Penguin Press.

Fforde, J.S. (1992), *The Bank of England and public policy, 1941–1958*, Cambridge: Cambridge University Press.

Fischer, S. (2016), 'Is there a liquidity problem post-crisis?', remarks at a conference sponsored by the Initiative on Business and Public Policy at the Brookings Institution, Washington DC, 15 November.

Fletcher, G.A. (1976), *The discount houses in London*, London: Macmillan.

Foucault, T., M. Pagano and A. Roell (2013), *Market liquidity: theory, evidence and policy*, Oxford: Oxford University Press.

Friedman, M. (1970), 'The counter-revolution in monetary theory', first Wincott memorial lecture, Institute of Economic Affairs.

Garbade, K. (2012), *Birth of a market*, Cambridge MA: MIT Press.

Garbade, K. (2014), 'Direct purchases of U.S. Treasury securities by Federal Reserve Banks', Federal Reserve Bank of New York Staff Report no. 684.

Gardner, R.N. (1969), *Sterling-dollar diplomacy*, new expanded edn, McGraw Hill.

Goldman Sachs (2015), 'A look at liquidity', Top of mind issue 37, 2 August.

Goodhart, C.A.E. (1972), *The business of banking 1891-1914*, London: LSE/Weidenfeld and Nicolson.

Goodhart, C.A.E. (1973), 'Monetary policy in the United Kingdom' in K. Holbik (ed.), *Monetary policy in twelve industrial countries*, Boston MA: Federal Reserve Bank of Boston.

Goodhart, C.A.E. (2015), 'Competition and Credit Control: some personal reflections', *Financial History Review*, 22(2), 235-46.

Goodhart, C.A.E. and A.D. Crockett (1970), 'The importance of money', BEQB 159-198.

Goodhart, C.A.E. and D.J. Needham (2017), 'Historical reasons for the focus on broad monetary aggregates in post-WW2 Britain, including the "Seven Years War" with the IMF', *Financial History Review*, 24(3), 331-56.

Goodson, H.F. (1962), 'The functioning of the London discount houses', in Institute of Bankers, The London Discount Market Today, the Ernest Sykes Memorial Lectures, February and March 1962.

Gowland, D.H. (1984), *Controlling the money supply*, 2nd edn, Croom Helm.

Hicks, J.R. (1989), *A market theory of money*, Oxford: Oxford University Press.

Howson, S.K. (1974), 'The origins of dear money, 1919-20', *Economic History Review*, 29(1), 88-107.

Howson, S.K. (1975), 'Domestic monetary management in Britain 1919-1938', Department of Applied Economics Occasional Paper 48, Cambridge: Cambridge University Press.

Howson, S.K. (1980), 'Sterling's managed float: the operations of the Exchange Equalisation Account 1932-39', Princeton Essays in International Finance no. 46.

Howson, S.K. (1987), 'The origins of cheaper money, 1945-7', *Economic History Review*, XL(3), 433-52.

Howson, S.K. (1988), 'Cheap money and debt management in Britain, 1932-51', in P.L. Cottrell and D.E. Moggridge (eds.), *Money and power*, London: Macmillan.

Howson, S.K. (1993), *British monetary policy 1945-1951*, Oxford: Oxford University Press.

International Monetary Fund (2015), Global financial stability report, October.

James, H. (1996), *International monetary cooperation since Bretton Woods*, Oxford: IMF and Oxford University Press.

Johnson, H.G. (1970), 'Recent developments in monetary theory – a commentary', in Croome and Johnson (1970).

Johnson, H.G. (1971), 'The Keynesian revolution and the monetarist counter-revolution', *American Economic Review*, LXI(2), 1–14.

King, W.T.C. (1946), 'The modern Goschen', *The Banker*, **LXXX**(250), 67–71.

King, W.T.C. (1947), 'The changing discount market', *The Banker*, **LXXXI**(254), 171–85.

King, W.T.C. (1962), 'The market's changing role', in Institute of Bankers, *The London Discount Market Today, the Ernest Sykes Memorial Lectures*, February and March 1962.

King, W.T.C. (1972), *History of the London discount market*, Cass.

Konstas, P. (1966), 'From bills only to Operation Twist: a study of Federal Reserve open market operations for the period 1953–64', PhD thesis, Oklahoma State University.

Kregel, J.A. (1995), 'Neoclassical price theory, institutions, and the evolution of securities market organisation', *Economic Journal*, **105**(429), 459–70.

Kynaston, D. (1983), 'The London Stock Exchange, 1870–1914: an institutional history', PhD thesis, University of London.

Kynaston, D. (2002), *The City of London, IV: a club no more, 1945–2000*, Pimlico.

Lees, D.S. (1953), 'The technique of monetary insulation, December 1932 to December 1937', *Economica*, **20**(80), 341–55.

Leijonhufvud, A. (1968), *On Keynesian economics and the economics of Keynes*, Oxford: Oxford University Press.

Leijonhufvud, A. (1981), *Information and coordination*, Oxford: Oxford University Press.

Macmillan Committee (1931a), Report of the Committee on Finance and Industry, Cmnd 3897, HMSO.

Macmillan Committee (1931b), Minutes of Evidence taken before the Committee on Finance and Industry, I, HMSO.

Martin, W. McC. (1953), 'The transition to free markets', remarks to a luncheon meeting of the Economic Club of Detroit, 13 April, available at FRASER, Federal Reserve Bank of St Louis.

Mayo, H.B. (1949), 'Newfoundland's entry into the Dominion', *Canadian Journal of Economics and Political Science*, **15**(4), 505–522.

Mehrling, P. (1998), 'The money muddle; the transformation of American monetary thought, 1920–1970', *History of Political Economy*, supplement 'From interwar pluralism to postwar neoclassicism', 293–306.

Mehrling, P. (2011), *The new Lombard Street*, Princeton NJ: Princeton University Press.

Meltzer, A.H. (2009), *A history of the Federal Reserve*, 2 book 1, 1951–69, Chicago IL: University of Chicago Press.

Meltzer, A. H. and G. von der Linde (1960), *A study of the dealer market for Federal Government securities, materials prepared for the Joint Economic Committee, Congress of the United States*, US Government Printing Office.

Meulendyke, A.-M. (1998), *US monetary policy and financial markets*, Federal Reserve Bank of New York.

Michie, R.C. (1999), *The London Stock Exchange – a history*, Oxford: Oxford University Press.

Moggridge, D.E. (1972), *British monetary policy 1924–1931: the Norman Conquest of $4.86*, Cambridge: Cambridge University Press.

Moran, M. (1984), *The politics of banking: the strange case of Competition and Credit Control*, New York: St Martin's Press.

Morgan, E.V. (1952), *British financial policy 1914–1925*, London: Macmillan.

Morgan, E.V. and W.A. Thomas (1962), *The Stock Exchange; its history and functions*, Elek Books.

Naef, A. (2017). 'Dirty float or clean intervention? The Bank of England on the foreign exchange market, 1952–72', unpublished manuscript.

Needham, D. (2014), *UK monetary policy from devaluation to Thatcher*, London: Palgrave.

Nevin, E. (1955), *The mechanism of cheap money*, University of Wales Press.

Nevin, E. and E.W. Davis (1970), *The London clearing banks*, Elek books.

Newton, C.C.S. (1984), 'The sterling crisis of 1947 and the British response to the Marshall plan', *Economic History Review*, 37(3), 391–408.

Nishimura, S. (1971), *The decline of inland bills of exchange in the London money market, 1855–1913*, Cambridge: Cambridge University Press

Norton, W.E. (1969), 'Debt management and monetary policy in the United Kingdom' *Economic Journal*, **79**(315), 475–94.

Odlyzko, A. (2016), 'Financialization of the early Victorian economy and the London Stock Exchange', https://papers.ssrn.com/sol3/papers.cfm?abstract_id=2787154.

Oliver, M. and A. Hamilton (2007), 'Downhill from devaluation: the battle for sterling 1968–72', Economic History Review, **60**(3), 486–512.

Osborne, J.A.C., ed. (1926), *The Bank of England 1914–1921*, 4 volumes. Archive document, reference BOE M7/156–159, available on the Bank of England archive internet site www.bankofengland.co.uk/archive/bank-of-england-1914-21-ww1.

Osborne, J.A.C. and R.E.H. Allport (1950), *War history of the Bank of England, 1939–45*. Archive document, reference BOE M5/533–539, available on the Bank of England archive internet site www.bankofengland.co.uk/archive/bank-of-england-1939-45-ww2.

Parker Tribunal (1958), *Proceedings of the Tribunal appointed to inquire into allegations that information about the raising of Bank Rate was improperly disclosed*, London: Her Majesty's Stationery Office.

Peden, G.C. (2000), *The Treasury and British public policy 1906–1959*, Oxford: Oxford University Press.

Pember and Boyle (1950 and 1976), 'British government securities in the twentieth century', and supplement, privately published.

Powell, J.H. (2015), 'Structure and liquidity in Treasury markets', remarks at the Brookings Institution, Washington DC, 3 August.

Pressnell, L.S. (1986), *External economic policy since the war: volume I: the post-war financial settlement*, London: HMSO.

Radcliffe Committee (1959), *Report of the Committee on the Working of the Monetary System*, Cmnd 827, London: HMSO.

Radcliffe Committee (1960a), *Principal memoranda of evidence*, 3 volumes, London: HMSO.

Radcliffe Committee (1960b), *Minutes of Evidence*, London: HMSO.

Reinhart, C. and K. Rogoff (2009), *This time is different: eight centuries of financial folly*, Princeton NJ: Princeton University Press.

Roberts, R. (2013), *Saving the City*, Oxford: Oxford University Press.

Roosa, R.V. (1967), 'Second lecture' in M. Friedman and R.V. Roosa, *The balance of payments: free versus fixed exchange rates*, American Enterprise Institute for Public Policy Research, Washington DC.

Sargent, T.J. and F. Velde (1995) 'Macroeconomic features of the French revolution', *Journal of Political Economy*, **103**,(3), 474–518.

Sargent, T. J. and N. Wallace (1981), 'Some unpleasant monetarist arithmetic', *Federal Reserve Bank of Minneapolis Quarterly Review*, Fall.

Sayers, R.S. (1936), *Bank of England operations 1890–1914*, P.S. King and Co.

Sayers, R.S. (1956), *Financial policy 1939–45*, London: HMSO and Longmans, Green.

Sayers, R.S. (1957), *Central banking after Bagehot*, Oxford: Oxford University Press.

Sayers, R.S. (1968), *Gilletts in the London money market 1867–1967*, Oxford: Oxford University Press.

Sayers, R.S. (1976), *The Bank of England 1891–1944*, 2 vols and appendices, Cambridge: Cambridge University Press.

Scammell, W. M. (1968), *The London discount market*, Elek Books.

Schenk, C.R. (2010), *The decline of sterling: managing the retreat of an international currency 1945–1992*, Cambridge: Cambridge University Press.

Self, R. (2006), *Britain, America and the war debt controversy*, Abingdon: Routledge.

Sheppard, D.K. (1971), *The growth and role of U.K. financial institutions, 1880–1962*, London: Methuen.

Shin, H.S. (2016), 'Market liquidity and bank capital', speech at AQR Asset Management Institute, London Business School, 27 April 2016, www.bis.org/speeches/sp160506.htm (last accessed 30 January 2018).

Sproul, A. (1980), *Selected Papers of Allan Sproul*, ed. L.S. Ritter, Federal Reserve Bank of New York.

Swanson, E. (2011), 'Let's Twist again: a high-frequency event-study analysis of Operation Twist and its implications for QE2', Brookings Papers on Economic Activity 151–95.

Tew, J.H.B. (1978), 'Monetary policy, part I', in F.T. Blackaby (ed.), *British economic policy 1960–74: demand management*, Cambridge: Cambridge University Press.

Thomas, W. and R. Young (1947), 'Problems of post-war monetary policy', *Postwar Economic Studies*, 8: Federal Reserve Policy. Board of Governors of the Federal Reserve System.

Tucker, P. (2009), 'The repertoire of official sector interventions in the financial system: last resort lending, market-making, and capital', speech given at Bank of Japan 2009 international conference, Tokyo.

United Kingdom (1951), *Reserves and liabilities, 1931 to 1945*, Cmnd 8354, London: HMSO.

Wainwright, D. (1990), *Government Broker: the story of an office and of Mullens and Co.*, Matham Publishing.

Walker, C.E. (1954), 'Federal Reserve policy and the structure of interest rates on government securities', *Quarterly Journal of Economics*, **68**(1), 19–42.

Weale, M.R. (2010), '"Default" on UK government debt was no such thing', *Financial Times*, 8 March.

Wicker, E.R. (1969), 'The World War II policy of fixing a pattern of interest rates', *Journal of Finance*, **24**(3), 447–58.

Wills, P.G.B. (2006), 'Moneybroking memories', Gilt-edged witness seminar – background documentation, Lombard Street Research, 22 March 2006.

Withers, H. (1910), 'The English banking system', US Senate National Monetary Commission document no. 492.

Wood, J.H. (2005), *A history of central banking in Great Britain and the United States*, Cambridge: Cambridge University Press, Studies in Macroeconomic History.

Wormell, J. (1985), *The gilt-edged market*, London: George Allen and Unwin.

Wormell, J. (1999), *The management of the national debt of the United Kingdom, 1900–1932*, Abingdon: Routledge.

Index

Howard Bodenhorn, *A History of Banking in Antebellum America: Financial Markets and Economic Development in an Era of Nation-Building* (2000)

Mark Harrison (ed.), *The Economics of World War II: Six Great Powers in International Comparison* (2000)

Angela Redish, *Bimetallism: An Economic and Historical Analysis* (2000)

Elmus Wicker, *Banking Panics of the Gilded Age* (2000)

Michael D. Bordo, *The Gold Standard and Related Regimes: Collected Essays* (1999)

Michele Fratianni and Franco Spinelli, *A Monetary History of Italy* (1997)

Mark Toma, *Competition and Monopoly in the Federal Reserve System, 1914-1951* (1997)

Barry Eichengreen (ed.), *Europe's Postwar Recovery* (1996)

Lawrence H. Officer, *Between the Dollar-Sterling Gold Points: Exchange Rates, Parity and Market Behavior* (1996)

Elmus Wicker, *Banking Panics of the Great Depression* (1996)

Norio Tamaki, *Japanese Banking: A History, 1859-1959* (1995)

Barry Eichengreen, *Elusive Stability: Essays in the History of International Finance, 1919-1939* (1993)

Michael D. Bordo and Forrest Capie (eds.), *Monetary Regimes in Transition* (1993)

Larry Neal, *The Rise of Financial Capitalism: International Capital Markets in the Age of Reason* (1993)

S. N. Broadberry and N.F.R. Crafts (eds.), *Britain in the International Economy, 1870-1939* (1992)

Aurel Schubert, *The Credit-Anstalt Crisis of 1931* (1992)

Trevor J.O. Dick and John E. Floyd, *Canada and the Gold Standard: Balance of Payments Adjustment under Fixed Exchange Rates, 1871-1913* (1992)

Kenneth Mouré, *Managing the Franc Poincaré: Economic Understanding and Political Constraint in French Monetary Policy, 1928-1936* (1991)

David C. Wheelock, *The Strategy and Consistency of Federal Reserve Monetary Policy, 1924-1933* (1991)

Printed in the United States
By Bookmasters